ENGLISH MIRACLE PLAYS

MORALITIES AND INTERLUDES

SPECIMENS AND EXTRACTS

POLLARD

FROM A SARUM HORAE
PARIS, P. PIGOUCHET FOR S. VOSTRE, 1502

ENGLISH MIRACLE PLAYS

MORALITIES AND INTERLUDES

SPECIMENS OF THE PRE-ELIZABETHAN DRAMA

EDITED, WITH AN INTRODUCTION

NOTES, AND GLOSSARY, BY

ALFRED W. POLLARD, M.A.

ST. JOHN'S COLLEGE, OXFORD

WITH ILLUSTRATIONS

EIGHTH EDITION, REVISED.

OXFORD

AT THE CLARENDON PRESS

LONDON : GEOFFREY CUMBERLEGE

TO THE

REV. WALTER W. SKEAT, LITT.D., LL.D.

ELRINGTON AND BOSWORTH PROFESSOR OF ANGLO-SAXON
IN THE UNIVERSITY OF CAMBRIDGE

THIS VOLUME IS GRATEFULLY DEDICATED

IN ACKNOWLEDGMENT OF THE HELP WHICH ITS EDITOR

IN COMMON WITH ALL STUDENTS OF OUR EARLIER LITERATURE

HAS RECEIVED FROM HIS WRITINGS

FIRST EDITION 1890
SECOND   1895
THIRD   1899
FOURTH   1904
FIFTH   1909
SIXTH   1914
SEVENTH   1923
EIGHTH   1927
REPRINTED   1946

PREFACE.

In the preface to the first edition of these specimens of the pre-Elizabethan drama (dated 24 May 1890) acknowledgement was made of 'obligations to Dr. Furnivall, Mr. Henry Bradley, Miss Toulmin Smith, Miss Emily Hickey, and Mr. York Powell for much kind help, and to Mr. Gurney and His Grace the Duke of Devonshire for permission to consult MSS.' Allusion was made to 'the small attention at that time paid to the subject in histories of English literature' and the hope was expressed that a small volume bringing together, out of several rather expensive texts, 'illustrations of the English dramatic literature of more than two centuries, with an unpretentious introduction and commentary, might fairly escape the charge of book-making, and be useful to many lovers of literature unable to make the subject their special study'. At the outset the book, though amiably reviewed, had a very poor sale: then (I record it with gratitude) large orders for it came regularly from the United States, and smaller ones from students of English in Germany. By the help of these a second edition was called for in 1894, and a third in 1898, and on both occasions the text and notes were carefully revised, and on the second some additional notes printed after p. 224 mainly as the result of suggestions by Dr. Henri Logeman and Dr. Eugen Kölbing. Since then I have done my best to keep the book up to date, though the steady increase in the literature as to these early plays has sometimes got ahead of me.

In the fourth edition my principal debt was to Mr. (now Sir) E. K. Chambers, whose fine book on *The Mediaeval Stage* (Clarendon Press, 1903) appeared just as I was beginning my revision. Some illustrations from fifteenth and sixteenth century sources were then added for the first time, and these have since been increased. Notes on them will be found at the end of the Introduction. In the fifth edition (1909) some of the corrections made were due to suggestions by Dr. Skeat; for some of those in the sixth (1914) I had to thank Dr. W. W. Greg. For the seventh edition (1923) the general introduction from p. xlix and the special introductions on Rastell and Heywood were re-written in the light of new knowledge as to the history of the Interlude mainly due to the researches of Dr. A. W. Reed. Most of the papers embodying these I had had the editorial pleasure of printing for him either in the third series of *The Library* or in the *Transactions* of the Biblio-graphical Society, and they had sunk so deep into me that I inadvertently brought up one of Dr. Reed's discoveries (the connexion between Rastell's first device as a printer and the play of the *Four Elements*) as a new idea of my own. Dr. Reed's papers have now been linked up, augmented, and revised in his admirable book *Early Tudor Drama: Medwall, The Rastells, Heywood and the Mori Circle* (Methuen, 1926), which should be consulted in pre-ference to the earlier versions.

In this eighth edition I record the localization and dating (Lincoln, *c.* 1405) of the *Castell of Perseverance* by Prof. W. K. Smart, whose correction to my dating of *Mankind* in the Early English Text Society edition of 1904 I had accepted in 1923. I also record Mr. A. R. Moon's very probable attribution of *Thersites* to Nicholas Udall, as set forth in *The Library* (Fourth Series, Vol. vii, Sept. 1926).

ALFRED W. POLLARD.

5 *January* 1927.

CONTENTS.

—◆◆—

INTRODUCTION.

§ I.

AT the outset of his enquiries almost every student of the modern drama is found instinctively peering through long centuries of darkness for some glimmerings of the brilliant torch-light of Greek tragedy. In this pious desire to connect new things with old, to link together the names of Æschylus and Shakespeare, the services of a motley crew are called into requisition, in which poets, philosophers, saints, mimes, jugglers, monks, nuns, bishops and tradesfolk have all to play their part; but the pedigree is like that of many a modern genealogy, clear at the beginning and the end, with a huge hiatus gaping between. Under the later Roman Empire the drama died a natural death, not because the Church condemned it, but by a lust for sheer obscenity and bloodshed which made true dramatic writing impossible. Until the theatres in which men were made to die and women to prostitute themselves, not in show but in reality, had long been closed and forgotten, the stage was something too vile and horrible for any attempt to Christianize it; nor could the innate dramatic instincts of mankind again find free play amid the unhealthy surroundings of a dying civilization. Yet one piece of positive evidence has long been quoted and re-quoted to the contrary. A drama entitled Χριστὸς Πάσχων, on the subject of the Passion of Christ and the sorrows of the Blessed Virgin, has been generally attributed to St. Gregory Nazianzene, a writer of the fourth century. Save for the absence of lyrical choruses, it is cast strictly upon the lines of Greek tragedy, and it is interesting to classical scholars because, together with a few verses from Æschylus (chiefly from the *Prometheus Vinctus*), the writer has incorporated into his play several hundred lines of Euripides, many of which have not been preserved in any other form. A cento such as this is necessarily destitute alike of dramatic appropriateness and religious feeling, and it is a pleasure to find some better reason for denying its authorship to St. Gregory than the doubt as to its strict orthodoxy, which, until quite recently, alone excited suspicion. To Dr. J. G. Brambs[1], the latest editor of the Χριστὸς Πάσχων, belongs the credit of a conclusive proof that the metre, prosody and grammar of this play are not those of St. Gregory, nor of any other writer of the fourth century, and cannot be reasonably attributed to an earlier period than some six hundred years later. The Χριστὸς Πάσχων, whether, as Dr. Brambs conjectures, the work of Joannes Tzetzes, or of one of his contemporaries, in any case thus ceases to be the dramatic landmark which it has long been represented, and falls into the same class with the plays of the learned nun Hroswitha, to which also a somewhat undue importance is generally attributed.

This Hroswitha[2] was a nun of Gandersheim in Saxony, and her six plays are planned in some measure on the comedies of Terence. Not that, like the author of the Χριστὸς Πάσχων with the Greek dramatists, she incorporated his verses into her own work, or made any attempt to imitate his metres; but that Terence, of whom it has been said that he 'bore a charmed life amid the monasteries of the middle ages,' appeared to the good nun undeservedly and dangerously popular, and she wished to show what much better comedies might be written to inculcate strict moral and religious teaching. That she succeeded in this attempt it is impossible to allow. What has been justly called her 'supersensuous modesty' (Hase)[3], is to modern readers infinitely more offensive than the license of her original. Her language is bald, and her characters without life or humanity. In one of her comedies a wicked Roman Governor goes to visit

---

[1] *Christus Patiens. Tragœdia Christiana Gregorio Nazianzeno falso attributa.* Recensuit Dr. J. G. Brambs. Lipsiæ, 1885.

[2] *Théâtre de Hrotswitha, religieuse allemande du X⁰ siècle.* Traduit en français avec le texte latin, revue sur le manuscrit de Munich. Par C. Magnin. Paris, 1845.

[3] *Miracle Plays.* An historical survey. Translated by A. W. Jackson. 1880.

the Christian virgins, whom, with some improbability, he has
caused to be imprisoned in the scullery of his palace. Suddenly
he is struck with madness, and addresses his embraces to the
pots and pans, covers himself with dirt, and is hustled by his
own bodyguard as a devil. This farcical scene is Hroswitha's
one attempt at humour ; for the rest her plays are written to
display the heroism of martyrs and the glories of chastity, and
deserve the credit due to goodness of intention, and little else.
Whether they were ever acted is a matter of controversy. On
the one hand some of her incidents could hardly have been
represented with modesty ; on the other, the really humorous
situation in the scullery is so baldly treated as to depend largely
upon acting for its effect, and throughout her plays the extreme
brevity of the diction and absence of any attempt at literary
grace, point to an appeal to an audience rather than to readers.
But the audience, it is needless to say, would have been confined to the nunnery and its benefactors, and there is no reason
to suppose that, whether acted or not, the half dozen plays of
the literary nun exercised the smallest influence on the history
of the drama. But what Hroswitha did at Gandersheim other
religious persons were doing in other monasteries, if not con-
temporaneously, at all events within the next hundred years,
but with all-important differences. The comedies of Hroswitha
are exotics, based, at however great a distance, on a heathen
model, coined in the main from her imagination, having nothing
to do with the services of the Church. The dramatic representations which we have next to describe are popular in their
aim, liturgical in their origin, taking as their subjects events
which belonged strictly either to sacred history or to accepted
legends.

Anyone who enters a Catholic Church at Christmas time
is likely to see near one of the altars a coloured illumination
representing the infant Saviour in His cradle, St. Joseph and
the Blessed Virgin watching Him, and an ox and an ass munch-
ing their food hard by. The children delight in it, and it brings
home to them the scene at the manger-bed at Bethlehem more
vividly than a thousand sermons. In the thirteenth century St.
Francis of Assisi, at his altar in the forest, represented that scene
still more realistically, with a real child, real men and women, a

real ox and ass. At any primitive little Italian town, when the members of the different religious gilds and confraternities walk in procession on Corpus Christi Day, little children toddle among them, dressed, some with a tiny sheepskin and staff to represent St. John the Baptist; others in sackcloth as St. Mary Magdalene; others in a blue robe, with a little crown, as the Blessed Virgin; others again with an aureole tied to their little heads, as the infant Saviour. Similar instances of the attempt to bring home to an unlettered people the reality of the chief events connected with the Christian religion might be multiplied indefinitely. The shepherds who, at Christmas time, come into Rome from the Abruzzi, and pipe before the pictures of the Virgin, or the German peasants who, down to the beginning of the present century, used to go round their village in the guise of the Three Kings from the East, illustrate the way in which the efforts of the Church were seconded by the common people. Not from vapid imitations of Euripides and Terence, but from such simple customs as these did the religious drama take its beginnings.

[1] All evidence points to Easter as the festival with which the earliest religious dramas were most intimately connected, and it is probable that the first form which the Easter Play assumed was that of a ceremony in which the crucifix was solemnly buried on Good Friday, and again disinterred on Easter Day amid a pompous ritual. Most commonly the 'sepulchre' in which the crucifix was deposited was a wooden erection placed within a recess in the wall or upon a tomb, but according to the interesting article 'Sepulchre,' in Parker's *Glossary of Architecture*, several English churches still contain permanent stone structures especially built for the purpose. Among the churches which Mr. Parker mentions are those at Navenby and Heckinton, Lincolnshire; Hawton, in Nottinghamshire; Northwold, in Norfolk; and Holcombe Burnell, in Devonshire. In the temporary structures the lower part generally contained a representation of sleeping soldiers, intended for the Roman guard, and in a curious account of the delivery by a certain Maister Canynge on July 4th, 1470, of 'a new sepulchre well gilt with golde and a civer

---

[1] The next few paragraphs are mainly quoted from an article on Easter Plays contributed to the *Guardian* by the present writer, May 22, 1889, improved with the help of Chambers's *The Mediaeval Stage.*

thereto,' to the vicar of St. Mary Redcliffe, Bristol, there is
mention of '4 knights armed, keeping the sepulchre, with their
weapons in their hands ; that is to say, 2 axes and 2 spears, with
2 pavés.' In this sepulchre both hell and heaven were represented, together with figures of angels and of still more sacred
persons. In Davis's *Antient Rites of Durham* we are told :—

'Within the church of Durham, upon Good Friday, there was a
marvellous solemn service, in which service time, after the Passion was
sung, two of the ancient monks took a goodly large crucifix all of gold
of the picture of our Saviour Christ, nailed upon the Cross. . . . The
service being ended, the said two monks carried the Cross to the *Sepulchre* with great reverence (which *Sepulchre* was set up that morning on
the north side of the Quire, nigh unto the High Altar before the service
time), and there did lay it within the said *Sepulchre* with great devotion.'

At the cathedral of Rouen there was a special service for the
occasion called '*Sepulchri Officium.*' Trace of the ceremony
still lingers in the custom of veiling the crucifix above the altar
from Holy Thursday to the first evensong of Easter. In its
original form it was of long continuance, and we are told that as
late as 1316 its popularity was so dangerous that in that year an
Archbishop of Worms ordained that thenceforth it should take
place within closed doors, and in the presence of the priests
only.

The first appearance of dramatic dialogue in the services of
the Church has been traced to the ninth century, when words
were fitted to the additional melodies (at first sung only to
vowel sounds) which it had become customary to insert, on
high festivals, in the Gregorian music of the Antiphons, more
especially in those of the Introit sung as the priest proceeds to
the altar to celebrate Mass. Of these interpolations or 'Tropes,'
as they were called, the most important in its dramatic influence
was that sung on Easter-day, leading up to the Introit *Resur-
rexi et adhuc tecum sum, Alleluia.* This is based on the
colloquy between the Angels at the tomb and the Three Maries
in the narratives of SS. Matthew and Mark ; in its earliest form
it ran :

> Quem quaeritis in sepulchro, Christicolae ?
> Iesum Nazarenum crucifixum, o caelicolae.

Non est hic : surrexit sicut praedixerat.
Ite, nuntiate quia surrexit de sepulchro.

In a trope in use at Winchester Cathedral at the end of the tenth century the form is slightly more elaborate, and the contemporary *Concordia Regularis*, an appendix to the Rule of St. Benedict drawn up at some date between 959 and 979 by Æthelwold, Bishop of Winchester, shows that at that Cathedral the colloquy had been transferred from the Easter Mass, to follow the third lesson at Matins, and describes the ceremonial the development of which was doubtless the cause of the transference. I quote the directions as translated by Mr. Chambers :

' While the third lesson is being chanted, let four brethren vest themselves. Let one of these, vested in an alb, enter as though to take part in the service, and let him approach the sepulchre without attracting attention, and sit there quietly with a palm in his hand. While the third respond is being chanted let the remaining three follow, and let them all, vested in copes, bearing in their hands thuribles with incense and stepping delicately [*pedetemptim*] as those who seek something, approach the sepulchre. These things are done in imitation of the angel sitting in the monument and the women with spices coming to anoint the body of Jesus. When therefore he who sits there beholds the three approach him like folk lost and seeking something, let him begin in a dulcet voice of medium pitch to sing *Quem quaeritis*. And when he has sung it to the end, let the three reply in unison *Ihesum Nazarenum*. So he, *Non est hic : surrexit sicut praedixerat. Ite, nuntiate quia surrexit a mortuis*. At the words of this bidding, let those three turn to the choir and say *Alleluia ! resurrexit Dominus !* This said, let the one, still sitting there and as if recalling them, say the anthem *Venite et videte locum*. And saying this let him rise and lift the veil, and show them the place bare of the cross, but only the cloths laid there in which the cross was wrapped. And when they have seen this, let them set down the thuribles which they bare in that same sepulchre, and take the cloth, and hold it up in the face of the clergy, and as if to demonstrate that the Lord has risen and is no longer wrapped therein, let them sing the anthem *Surrexit Dominus de sepulchro*, and lay the cloth upon the altar. When the anthem is done, let the priest sharing in their gladness at the triumph of our King, in that, having vanquished death, He rose again, begin the hymn *Te Deum laudamus*. And this begun, all the bells chime out together.

Here we already have a drama, but elaboration once begun steadily continued, as is proved by the more developed variation on the same theme printed in our first appendix from Thomas

Wright's edition of a thirteenth-century manuscript preserved at Orleans.

An early Christmas play on the subject of the Slaughter of the Innocents (*Interfectio Puerorum*), which has been handed down to us in the same manuscript, is cast upon very similar lines to the Mystery of the Resurrection printed in our Appendix. The part of the Holy Innocents (the fact that they were under two years of age is neglected!) was taken by the choir boys, the other characters, including the women, would be played by the clergy. In one part of the church (pews, it will be remembered, were a later invention) is erected a manger; in another a throne for Herod; a distant corner is supposed to represent Egypt. With this simple stage-arrangement the action proceeds. The story is set forth in the fewest possible words, interspersed with anthems for the choristers. Towards the end of the play the boys (having arisen from the dead) enter the choir; the throne of Herod is taken by another actor, who represents Archelaus; an angel bids the Holy Family return from Egypt, and then the Precentor begins the *Te Deum* and the performance is over.

The manuscript which has preserved for us these two plays contains also eight others, four of which are concerned with the miracles of St. Nicholas, while the rest have as their respective subjects the Adoration of the Magi, the Appearance of Christ to the two disciples on the road to Emmaus, the Conversion of St. Paul, and the Raising of Lazarus. All ten plays have the same characteristics. They are all intended to be performed in church, introducing anthems and hymns from the office of the day, and requiring only the simplest stage-machinery. They are all written with great brevity and simplicity, partly in prose, partly in classical metres, partly in monkish rimes. A knowledge of classical Latin is indicated by adaptations from Virgil in two of the plays, and by the tag from Sallust (*Incendium meum ruina restinguam*), which is put into the mouth of Herod in the *Interfectio Puerorum*; but the plays themselves have no pretensions whatever to any literary merit.

As has already been said, the Orleans manuscript, in which the plays we have been considering are preserved, belongs to the thirteenth century. Its contents, however, were probably

composed before the year 1200, and may thus be reckoned as contemporaneous with those of Hilarius, with which we have next to deal. Of this Hilarius, both of his works and of what little is known of his life, an excellent account is given in the third volume of Professor Morley's *English Writers*, and a shorter one in his *Sketch of English Literature*, so that the less need be said here. He is thought, on good grounds, to have been an Englishman, and we know from his writings that he was a pupil of the celebrated Abelard. Of his three plays (all in Latin), that on the history of Daniel was composed in collaboration with two other writers, and was probably intended for representation at Christmas. Another is on the Raising of Lazarus ; while the third, which is printed in our Appendix, has for its subject a miracle wrought by St. Nicholas in defence of the honour of an image of himself, under the care of which a heathen is supposed to deposit a treasure for safe keeping. The treasure is stolen by robbers, and the heathen on his return upbraids and beats the image which has played him so false. Smarting under the blows, St. Nicholas appears to the robbers, and in a speech, of which, from what we know of Hilarius, there is no reason to suppose the humour unconscious, forces them to restitution. The heathen returns again, and in his joy makes honourable amends to the saint, and is converted to Christianity. This play is noteworthy for its refrains in old French. Similar French refrains are found in Hilarius' play on the Raising of Lazarus, and are extended to short speeches in the Mystery of the Ten Virgins, another early French play. Similarly German and Latin are mingled in the episode of the anointing of the feet of Christ by St. Mary Magdalene, in a play written about this time in Germany. These refrains and short speeches paved the way for the composition of whole plays in the vernacular, of which in France we find very early specimens, e. g. the Norman play on the subject of *Adam*, which belongs to the thirteenth century.

§ 2.

Before the Norman Conquest we have no reason to suppose that dramatic representations were known in England. The performance of the earliest play of which we have any mention

must probably be assigned to the reign of William Rufus. According to Matthew of Paris (writing *circ.* 1240), a certain Geoffrey, who afterwards became Abbot of St. Albans, while yet a secular person, was invited from France to take the mastership of the Abbey School. His arrival was delayed, and in the meanwhile the school was given to another. He therefore settled for a while at Dunstable, and while there borrowed from the sacristan of St. Albans copes (*capæ chorales*) in which to array the performers of a Miracle Play in honour of Saint Katharine. During the performance of the play these copes were destroyed by fire, and Geoffrey took this disaster so much to heart, that he abandoned the world and entered the Abbey of St. Albans as a monk. By 1119 he had risen to be its Abbot, and it is by reckoning back from this year that we arrive at the end of the eleventh century as the probable date of the performance of his unlucky play. A century later such representations had become common. William Fitzstephen, who wrote *circ.* 1182, in his *Life of Saint Thomas à Becket*, contrasts with the theatrical spectacles of ancient Rome the 'holier plays' of London, in which were represented the miracles and sufferings of the confessors and martyrs of the Church : *repræsentationes miraculorum quæ sancti confessores operati sunt, sive repræsentationes passionum quibus claruit constantia martyrum.* The word *miraculorum* in this quotation, and the phrase *quæ miracula vulgariter appellamus*, used by Matthew Paris in writing of the play of St. Katharine, reminds us of a distinction between *Miracle Plays* and *Mysteries*, of which a great deal is made in all text-books of English Literature, but which in England had no existence in fact during the centuries in which the sacred drama chiefly flourished. 'Properly speaking,' says Professor Ward (*English Dramatic Literature*, vol. i. p. 23), '*Mysteries* deal with Gospel events only, their object being primarily to set forth, by an illustration of the prophetic history of the Old Testament, and more particularly of the fulfilling history of the New, the central mystery of the Redemption of the world, as accomplished by the Nativity, the Passion, and the Resurrection. *Miracle Plays*, on the other hand, are concerned with incidents derived from the legends of the saints of the Church.' The distinction in itself is, as Professor Ward

remarks, a legitimate one, but it is rendered rather confusing by
the fact that, while in England we have no single extant example
of a pure Miracle Play as thus defined, all dramatic representations
on this subject were called by this name, and the word *mystery*
is said to have been first applied to them in this country by
Dodsley, in the preface to his collection of Old Plays, early in
the eighteenth century[1]. But the English preference for the
word *miracula* must have had some basis in fact, and its
predominance gives a certain plausibility to the theory of Professor Ten Brink (*Gesch. der alt. eng. Litt.* § 248), that in the
development of the sacred drama legendary subjects preceded
Biblical, and those drawn from the Old Testament the ones
taken from the New. The theory, however, is not one to be
hastily accepted, partly because the motives of reverence to
which it is assigned appeal far more to the modern mind than
to mediæval simplicity, and partly because it hardly fits in
with the existence of the liturgical dramas for Christmas and
Easter, to which attention has already been drawn. On the
other hand, it may be taken as certain that the sacred drama
had no independent origin on English soil, but was introduced
into this country after the Norman Conquest. It is thus
probable that towards the beginning of the twelfth century the
miracles of the saints formed the favourite theme of the French
playwrights in England, and that the English preference for the
word *miracle* over that of *mystère* was due to the fact that it
was to this class of play that English audiences were first
introduced.

[1] The *Ludus de Sancta Katharina* at Dunstable, pageants on the
subject of the lives of St. Fabyan, St. Sebastian and St. Botulf, performed in London, plays at Windsor and Bassingbourne on St. George,
and the *Ludi beatæ Christinæ* at Bethersden, Kent, are the only Miracle
Plays, in the scientific use of the term, of which I can find mention of
the performance in England, and none of these unfortunately now survive.
The classification of the play of St. Paul in the Digby MS. is perhaps
doubtful; the play of St. Mary Magdalene, from which extracts are given
in this volume, as introducing the character of Christ and the Resurrection, is at least in part a mystery. But, as remarked in the preface
to it in my notes, this interesting play unites in itself all the features
which are commonly assigned respectively to Miracle Plays, Mysteries
and Moralities.

Of Miracle Plays written in Latin none now exist of which it can be said with any probability that they were acted in England. An early play on the subject of the creation and fall of *Adam*, which was stated by its first editor, M. Luzarche, to be written in Anglo-Norman, is now regarded as purely Norman, and although it is highly probable that French plays were written and acted in England during the twelfth and thirteenth centuries, we are in possession of no trustworthy evidence on the subject. According to statements made at the end of the sixteenth century in the *Banes* or proclamation of the Chester Plays, this great cycle dates in some form from the mayoralty of Sir John Arneway, whose term of office, which really covered the years 1268–1276, is elsewhere in this connexion transferred to 1328. Sir E. K. Chambers has ingeniously suggested that Arneway's name has been confused with that of a Richard Erneis or Herneys who held office from 1327 to 1329, and with this correction the tradition is probable enough. The composition of the cycle is attributed in the Banns to ' one Done Rondall, moonke of Chester Abbe,' i. e. to the famous Randall or Randulf Higden, the author of the *Polychronicon*, who was a monk of St. Werburgh's Abbey at Chester from 1299 to his death in 1364, and whose zeal for the English tongue would make him a very fitting author of one of the first English cycles. It is probable, however, that Chester did not stand alone, but that dramatic composition began at an early date also in the East-Midlands [1]. *The Harrowing of Hell*, an East-Midland poem in dialogue, quoted in full in our Appendix, though not itself a Miracle Play, undoubtedly shows that dramatic influences had been at work before its composition, and three extant manuscripts of it date from the reign of Edward II. The East-Midland play of *Abraham and Isaac* (also quoted from in the Appendix), discovered by Miss Lucy Toulmin Smith, at Brome Hall in Suffolk, may be assigned to the fourteenth century, and about the year 1350 a *Ludus Filiorum Israel* was performed at Cambridge. Passing from the East-Midlands northwards, we are confronted with the great York cycle of plays dating from about 1360, with the

---

[1] In the geographical grouping of the plays I follow Professor Ten Brink (*Gesch. der alt. eng. Lit.* § 251).

closely related 'Towneley' or Wakefield cycle of a little later period, and with the lost Beverly cycle, some remnants of which may possibly be preserved in the fragments lately printed by Prof. Skeat[1] from an early fifteenth century MS. Further north still we find another at Newcastle, of which one play (*The Building of the Ark*) still remains. Westwards, again, in the fifteenth century, Chester became a kind of dramatic metropolis for Preston, Lancaster, Kendall and Dublin. Southwards, the fame of Coventry gradually overshadowed that of all its rivals, and we hear of plays performed at Tewkesbury, at Reading, and at Witney. Throughout the fourteenth, the fifteenth and the sixteenth centuries, we have continuous evidence of the popularity[2] and frequent production of Miracle Plays in nearly

---

[1] *Academy*, Jan. 4 and 11, 1890.

[2] The plays did not always meet with approval. I quote from a Wycliffite sermon against them the apology which the preacher puts into the mouths of their defenders. It gives a good summary of medieval views on the subject, and, inferentially, of the nature of the preacher's attack.

'But here aȝenis thei seyen that they pleyen these myraclis in the worschip of God, and so dyden not these Jewis that bobbiden [mocked] Crist. Also, ofte sithis by siche myraclis pleyinge ben men converted to gode lyvynge, as men and wymmen seyng in myraclis pleyinge that the devil by ther array, by the which thei moven eche on othere to leccherie and to pride, makith hem his servauntis to bryngen hemsilf and many othere to helle, and to han fer more vylenye herafter by ther proude aray heere than thei han worschipe heere, and seeynge ferthermore that al this wor[l]dly beyng heere is but vanité for a while, as is myraclis pleyng, wherthoru thei leeven ther pride, and taken to hem afterward the meke conversacioun of Crist and of his seyntis, and so myraclis pleyinge turneth men to the bileve, and not pervertith. Also ofte sythis by siche myraclis pleyinge men and wymmen, seynge the passioun of Crist and of his seyntis, ben movyd to compassion and devocioun wepynge bitere teris, thanne thei ben not scornynge of God but worschipyng. Also, prophitable to men and to the worschipe of God it is to fulfillen and sechen alle the menes by the whiche men mowen seene synne and drawen hem to vertues; and sythen as ther ben men that only by ernestful doynge wylen be convertid to God, so ther ben othere men that wylen be convertid to God but by gamen and play; and now on dayes men ben not convertid by the ernestful doyng of God ne of men, thanne now it is tyme and skilful to assayen to convertyn the puple by

every part of England. During this period we have record of
the performance of plays in nearly a hundred English towns and
villages, some of them quite small places. In London, in 1378,
the choristers of St. Paul's prayed for the suppression of the
performances of 'unexpert people'; in 1391 the Parish Clerks
played for three days at Skinners' Well near Smithfield, and we
have record of another play at the same place in 1407, which
lasted no less than eight days. In 1416 a play of St. George of
Cappadocia was performed before Henry V. and the Emperor
Sigismund at Windsor, and in the following year the English
Bishops at the Council of Constance entertained first the
Burghers and afterwards their fellow-councillors with a Christmas play, representing the Nativity, visit of the Magi, and
Slaughter of the Innocents. Similar references might be almost
indefinitely multiplied.

From the mention of the *ludi sanctiores* in William Fitzstephen (circ. 1182), to the prayer of the choristers of St. Paul's
in 1378, we have no reference to Miracle Plays in London.
During these two centuries a great change had been wrought
in the plays and the manner of their performance, with the
gradual evolution of which we are only imperfectly acquainted.
Originally, as we have seen, they were acted in, or in the
precincts of, churches, and by the priests and their assistants.
But the apparently instantaneous popularity of the plays led to
a demand for their extension, which gradually resulted in the
exclusion of the original performers from all participation in
them. In the shows and processions which formed so prominent
a feature in medieval life, allegorical personages and symbols
had from very early times played a part. In the procession of

pley and gamen, as by myraclis pleyinge and other mauer myrthis.
Also, summe recreatioun men moten han, and bettere it is, or lesse yvele,
that thei han theyre recreacoun by pleyinge of myraclis than by pleyinge
of other japis. Also, sithen it is leveful to han the myraclis of God
peynted, why is not as wel leveful to han the myraclis of God pleyed,
sythen men mowen bettere reden the wille of God and his mervelous
werkis in the pleyinge of hem than in the peyntynge, and betere thei ben
holden in mennus mynde and oftere rehersid by the pleyinge of hem than
by the peyntynge, for this is a deed bok, the tother a qu[i]ck.'—MS. of
the end of the fourteenth century in library of St. Martin's-in-the-Fields,
quoted in Wright and Halliwell's *Reliquiæ Antiquæ*, vol. ii. p. 45.

a gild the patron saint would form a prominent figure, and on the occasion of royal entries and rejoicings his representative would act as the spokesman of the craft from one of the gaily decorated scaffolds, which were erected at different points along the route. As the Miracle Plays grew in popularity and the desire arose for greater elaboration in stage-effects, performances in churches became increasingly impossible. The churchyard, which was next tried, was equally unsuitable, for the crowds of spectators desecrated the graves. Gradually, therefore, the players left the church and its precincts, and performed in any convenient open spaces about the town. When this practice became the rule the members of the trade-gilds entered the lists as competitors with the clergy, while the wandering jugglers or *histriones* were ready to supplement by their aid the dramatic deficiencies of either party. At the same time, now that the plays were more and more dissevered from the services of the Church, the Ecclesiastical authorities began to feel grave doubts as to the advisability of the participation of the clergy in such performances. Even if the prohibition of clerical 'ludi theatrales' by Innocent III in 1207 refers to the Feast of Fools rather than to plays, it indicates increased strictness, and Church feeling on the subject is well summed up in a passage in the *Manuel des Pechés*, written in Norman-French about the end of the thirteenth century, and quoted here in its translation under the name of the *Handlyng Synne*, by Robert Mannyng of Brunne, in or about the year 1303.

> 'Hyt ys forbode hym yn the decre
> Miracles for to make or se;
> For miracles, ȝyf you begynne,
> Hyt ys a gaderynt, a syght of synne.
> He may yn the Cherche, thurgh thys resun,
> Pley the resurrecyun;
> That is to seye, how god ros,
> God and man yn myght and los,
> To make men be yn beleve gode,
> That he ros with flesshe and blode;
> And he may pleye withoutyn plyght
> How god was bore yn thole nyght,
> To make men to beleve stedfastly
> That he lyght yn the vyrgyne Mary.

3yf thou do hyt in weyys or grenys.
A syght of synne truly hyt semys.'   Ed. Furnivall.

The compromise which these lines represent was of no long
duration.   The spirit of the times was all in favour of the open-
air performances in the highways and public greens, and no
English play which has been preserved to us contains any
marks of its representation by clerical actors.

Eight years after the appearance of Robert of Brunne's
Handlyng Synne, a great impetus was given to the Miracle
Plays by a decree of the Council of Vienne (1311).   The feast
of Corpus Christi, instituted by Pope Urban in 1264, owing to
his death in the same year, had never been observed.   Its
due celebration on the Thursday after Trinity Sunday was now
strictly enjoined, and was adopted by the trade-gilds in many
towns as their chief festival of the year.   The custom of linking
several plays on kindred subjects into one grand performance
was now greatly extended, in order to provide each craft, or
group of crafts, with a separate scene.   There was nothing in
the nature of the festival, as there is in those of Christmas and
Easter, to limit the thoughts of Christians to particular events
in the Bible narrative, and the fact that the Thursday after
Trinity Sunday mostly falls within a few weeks of the longest
day, also lent itself to the performance of those great cycles 'of
mater from the beginning of the world' to the Day of Judgment,
four of which have come down to us as the most important
remains of the English religious drama.

The manner of performance of the Miracle Plays has often
been described.   In order to enable as large a number of people
as possible to be spectators, each play was repeated several
times in different parts of the town, called 'stations,' and to this
end moveable scaffolds were constructed, which could be drawn
by horses from point to point.   With this much premised, there
can be no difficulty in understanding the oft-quoted account
by Archdeacon Rogers (obiit, 1595), who witnessed one of
the last performances of the Whitsun plays at Chester, the year
before his death.

'Every company,' he writes, 'had his pagiant, or parte, which
pagiants weare a high scafolde with two rowmes, a higher and
a lower, upon four wheeles.   In the lower they apparelled

them selves, and in the higher rowme they played, beinge all open on the tope, that all behoulders mighte heare and see them. The places where they played them was in every streete. They begane first at the abay gates, and when the firste pagiante was played it was wheeled to the highe crosse before the mayor, and so to every streete ; and soe every streete had a pagiant playinge before them at one time, till all the pagiantes for the daye appoynted weare played : and when one pagiant was neere ended, worde was broughte from streete to streete, that soe they mighte come in place thereof excedinge orderlye, and all the streetes have theire pagiantes afore them all at one time playeinge togeather ; to se which playes was greate resorte, and also scafoldes and stages made in the streetes in those places where they determined to playe theire pagiantes.'

It will be noted that the word pageant, which is ultimately connected with the Greek πῆγμα, and is found spelt in every conceivable way, is primarily applied to the moveable scaffold on which the play was acted, and only secondarily to the performance itself. In some cases, e.g. in that of the *Trial of Christ*, for the proper performance of a play two scaffolds would be required, and the actors would go from one to another, as between the judgment halls of Pilate and Herod. Messengers also would ride up to a scaffold through the town, and there are stage directions such as that 'here Herod shall rage on the pagond and also in the streete.' In the more elaborate performances some attempt was made at scene shifting, as is indicated by directions in the Coventry Play of the *Last Supper*.

'Here Cryst enteryth into the hous with his disciplis and ete the Paschal lomb ; and in the mene tyme the cownsel-hous beforn seyd xal sodeynly onclose, schewyng the buschopys, prestys, and jewgys syttyng in here astat, lyche as it were a convocacyon.'

And again,

'Here the buschopys partyn in the place, and eche of hem takyn here leve, be contenawns, resortyng eche man to his place with here meny to make redy to take Cryst ; and than the place ther Cryst is in xal sodeynly unclose round abowt, shewyng Cryst syttyng at the table and hese dyscypules eche in ere degré, Cryst thus seyng,' &c.

In simpler performances a different part of the stage was accepted as a different scene, and actors who were not taking part in the dialogue remained in view of the spectators. The dresses, as was long the custom on the English stage, aimed rather at splendour than appropriateness, save in the hideous attire assigned to the demons. God was represented in a white coat, and until the injurious effects of the process were understood, the actor who played this part used to have his face gilded.

In the accounts of the gilds and municipalities there are numerous entries for the purchase of these dresses, for the housing and repair of the pagond, for meat and drink for the actors during rehearsals, and for their fees for the performance. In his *Dissertation on the Coventry Mysteries* (pp. 15, 16), Mr. Sharp quotes in full the expenses incurred by the Smiths in 1490 in rehearsing and exhibiting their pageant of the *Trial, Condemnation, and Passion of Christ.* They are as follows :

' This is the expens of the furste reherse of our players in Ester weke.

Imprimis in Brede, iiij^d.

Itm̃ in Ale, viij^d.

Itm̃ in Kechyn, xiij^d.

Itm̃ in Vynegre, j^d.

Itm̃ payd at the Second Reherse in Whyttson weke, in brede, Ale and Kechyn, ij^s. iiij^d.

Itm̃ for drynkynge at the pagent in having forth in Wyne and ale, vij^d.

Itm̃ in the mornynge at diner and at Sopper in Costs in Brede, vij^d.

Itm̃ for ix galons of Ale, xviij^d.

Itm̃ for a Rybbe of befe and j gose, vj^d.

Itm̃ for kechyn to dener and sopp, ij^s. ij^d.

Itm̃ for a Rybbe of befe, iij^d.

Itm̃ for a quarte of wyne, ij^d.

Itm̃ for another quarte for heyrynge of procula is gowne, ij^d.

Itm̃ for gloves ij^s. vj^d.

Itm̃ spent at the repellynge of the pagantte and the expences of havinge it in and furthe, xiiij^d.

Itm̃ in paper, ob.

Md payd to the players for corpus xisti daye.

Imprimis to God, ij^s.

Itm̃ to Cayphas, iij^s. iiij^d.

Itm̃ to Heroude, iij^s. iiij^d.

Itm̃ to Pilatt is wyffe, ij^s.

Itm̃ to the Bedull, iiij^d.

Itm̃ to one of the Knights, ij^s.

Itm̃ to the devyll and to Judas, xviij^d.
Itm̃ to Petur and malchus, xvj^d.
Itm̃ to Anna, ij^s. ij^d.
Itm̃ to Pilatte, iiij^s.
Itm̃ to Pilatte is sonne, iiij^d.
Itm̃ to another knighte, ij^s.
Itm̃ **to** the Mynstrell, xiiij^d.'

To meet these expenses a yearly rate, varying in the different gilds from a penny to fourpence, was levied on every craftsman. The spending of this rate (called pageant-silver), and of any additions to it through fines, &c., was entrusted to pageant-masters, who were annually elected, and had before leaving office to account for all monies received. The payments to the players (supers like the Bedull and Pilate's son, who received fourpence, being excluded) began at Coventry at fourteenpence, and reached in some cases as much as four shillings, no inconsiderable sum in 1490, when a rib of beef could be bought for threepence, and ale was twopence a gallon. At any rate there was no lack of candidates for the honour of acting, and one of the duties of the pageant-master was to examine into the qualifications of these trade-folk actors. In York this duty was taken up by the Council itself, who on April 3, 1476, ordained :

‘ That yerely in the tyme of lentyn there shall be called afore the maire for the tyme beyng iiij of the moste connyng discrete and able players within this Citie, to serche, here, and examen all the plaiers and plaies and pagentes thrughoute all the artificers belonging to Corpus Xti Plaie. And all such as thay shall fynde sufficiant in personne and connyng, to the honour of the Citie and worship of the saide Craftes, for to admitte and able ; and all other insufficiant personnes, either in connyng, voice, or personne, to discharge, ammove, and avoide.

‘ And that no plaier that shall plaie in the saide Corpus Xti plaie be conducte and reteyned to plaie but twise on the day of the saide playe [i.e. shall not take more than two different characters] ; and that he or thay so plaing plaie not overe twise the saide day, vpon payne of xl*s*. to forfet vnto the chaumbre as often tymes as he or thay shall be founden defautie in the same.'

From this it will be seen that in the larger towns, at any rate, the plays were most carefully rehearsed and prepared, and that Shakespeare's caricature of the tradesman-amateur in Bottom and his fellows cannot fairly be applied to these performances. On this part of our subject it only remains to quote the York Proclamation as to the performance of the Corpus Christi plays, which not only illustrates the importance which was attached to them, but gives us the interesting information that the plays began between four and five a.m. The Proclamation belongs to the year 1415, after the performance of the plays had been transferred from the festival of Corpus Christi to its vigil. It is given here as transcribed by Miss Toulmin Smith for her edition of the York Plays.

' Proclamacio ludi corporis cristi facienda in vigilia corporis cristi.

' Oiez &c. We comand of ye Kynges behalue and ye Mair and ye Shirefs of yis Citee yat no mann go armed in yis Citee with swerdes ne with Carlill-axes, ne none othir defences in distorbaunce of ye Kingis pees and ye play, or hynderyng of ye processioun of Corpore Christi, and yat yai leue yare hernas in yare Ines, saufand knyghtes and sqwyers of wirship yat awe haue swerdes borne eftir yame, of payne of forfaiture of yaire wapen and inprisonment of yaire bodys. And yat men yat brynges furth pacentes yat yai play at the places yat is assigned yerfore and nowere elles, of ye payne of forfaiture to be raysed yat is ordayned yerfore, yatis to say xl*s*. And yat menn of craftes and all othir menn yat fyndes torches, yat yai come furth in array, and in ye manere as it has been vsed and customed before yis time, noght haueyng wapen, careynge tapers of ye pagentz. And officers yat ar keepers of the pees of payne of forfaiture of yaire fraunchis and yaire bodyes to prison : And all maner of craftmen yat bringeth furthe ther pageantez in order and course by good players, well arayed and openly spekyng, vpon payn of lesyng of C*s*. to be paide to the chambre without any pardon. And that euery player that shall play be redy in his pagiaunt at convenyant tyme, that is to say, at the myd howre betwix iiijth and vth of the cloke in the mornynge, and then all oyer pageantz fast followyng ilk one after oyer as yer course is, without tarieng. Sub pena facienda camere vi*s*. viii*d*.'

§ 3.

In approaching the consideration of the four great cycles of Miracle Plays still extant (the York, Towneley, Chester and Coventry), it must be remembered that no one of them, in the form in which it has come down to us, can be regarded as a homogeneous whole, the work of a single author. So little attention has as yet been devoted to these plays, that the relations of the different cycles to each other, and of the

different parts of the same cycle to the whole, have as yet been
very imperfectly worked out[1]. It is plain, however, that the
dramatists borrowed ideas and sometimes whole scenes from
each other, and that the plays were frequently rewritten, often
to the great detriment of the original metre. The connection of
the plays with the trade-gilds was in itself a great cause of
confusion. Where a city was prosperous new gilds would arise,
and the original plays have to be subdivided in order to give
them a share in the performance. When, on the other hand,
the means or the enthusiasm of the gilds was on the decline, two
or more plays would have to be run together. The manuscript
of the York cycle, which dates from about 1430–40 contains
forty-eight plays : in 1415 there had been fifty-one, and another
list, probably a few years earlier, gives fifty-seven. The process
of subdivision had probably reached its height about the end of
the fourteenth century, and the tendency thenceforward would
be to amalgamation or excision. In the Chester cycle, of
which we have no complete manuscript earlier than 1591, the
number of the plays is only twenty-five, and marks of amalgamation are easily traced. Thus each cycle as it has come
down to us must be regarded rather as an organic growth than
as the work of a single author.

From whatever point of view we regard them, whether as
to antiquity, length, or serious interest, the York Plays, which
have been the last to receive the honours of print, have the first
claim on our attention. The date of the composition of the
cycle as a whole is referred by Miss Toulmin Smith to the years
1340–1350. The plays are forty-eight in number, and they
follow the Bible narrative very closely, though with the occasional
introduction of apocryphal legends from the pseudo-gospels and
similar sources. It will be convenient, therefore, to take the
York cycle as our standard of comparison, and in order to give
the fullest idea of its contents the *Ordo Paginarum* of 1415
is here subjoined in a translation, that of Drake (the author
of the *Eboracum*), slightly emended from the Latin text printed
by Miss Toulmin Smith.

---

[1] In an article in *Anglia*, Bd. xi. (1889) Dr. A. Hohlfeld had made
a good beginning. Since 1890, when this remark was written, much
excellent work has been done in a long series of papers.

'The order of the Pagents of the Play of Corpus Christi, in the time of the mayoralty of William Alne, in the third year of the reign of King Henry V., anno 1415, compiled by Roger Burton, town clerk.

1. Tanners ... { God the Father Almighty creating and forming the heavens, angels and archangels, Lucifer and the angels that fell with him to hell.

2. Plasterers ... { God the Father, in his own substance, creating the earth and all which is therein, by the space of five days.

3. Cardmakers { God the Father creating Adam of the clay of the earth, and making Eve of Adam's rib, and inspiring them with the breath of life.

4. Fullers ... { God forbidding Adam and Eve to eat of the tree of life.

5. Coopers ... { Adam and Eve and a tree betwixt them; the serpent deceiving them with apples; God speaking to them and cursing the serpent, and with a sword driving them out of paradise.

6. Armourers ... { Adam and Eve, an angel with a spade and distaff assigning them work.

7. Gaunters [Glovers] } Abel and Cain offering victims in sacrifice.

8. Shipwrights { God warning Noah to make an Ark of floatable wood.

9. Pessoners [Fishmongers] and Mariners } Noah in the Ark, with his wife; the three sons of Noah with their wives; with divers animals.

10. Parchment-makers Bookbinders } Abraham sacrificing his son Isaac on an altar, a boy with wood and an angel.

11. Hosiers ... { Moses lifting up the serpent in the wilderness; King Pharaoh; eight Jews wondering and expecting.

12. Spicers ... { A Doctor declaring the sayings of the prophets of the future birth of Christ. Mary; an angel saluting her; Mary saluting Elizabeth.

13. Pewterers Founders { Mary, Joseph wishing to put her away; an angel speaking to them that they go to Bethlehem.

14. Tylers ... ... { Mary, Joseph, a midwife; the Child born, lying in a manger betwixt an ox and an ass, and an angel speaking to the shepherds, and to the players in the next pageant.

15. Chandlers ... { The shepherds talking together, the star in the East; an angel giving the shepherds the good tidings of the Child's birth.

16, 17. Orfevers [Goldsmiths] Goldbeaters Monemakers	The three kings coming from the East, Herod asking them about the child Jesus; the son of Herod, two counsellors, and a messenger. Mary with the Child, a star above, and the three kings offering gifts.
41. [Misplaced in the MS.] Formerly the Hospital of St. Leonards, now the Masons.	Mary with the Child, Joseph, Anna, the midwife with young pigeons; Simeon receiving the Child in his arms, and two sons of Symeon.
18. Marshals [Shoers of horses.]	Mary with the Child, and Joseph fleeing into Egypt at the bidding of an angel.
19. Girdellers Nailers Sawyers	Herod commanding the children to be slain; four soldiers with lances; two counsellors of the king, and four women lamenting the slaughter of the children.
20. Spurriers Lorymers [Bridle makers]	The Doctors, the Child Jesus sitting in the Temple in their midst, questioning and answering them. Four Jews, Mary and Joseph seeking Him, and finding Him in the Temple.
21. Barbers ...	Jesus, John the Baptist baptizing Him.
[Omitted in the MS.] Vintners	Jesus, Mary, bridegroom with bride, the Ruler of the Feast with his household, with six water-pots, in which the water is turned into wine.
22. Fevers [Smiths]	Jesus upon the pinnacle of the Temple, Satan tempting Him, with stones, and two angels ministering.
23. Curriers ...	Peter, James and John; Jesus ascending into the mountain and transfiguring Himself before them; Moses and Elias appearing, and a voice speaking from a cloud.
[Omitted in the MS.] Ironmongers	Jesus, and Simon the Leper asking Jesus to eat with him; two disciples, Mary Magdalen washing the feet of Jesus with her tears and wiping them with her hair.
24. Plumbers Pattenmakers	Jesus, two Apostles, the woman taken in adultery, four Jews accusing her.
Pouchmakers Bottlers Capmakers	Lazarus in the tomb, Mary Magdalene, Martha, and two Jews in wonderment.
25. Skinners ...	Jesus upon an ass with its foal, xii Apostles following Jesus, six rich and six poor men, eight boys with branches of palms, singing *Benedictus*, &c., and Zacchæus climbing into a sycamore-tree.

26. Cutlers
    Bladesmiths
    Sheathers
    Scalers
    Bucklemakers
    Horners
    } Pilate, Caiaphas, two soldiers, three Jews, Judas selling Jesus.

27. Bakers ...   ...
    { The paschal lamb, the Lord's supper, the xii Apostles, Jesus girt with a linen towel washing their feet; the institution of the Sacrament of Christ's Body in the New Law ; the communion of the Apostles.

28. Cordwaners
    { Pilate, Caiaphas, Annas, fourteen armed soldiers, Malchus, Peter, James, John, Jesus, and Judas kissing and betraying Him.

29. Bowyers
    Fletchers
    [Arrow-feather-ers]
    } Jesus, Annas, Caiaphas, and four Jews persecuting and scourging Jesus. Peter, the woman accusing Peter, and Malchus.

30. Tapisers
    Couchers
    } Jesus, Pilate, Annas, Caiaphas, two counsellors and four Jews accusing Christ.

31. Littesters ...
    { Herod, two counsellors, four soldiers, Jesus and three Jews.

32. Cooks
    Waterleaders
    } Pilate, Annas, Caiaphas, two Jews, and Judas bringing back to them the thirty pieces of silver.

33. Tilemakers
    Millers
    Turners
    Hayresters
    [Workers in Horse Hair?]
    Bollers
    [Bowlmakers?]
    } Jesus, Pilate, Caiaphas, Annas, six soldiers carrying spears and ensigns, and four others leading Jesus from Herod, desiring Barabbas to be released and Jesus to be crucified, and then binding and scourging him, placing a crown of thorns upon his head; three soldiers casting lots for the vest of Jesus.

34. Tunners   ...
    { Jesus, covered with blood, bearing His cross to Calvary ; Simon of Cyrene, Jews compelling him to bear the cross ; Mary, the mother of Jesus, the Apostle John informing her of the condemnation of her Son and of His journey to Calvary ; Veronica wiping blood and sweat from the face of Jesus with the napkin on which is imprinted Jesu's face ; and other women lamenting Jesus.

35. Pinners
    Latoners
    Painters
    { The Cross, Jesus stretched upon it on the earth, four Jews scourging and dragging Him with ropes, and afterwards uplifting the Cross and the body of Jesus nailed to it, on Mount Calvary.

36. **Butchers** **Poulterers**	The cross, two thieves crucified, Jesus hung on the cross between them, Mary the mother of Jesus, John, Mary, James and Salome. Longeus with a lance, a slave with a sponge, Pilate, Annas, Caiaphas, a centurion, Joseph of Arimathea and Nicodemus laying Him in the tomb.
37. **Sellers** [Saddlers] **Verrours** [Glaziers] **Fuystours** [Makers of Saddle Trees]	Jesus despoiling Hell, twelve spirits, six good and six bad.
38. **Carpenters** ...	Jesus rising from the tomb, four soldiers armed, and the three Maries lamenting. Pilate, Caiaphas [and Annas. A young man clad in white, sitting at the tomb, talking to the women].
39. **Winedrawers**	Jesus, Mary Magdalene with spices.
40. **Broggours** [Brokers.] **Woolpackers**	Jesus, Luke and Cleophas in the guise of pilgrims.
42. **Escriveners** **Luminers** [Illuminators] **Questors** [Pardoners] **Dubbers** [Refurbishers of cloths]	Jesus, Peter, John, James and other apostles. Thomas feeling the wounds of Jesus.
43. **Talliaunders** [Tailors]	Mary, John the Evangelist, two Angels, and eleven Apostles; Jesus ascending before them and four angels carrying a cloud.
44. **Potters** ...	Mary, two Angels, eleven Apostles, and the Holy Spirit descending on them, and four Jews in wonderment.
45. **Drapers** ...	Jesus, Mary, Gabriel with two angels, two virgins and three Jews of the kindred of Mary, eight Apostles, and two devils.
[Omitted in MS.] **Linen-weavers**	Four apostles carrying the bier of Mary; Fergus hanging upon the bier, with two other Jews, [and one angel].
46. **Weavers of Woollen**	Mary ascending with a crowd of Angels, eight Apostles, and Thomas the Apostle preaching in the desert.

47. **Hostlers**	...	Mary, Jesus crowning her, singing with a crowd of angels.
48. **Mercers**	...	Jesus, Mary, twelve Apostles, four angels with trumpets and four with a crown, a lance and two scourges; four good spirits and four evil spirits, and six devils.

The next cycle which we have to consider is that of the Towneley Plays, so called from the only known manuscript in which they exist having been long in the possession of the Towneley family, from whom it passed *via* Major E. Coates, M.P., into the H. E. Huntington Library. This cycle has also been quoted as the Widkirk, Woodkirk, or Wakefield plays. The authority for the name Widkirk is a tradition of the Towneley family (recorded by Mr. Douce in the Towneley Catalogue for 1814), by which the plays are supposed to have formerly 'belonged to the Abbey of Widkirk, near Wakefield, in the County of York.' Widkirk, however, as Prof. Skeat showed in the *Athenæum* of Dec. 2, 1893, is only an earlier spelling for Woodkirk, the old form naturally surviving in the mouths of the country people. Woodkirk itself is about four miles to the north of Wakefield, and here there was a cell of Augustinian Canons, in dependence on the house of St. Oswald, at Nostel. To these Canons, therefore, the plays were at one time assigned, though it would be difficult to find any reason for the attribution apart from the popular desire to trace as much medieval literature as possible to 'the monks.' With Wakefield the connection of these plays is beyond a doubt. Thus at the head of the first play in the series is written in a large hand 'Wakefelde, Barkers'; at the head of the second 'Glover Pag[eant]'; at the head of the third 'Wakefeld,' and before the play of the *Travellers to Emmaus* 'Fysher Pageant.' There is also an allusion (in the second play of the *Shepherds*) to the 'shroges,' or rough moorland of Horbery, a village two or three miles to the south-west of Wakefield. Plainly, therefore, several of these plays were acted by the Trades of Wakefield, and the trend of opinion is certainly in favour of regarding the whole cycle as the trade-plays of that town. It is certain in any case that the cycle is a composite one, as five of the plays reproduce, often in a corrupted form,

Nos. 11, 20, 37, 38, 48, in the York cycle, and the plays differ greatly in style and metre. Their composition must cover a wide range of time, those in the metre of the Shepherds' Play here printed being the latest of all. They were probably added at the beginning of the fifteenth century by a new editor of very unusual humour and dramatic power. The cycle, as we have it, consists of thirty-two plays, of which two, *The Raising of Lazarus* and *The Hanging of Judas*, are inserted at the end of the MS. out of their right order. Twelve leaves have been lost from the MS. at the end of the *Creation*, and another twelve after the *Ascension*, besides other probable losses. We can only note, therefore, that in our text there is nothing to answer to the York Plays 22, 23, 24 part i, 25–27, 29, 39, 44–47; but it is most probable that if a complete manuscript should ever be recovered its contents would be found to correspond very closely indeed to the York cycle. As compared with the other plays which have come down to us, these two Northern cycles are distinguished by their vigour and originality. They have little pathos, but much humour, and are especially rich in those interpolations on the Scripture narrative, in which the dramatists felt themselves freed from the restraints by which they were hampered in dealing with sacred personages.

Of the origin of the Chester cycle something has already been said, and a short account of the extant MSS. will be found in the notes to the two extracts here printed. The MSS. are all of them late, but they appear to be based on a text of the beginning of the fifteenth century. The composition of the cycle probably dates from some fifty or sixty years earlier. The fame of cycles appears to have spread to Chester, and to have awakened the ambition of a local playwright. As regards metre and form the cycle shows exceptional unity. It is mainly written in eight-line stanzas, the author, as Dr. Hohlfeld points out, at the beginning of each play making a manful attempt to content himself with two rimes (aaabaaab), but soon drifting into the use of three (aaabcccb). In some of the Chester plays

[1] *The Departure of the Israelites from Egypt; Christ with the Doctors in the Temple; The Harrowing of Hell; The Resurrection*, and *The Judgment.*

(notably in that of *Jesus in the Temple*) we can trace the influence of the Yorkshire cycles, and the play on the sacrifice of Isaac is closely connected with the Brome play on the same subject (see Appendix IV) first printed by Miss Toulmin Smith. But if it be true, as Professor Ten Brink suggests, that the Chester cycle is both less important and less original than those of York and Wakefield, and that its best, both of pathos and humour, appears to be borrowed, it must be allowed on the other hand that its author was possessed of an unusual share of good taste. There is less in the Chester plays to jar on modern feelings than in any other of the cycles. The humour is kept more within bounds, the religious tone is far higher, and though the plays are not spoilt by any obtrusive didacticism such as we find in the ' Coventry ' cycle, the speeches of the Expositor at the end of each play show that a real effort was made to serve the religious object to which all Miracle plays were ostensibly directed. On a comparison of the contents of this cycle with that of York we note that fresh subjects are introduced in the histories of Lot and of Balaam, in the play on Ezekiel, which contains prophecies of the end of the world and the Fifteen Signs of Doom, and in the very curious embodiment of the medieval legends on the coming of Antichrist. On the other hand, there is no play of the Exodus, the plays on the history of the Blessed Virgin are represented only by a *Salutation* and the *Nativity of Christ* (in the course of which the Emperor Octavian is introduced giving his orders for all the world to be taxed), and there is no play on the Assumption. Like those of York, the Chester plays were enacted by the members of the Trade-Gilds, not, however, on the feast of Corpus Christi, but at Whitsuntide.

The fourth cycle of plays which we have to consider is contained in a manuscript, the greater part of which was written in the year 1468, and which now belongs to the Cottonian Collection in the British Museum. On the fly-leaf of this manuscript, which was probably purchased by Sir Robert Cotton about 1630, is written in the handwriting of his librarian, Dr. Richard James, the following note:—*Contenta Novi Testamenti scenice expressa et actitata olim per monachos sive fratres mendicantes : vulgo dicitur hic liber Ludus Coventriæ, sive Ludus Corporis*

Christi: scribitur metris Anglicanis. Early allusions to plays acted 'by the Grey Friars at Coventry' are now referred to performances by the gilds *near* the Franciscan friary. It seems probable that James misunderstood the word *by*, and then rashly identified these plays with those supposed to have been performed by the Friars.

The lengthy prologue to these plays contains at its end a passage —

> A Sunday next, yf that we may,
> At six of the belle, we gynne our play
> In N—— towne;

which points to the performances of a strolling company. The list of the plays in the prologue, however, makes no mention of several which are found in the manuscript, and Dr. W. W. Greg has shown (*Problems of the English Miracle Plays*, 1914, pp. 108–43) that this must be regarded as a much revised amalgamation from three different sources, written in different metres, put together in 1468 for private reading, not for acting. The linguistic evidence connects this composite collection not with Coventry, but with the Eastern counties. As Prof. Ten Brink has pointed out (*Gesch. der alt. Eng. Litt.* § 275), the dialect and scribal peculiarities of these plays belong rather to the North-East Midlands than to the neighbourhood of Coventry, and in the fifteenth century, to the early part of which the composition of this cycle must be attributed, it was in the East-Midlands that the writers of Miracle plays and Moralities were most busily at work. In language, in metre, in tone, in the elaborate stage directions, in the proclamation of the play by the wandering banner-bearers or *vexillatores*, this composite collection is linked up with the later Miracle plays, such as the Croxton play on the *Sacrament*, and the play of *Mary Magdalen*, and with the early Moralities such as the *Castell of Perseverance*, all of which are of East-Midland origin, and to the East-Midlands I have no doubt that it must now be assigned.[1] As divided by its editor, Mr. Halliwell Phillipps, the cycle consists of forty-two plays, which, as we learn from a passage in the twenty-ninth,

---

[1] It is worth noting in this connection that the beautiful speech of Christ on the Resurrection morning, beginning 'Earthly man that I have wrought,' is taken almost word for word from the old East-Midland dramatic poem of the *Harrowing of Hell*.

were not all of them performed in any one year. Comparing the plays with those of the York cycle, we note that a long didactic play on the Giving of the Law takes the place of that of the Exodus (11), that the thirteenth York play is expanded into a series of seven, dealing with the history of S. Joseph and the Blessed Virgin up to the time of the Nativity, that there is no play on the Transfiguration, and that the three York plays on the Death of Mary, her Appearance to St. Thomas, Assumption and Coronation, are represented by a single long play on the Assumption. In this cycle the didactic speeches elsewhere assigned to a 'Doctor' or 'Expositor' are delivered by an allegorical personage called Contemplacio. Death is personified, and a play on the Salutation is prefaced by a long prologue in heaven, in which the speakers are (besides Deus Pater and Deus Filius), Veritas, Misericordia, Justicia, and Pax[1]. This tendency towards the personification of abstract ideas is a mark of late date in the history of the Miracle play, and helps to link this cycle to the earlier Moralities, of which we shall soon proceed to speak. Taken as a whole[2], these so-called Coventry plays show the least dramatic power of any of the four cycles which we have examined. Their interest is mainly didactic, and they are especially concerned with the doctrine of the Holy Trinity and with the honour due to the Blessed Virgin. But they are not without vigour, and their refusal of humorous episodes is not to be reckoned against them.

§ 4.

In the English Miracle plays which we have been examining, as in the religious dramas of other European countries, two distinct centres of interest offer themselves for examination. The student of the history of religious thought will investigate the respective influences in the composition of these plays of the Bible narrative, the Apocryphal Gospels, and the Medieval Legends. He will be interested in the position assigned to the

---

[1] This scene, which forms one of our extracts, closely resembles one at the end of the *Castell of Perseverance*. A similar heavenly conference occurs in the French *Mystère du Vieil Testament* in a play on the sacrifice of Isaac.

[2] Some exceptions must be made. Thus the plays on the *Woman taken in Adultery* and the *Death of Herod* are both vividly dramatic.

Blessed Virgin, in the reality with which the truths of the Christian Faith have been apprehended, and in the underlying meaning of the irreverence and prurience with which the most sacred subjects are occasionally handled. This is a line of investigation well worthy of pursuit, but which the scope of this volume absolutely forbids. Such an investigation must take as its field the whole remains of the religious drama in this country, viewed in connection with the contemporary literature both at home and abroad. Nor could its results be adequately supported except by selections at least ten times as long as those which are here presented. For us, therefore, the interest of these plays comes primarily from their dramatic side, and their importance in the history of medieval thought can only be made the subject of incidental illustration. It is this principle which has come to our help in the selection of typical extracts, which otherwise would have been a task of almost insuperable difficulty. Thus our first extract (The Creation, and Fall of Lucifer) may be taken as exemplifying the power of these primitive playwrights in developing a great historical situation; the second, that of Noah's Flood, their development of a humorous incident (the controversy between Noah and his wife) within the limits of the Miracle play proper; while our third extract, on the Sacrifice of Isaac, exhibits the treatment of the most tragic and pathetic incident, with one exception, with which the playwrights were concerned. They may thus be taken as representing the nearest approach which the religious drama could properly make to the Histories, Comedies, and Tragedies of the great days of Elizabeth, an approach so distant as to demonstrate that had all foreign influences been excluded, the development of the drama in England would have been almost indefinitely delayed. Yet our fourth extract, the Shepherd's Play (No. 2) from the Towneley manuscript, may give us reason to believe that, however great the time which would have been needed for its unaided evolution, the seed, at least of Comedy, had reached a considerable stage of development before the influence of classical and Italian models quickened the progress of the drama to a speed in which the shares of its respective factors becomes difficult to distinguish.

In any exhaustive treatment of the history of the Miracle

play, one of the most important lines of investigation would be concerned with the characters with whom the medieval dramatist felt himself free to deal as he pleased. These characters are almost exclusively those of persons to whom neither Scripture nor legend ascribed either name or individuality. Cain's 'Garcio' or Servant, Noah's Wife, the Detractors of the Blessed Virgin, the Shepherds, the Soldiers sent to slay the Holy Innocents, the Pharisees who brought before Christ the Woman taken in Adultery, the Woman's Lover, the Beadle of Pilate's Court, the Workmen who set up the Cross, the Soldiers who watch at the Tomb,—it is in the treatment of these nameless characters that some of the most dramatic touches are bestowed. They are obviously introduced for the sake of relief, and in the York plays it is in the intervals of the torturing and crucifixion of Christ that these interludes, all more or less humorous, are most frequently introduced. Pilate toys with his wife in open court, and to the intense amusement of the spectators is reproved by his Beadle, just before Jesus is led in fresh from the buffettings in the Hall of Annas; the despair of Judas is followed by a scene in which a Squire is cheated of his title-deeds to Calvary-Locus; the soldiers who set up the Cross wrangle together through a hundred lines over their work. These interludes are to us at times inexpressibly painful, but dramatically they are good art, and were welcomed by their spectators as a relief to the extreme tension of feeling which the protracted exhibition of Christ's Passion could not fail to excite. On the same principle the rough sport of the Shepherds is made to introduce the touching scenes of the Manger Bed at Bethlehem, and it is to this desire for dramatic relief that we owe the story of Mak and his sheep-stealing, our first English Comedy.

§ 5.

If of all the sacred dramas of whose performance in England we possess a record the full text had been handed down to us, the field for investigation would have been so vast as to frighten rather than attract enquirers[1]. There is, however, at least one

---

[1] This seems to have happened in France, where, according to Mr. Stoddart's Bibliography, fifteen MSS. containing plays or cycles, extending from 4000 to 37,000 lines apiece, are still awaiting a printer.

play of which the most faint-hearted student must bitterly regret
the loss. 'Once on a time[1],' we are told, 'a play setting forth
the goodness of the Lord's Prayer was played in the city of
York; in which play all manner of vices and sins were held up
to scorn, and the virtues were held up to praise.' This play is
alluded to by Wyclif[2], and we have a few details respecting a
gild which was formed in York for the special purpose of its
maintenance. In her introduction to the *York Plays*, Miss Lucy
Toulmin Smith describes a compotus Roll of this gild *Oracionis
domini*, 'dated Michaelmas, 1399, which shows that there were
then over 100 members and their wives, and that they possessed
rents and receipts amounting to £26 5s. 11½d.' The Roll
contains a special mention of a *ludus Accidie* 'holding up to
scorn' the vice of sluggardy. The gild was dissolved by
Henry VIII, but in 1558 the play was performed at the expense of the city in place of the Corpus Christi plays, and this
happened again in 1572. In that year, however, Grindal was
Archbishop of York, and demanded that a copy of the play
should be submitted to him. The copy was sent, and its return
requested three years later, but thenceforward we hear of it no
more. The loss is irreparable, for this is the earliest *Morality
Play* of which we have any mention, and must have preceded
by some forty years the *Castell of Perseverance*, its earliest
extant successor. Besides the play of the *Lord's Prayer*, we
know of the performance at York of a *Creed Play*, which also
must have been rather a Morality than a Miracle play. 'It was
performed,' Miss Smith tells us, 'about Lammas-tide every
tenth year, and five such performances, beginning in 1483, are
recorded; the last of these, in 1535, superseded the usual
Corpus Christi plays. A performance was proposed in 1568,
but the question was referred to Dean Hutton, whose opinion
was adverse, and we know nothing more as to the play.'

The loss of these two plays of the *Lord's Prayer* and the
Creed cannot be too deeply regretted; we may be grateful,

---

[1] *English Gilds*, by Toulmin Smith, p. 137, Preamble to ordinances
of Gild of the Lord's Prayer. (Quoted by Miss Toulmin Smith).

[2] '& herfore freris han tauȝt in Englond þe Paternoster in Engliȝcsh
tunge, as men seyen in þe playe of Yorke,' *De officio pastorali*. Cap. XV
(written about 1378), ed. F. D. Matthew for E. E. T. S.

however, even for the bare record of their existence, which helps us to a clearer notion of the origin and nature of the Morality play than we could otherwise obtain. In its later development the Morality became dull, narrow, and essentially sectarian, and its heavy didactics were only relieved by the insertion of scenes of low humour, of which the humourousness is far from apparent. But in its earlier days the Morality was not wholly unworthy to be ranked with the Miracle plays, to which it formed a complement. The Miracle play takes as its basis the historical books of the Bible and the legends of the Church, but these alone do not furnish a complete answer to the questions 'What must I do—What must I believe—to be saved?' and in the two centuries during which the popularity of the sacred drama was at its height, various plays were written in which the moral and sacramental teaching of the Church are assigned the prominence which in the Miracle play is occupied by its history. We know that in the play of the *Lord's Prayer* 'all manner of vices and sins were held up to scorn, and the virtues were held up to praise,' and in the contest between the personified powers of good and evil, the Seven Cardinal Virtues and the Seven Deadly Sins, for the possession of man's soul, we have the essence of the Morality play. This contest naturally involved the use of personifications, for the medieval playwright was too simple-minded to anticipate the method of Ben Jonson, by representing men and women living human lives with human relationships, and at the same time embodying a single humour or quality, to the exclusion of all others. We must not, however, regard the use of personification as involving a dramatic advance. It was essential to the scheme of the Morality, and must have been present no less in the fourteenth century plays, of which we hear at York, than in their successors. In itself, as tending to didacticism and unreality, personification is wholly undramatic, and the popularity of the later Morality significantly coincides with the dullest and most barren period in the history of English literature.

It is remarkable that most of the early Morality plays which have come down to us, together with the contemporary Miracle plays, to which they exhibit the closest affinity, are connected with the East-Midland district, throughout which, during the fifteenth century, the popularity of the religious drama appears to have been very great. Reasons have already been assigned for connecting with this district the cycle of Miracle plays usually attributed to the Grey Friars of Coventry, and in this cycle the influence of the Morality is shown in the personifications in the Council in Heaven (quoted in our specimens), and in the appearance of Death at the Court of Herod, and also in the unflinching didacticism which devoted an entire scene to an exposition of the Ten Commandments. The play of *S. Mary Magdalen*, from which also extracts are given in this volume, shows even stronger proofs of the influence of the Morality in the appearance of Good Angel and Bad Angel, and of the World and the Flesh as no less real personages than the Devil himself. Again, the Croxton play of the *Sacrament*, which should certainly be connected with the Norfolk rather than with any other Croxton, although not a Morality and introducing no personifications, is yet allied to the Morality in its endeavour to bring the sacramental teaching of the Church within the scope of the religious drama. The subject of the play and its treatment by the dramatist are both so painful that it is difficult to award this drama the attention which, as dealing with a modern legend and introducing almost contemporary characters, it in some respects deserves. The medieval hatred of the Jews gave rise to a succession of legends of their obtaining possession of the Consecrated Host, and by fire and sword endeavouring to torture afresh the Christ believed by devout worshippers to be there present. In a Yorkshire church a fresco has recently been uncovered in which is commemorated such an attempt on the part of some Flemish Jews in the fourteenth century. The Croxton play[1] deals with a miracle 'don in the forest of Aragon. In the famous cite Eraclea, the yere of ow^r lord God m.cccc.lxi.' It introduces Aristorius, a Christian merchant, who for one hundred pounds procures the Host for the Jews ; Ser Isoder, his chaplain ; Jonathas, Jason, Jasdon, Masphat and Malchus, five Jews, of whom the first is the chief ; a Bishop, and a Quack

---

[1] Edited by Mr. Whitley Stokes, from the MS. in Trinity College, Dublin, in the Appendix to the *Transactions of the Philological Society* for 1860, 61.

Doctor[1], with Colle, his servant, who are called in to heal the
hand of Jonathas, withered as a result of his sacrilege, and
indulge in much buffoonery. The play has absolutely nothing
to recommend it. It is without dignity, pathos or dramatic
power, and its incongruous humour is of the lowest kind. Only
one other point need be noted in connection with it, that its
performance, although localised at Croxton (whether perma-
nently or not, we cannot say), was announced throughout the
neighbouring villages by *vexillatores* or banner-bearers, of the
same kind as those who advertised the plays of the itinerant
actors who represented the ' Coventry ' cycle and the *Castell of
Perseverance.*

§ 6.

We at length approach the consideration of the earliest extant
Morality play, the *Castell of Perseverance.* This is important
not only for its date (*c.* 1405, see p. 198), but for the completeness
with which it develops the central ideas underlying all the
plays of this class. Thus in the initial proclamation the second
banner-bearer announces :

> The cause of our comynge you to declare
> Every man in hymself for sotne he it may fynde,
> Whou mankynde into this world born is ful bare
> And bare schal beryed be at the last ende ;
> God hym *y*evyth two aungel ful *y*ep and ful *y*are,
> The good aungel and the badde to hym for to lende ;
> The goode techyth hym goodnesse, the badde synne and sare,
> Whanne the ton hath the victory the tother goth behende.
> Be skyll
> The goode aungel coveytyth evermore man's salvacion,
> And the badde bysyteth hym euere to hys dampnacion,
> And God hathe gevyn man fre arbitracion
> Whether he wyl hym[self] save hy[s soul?].

His comrades take up the story :

> Spylt is man speciously whanne he to synne assent,
> The bad aungel thanne bryngeth hym iij enmys so stout,
> The werlde, the Fende, the foul Flesche, so joly and jent ;
> Thei ledyn hym fful lustyly with synnys al abowt.

---

[1] The appearance of the Quack Doctor is particularly interesting,
because of his survival in the Christmas mummings and plays of St.
George and the Dragon, which are still acted in some country villages.

To trace the spiritual history of *Humanum Genus* (Mankind, or the Typical Man) from the day of his birth to his appearance at the Judgment Seat of God, to personify the foes by whom his pathway is beset, the Guardian Angel by whose help he resists them, and the ordinances of Confession and Penance by which he is strengthened in his conflict, this was the playwright's object; and, however dramatically impossible, it was certainly a worthy one. The opening pageant of *Mundus*, *Belyal* and *Caro*, the World, the Devil, and the Flesh, each boasting of his might; the appearance of *Humanum Genus*, naked save for the chrism cloth on his head, and conscious of his helplessness; the first struggle for his soul of his Good and Bad Angels, and the victory of the latter, make up an impressive prologue, which ends with the lament of *Bonus Angelus*, chanted to music:

> Mankynde hath forsakyn me,
> Alas, man, for love of the!
> Ya for this gamyn and this gle
> Thou schalt groechyn and grone.

In the next division of the play Mankind is presented to *Mundus*, to whom he professes allegiance, and is confided to the care of Pleasure, Folly, and Backbiting (*Voluptas*, *Stultitia*, *Detraccio*), and ultimately to *Belial* and *Caro*, and the Seven Deadly Sins, each of whom enters with an appropriate speech. Then Mankind's Good Angel calls to his aid *Confessio* and *Schrift*, and with the help of *Penitencia* the sinner is converted and reconciled, and safely lodged in the Castle of Perseverance, there to await the fresh assaults of his enemies. These are not long delayed. In what we may call Act III, *Detraccio* brings the news of Mankind's conversion to *Caro*, and after brief counsel they report what has happened to *Mundus*. But if the forces of Hell are mustering, those of Heaven are not idle. *Caritas*, *Abstinencia*, *Castitas*, *Solicitudo*, *Largitas*, and *Humilitas*, successively come on the scene, each with his exhortation. That of *Solicitudo* is perhaps the best worth quoting, and may serve as a specimen of the rest:

> In besynesse man loke thou be
> With worthi werkes goode and thykke,
> To slawthe if thou cast the
> It schal the drawe to thoutes wyckke.

It puttyth a man to pouerte
And pullyth hym to peynys prycke.
Do sumwhat alwey for love of me,
Thou thou schuldyst but thwyte a stycke.
    With bedys sumtyme the blys,
Sum tyme rede and sum tyme wryte,
And sum tyme pleye at thi delyte;
The devyl the waytyth with dyspyte,
    Whanne thou art in Idylnesse.

But the *Deadly Sins* are advancing to the attack, led by *Belial*, whose banner is borne by *Pride*, while *Caro* is apparently on horseback, and *Gula* flourishes a long lance. The Virtues meet their assault with roses [1], the emblem of Christ's Passion, and the Vices are driven back. Then *Mundus* calls *Avaritia* or *Covetyse* to the rescue, and by him *Humanum Genus* is lured from the Castle. Old Age is creeping upon him, and he yields to its besetting sin :

Penyman best may spede,
He is a duke to don a dede

is his argument, and, despite the laments of his Good Angel and the warnings of *Solicitudo* and *Largitas*, he gives himself over to sin, and the division of the play ends with the exultation of *Mundus* over his fall.

In Act IV (the divisions are my own) *Humanum Genus* receives his reward in the shape of a thousand marks. To the gift, however, there is a stipulation attached :

Lene no man hereof for no karke,
Thou he schuld hange be the throte,
Monk nor frere, prest nor clerke,
Ne helpe therwith chyrche nor cote,
    Tyl deth thi body delve.
Thou he schuld sterve in a cave,
Lete no pore man therof have,
In grene gras tyl thou be grave
    Kepe sum what for thi selve.

---

[1] Thus *Ira*, after threatening *Patientia* with 'styffe stones,' presently cries out :

I am al beten blak and blo
With a rose that on rode was rent.

The money is hid in the ground and there abides. But Death is making ready to strike *Humanum Genus* down, and *Mundus* sends *Garcio* to claim the money as his inheritance.

> What devyl! thou art not of my kyn,
> Thou dedyst me nevere no maner good,
> I hadde lever sum nyfte, or sum cosyn,
> Or sum man hadde it of my blod:
> I trowe the werld be wod

is the exclamation of *Humanum Genus*, but he laments in vain. Bereft of his goods and in terror for his soul, he awaits Death, and amid his prayers to *Misericordia* and the gibes of his Bad Angel his spirit takes its flight, to become in the 'fifth Act' the subject of an argument in heaven between *Misericordia, Justitia, Veritas, and Pax*, similar to the one quoted from the 'Coventry' plays. 'Lete hym drynke as he brewyit' is the plea of Justice, but Mercy appeals to Christ's Passion, and the decision of *Pater sedens in trono* is merciful.

The *Castell of Perseverance* cannot escape the charge of prolixity. At a rough guess it contains about 3500 lines, nearly as many as all but the longest of Shakespeare's tragedies. The language, again, is without grace, and too often sacrifices clearness to the desire for alliteration. But with all its faults the play is a fine one, dealing with man's salvation in no unimpressive fashion, and distinguished by a logical development and unity of purpose, which is found in the great cycles of Miracle plays when regarded as dramatic entities, but nowhere else. As the stage directions, quoted in the short Introduction in the Notes, sufficiently show, it was intended to be presented with something of the elaborateness of the Miracle plays, and it is altogether a very noteworthy production. The manuscript of which it forms part, and which by the kindness of its owner, Mr. Gurney, I had the pleasure in 1904 of helping Dr. Furnivall to edit for the Early English Text Society, contains also two other plays, the examination of which need not detain us long[1]. They are full of interesting points, but are inferior in every way to the

---

[1] The manuscript of these plays has also itself been excellently reproduced by the collotype process for Mr. J. S. Farmer. The title by which they are generally known, the Macro Moralities, is due to their having once belonged to a Mr. Cox Macro.

play we have been considering. The first of them is called by
Mr. Collier *Mind, Will, and Understanding*, but by Dr.
Furnivall[1] *A Morality of the Wisdom that is Christ. Ever-
lasting Wisdom* discourses to *Anima* on the means of grace,
Mind, Wyll, and *Understanding* declare themselves as the
three parts of the soul, and are seduced by *Lucyfer* in the guise
of a 'proud gallant.' When they have loudly expressed their
determination to be wicked *Wisdom* re-enters, and with *Wisdom
Anima*, now 'in the most horrible wyse, fowlere than a fende,'
and with little devils running from under her skirts. *Mind,
Wyll*, and *Understanding* are converted, and *Wisdom* delivers
a long discourse on the nine works specially pleasing to God.
A curious passage on the evils of the age, especially the practice
of maintenance, forms the most noteworthy portion of the text of
the play, but it is probable that the spectators were best pleased
with the rich dresses of the actors, and the dumb shows by
which the representation was diversified. Thus in one part of
the play a procession was formed of the *Five Wyttes* (or, as we
should say, *five senses*) as 'five vyrgynes, with kertyllys and
mantelys, and chevelers and chappelettes,' singing an anthem,
'and they goyng befor, *Anima* next, and her folowynge *Wysdom*,
and aftyr hym *Mynde, Wyll*, and *Undyrstondynge*, all iii in
wyght cloth of golde, cheveleryde and crestyde in sute ;' and in
another place there enters a dumb show of 'six dysgysyde in
the sute of *Mynde*,' viz. *Indignation, Sturdiness, Malice, Hasti-
ness, Revenge* (or *Wreche*) and *Discord*, 'with rede berdes and
lyons rampaunt on here crestes and yche a warder in his honde.'
Apart from these scenic diversions the play must have been dull
enough, for of dramatic action there is none, and the speeches
are terribly long and didactic.

The third play in Mr. Gurney's MS., called by Mr. Collier
Mankind, is the least seriously didactic of the Moralities. It
tells of a struggle between *Mercy* and *Mischief* for the soul
of *Mankind*. *Mischief* is aided by *Nought, New Gyse* and
Nowadays, whose assaults *Mankind* repulses by a threat to
'ding' them with his spade. But when *Titivillus*, a more potent
devil, appears on the scene, *Mankind* yields to his temptations,

---

[1] In his edition for the New Shakspere Society of a part of the play
as it survives in the Digby MS.

declaring 'Of labure and preyere I am nere yrke of both.'
Mischief triumphs over *Mercy*, and *Mankind* is nearly persuaded
to hang himself, but is rescued and reconciled by *Mercy*. This
play was probably written in the early spring of 1471, and we
shall have to speak of it again as foreshadowing the development
of the Interlude and the less distinctively religious Moralities.

Of Moralities handed down to us in printed editions, that of
Everyman, though now known to be only a translation from the
Dutch *Elkerlijk*, claims the first place. It was printed at least
four times early in the 16th century, twice by Richard Pynson
and twice by John Skot. Though planned on a far less extensive
scale than the *Castell of Perseverance*, it is distinguished by the
same breadth of motive as the earlier play, and both in language
and treatment it is thoroughly dramatic. Its plot, as Prof.
Ten Brink has noted, is derived from the old Buddhist parable
known to Europeans through the legend of Barlaam and
Josaphat. The extracts given in the present volume are so long,
comprising nearly half the play, that no further analysis is
needed. It is sufficient here to note its prominent introduction
of Catholic teaching on the subject of the seven sacraments,
and its exaltation of the priesthood.

> For preesthode excedeth all other thynge;
> To us holy scripture they do teche
> And converteth man fro synne heven to reche;
> God hath to them more power gyven
> Than to any aungell that is in heven.
>
> ll. 728, sqq.

And again—

> Ther is no emperour, kyng, duke ne baron,
> That of God hath commissyon,
> As hath the leest preest in the worlde beynge,
> For of the blessed sacramentes pure and benynge
> He bereth the kayes, and thereof hath cure
> For mannes redempcion, it is ever sure.
>
> ll. 709, sqq.

Prof. Ten Brink is inclined to place this play as early as the
reign of Edward IV, and it is certain that it must have been
composed before the end of the 15th century.

Only once again, in 'a proper new interlude of the *World and
the Child*, otherwise called *Mundus et Infans*,' do we find the

Morality concerned with issues that touch the whole of human nature. Though called a 'new interlude' when printed by Wynkyn de Worde in 1522, this remarkable play, by its language, its strong alliteration, and its bragging speeches, cast almost in Herod's vein, is manifestly of a much earlier date, and cannot be assigned to a later reign than that of Henry VII. It traces the career of man through its successive stages of Infancy, Boyhood, Youth, Manhood, and Age. In Infancy he is called by his mother Dalliance, in Boyhood *Mundus* gives him the name of Wanton, in Youth he is called Love-Lust and Liking. When 'one and twenty winter is comen and gone' *Mundus* thus addresses him (Roxburghe Club reprint, 1817):

Now welcome, Love-Lust and Lykynge !
For thou hast ben obedyent to my byddynge
I encreace the in all thynge,
And myghty I make the a man.

Manhode Myghty shall be thy name.
Bere the prest in every game,
And wayte well that thou suffre no shame,
Neyther for londe nor for rente :
Yf ony man wolde wayte the with blame,
Withstonde hym with thy hole entent
Full sharpely thou bete hym to shame
With doughtynesse of dede :

For of one thynge, Manhode, I warne the
I am moost of bounte,
For seven kynges sewen me
Bothe by daye and nyght.
One of them is the kynge of pryde,
The kynge of envy, doughty in dede,
The kynge of wrathe that boldely wyll abyde,
For mykyll is his myght.

The kynge of covet[ise] is the fourte :
The fyfte kynge he hyght slouthe,
The kynge of glotony hath no Jolyte
There poverte is pyght :
Lechery is the seventh kynge,
All men in hym have grete delytynge,
Therfore worshyp hym above all thynge,
Manhode with all thy myght.

Manhood promises obedience to *Mundus* in all things, but now
Conscience comes on the scene and *Manhood* is persuaded,
though not without considerable reluctance, to profess himself
his servant. His conversion, however, is very half-hearted,
for he says of *Mundus,*

> But yet wyll I hym not forsake,
> For mankynde he dothe mery make:
> Thoughe the worlde and conscyence be at debate,
> Yet the worlde will I not despyse,
> For bothe in chyrche and in chepynge,
> And in other places beynge,
> The world fyndeth me all thynge
> And dothe me grete servyse.

Weakened by this determination to serve two masters, *Mankind*
falls an easy victim to the wiles of *Folly*, and it is not until his
name is changed to *Age* that he learns the lessons of *Perseverance*, and receives from him his final appellation, *Repentance*.
There is little action about the play, and such rough eloquence
as it may have originally possessed, is sadly marred by the
obvious imperfections of the form in which it has come down to
us. It remains, however, a notable play, and stands a head
and shoulders higher than any of its successors.

§ 7.

Since the fifth edition of this book in 1914 the rediscovery of
Medwall's *Fulgens and Lucres* has rehabilitated the old explanation of an Interlude as a play interposed in the pauses of some
other entertainment, in opposition to the meaning assigned to it
by Sir E. K. Chambers (*The Mediaeval Stage,* ii. 181 sq.) of
a play in dialogue between two or more performers. *Fulgens*
was written about 1495 by Thomas Medwall, chaplain to Cardinal
Morton, to be played in two parts in a hall, between three bouts
of eating and drinking, to which the guests are liberally invited.
Medwall's other extant interlude, *Nature*, is also in two parts,
no doubt with the same intention. The two plays thus stand at
the head of the movement of the drama during this period, from
the publicity of the street to the halls of large houses, or in fine
weather to a stage in a garden. Except when in two parts the
new plays seldom greatly exceed a thousand lines, they required

no stage accessories, and could mostly be performed by from four to six players dividing the parts among them. The later Moralities, while remaining didactic, compromise with the new style. In place of the whole of man's life in its relation to its eternal issues, they deal with mere fragments of it, and their moral teaching is confined to exhortations against the besetting sins of youth, and to the praise of learning and studiousness. In other plays for the sacramental teaching of the Church there is substituted the Reformation controversy, and these polemics of the stage were carried to such a length as to draw down on themselves the royal prohibition. The word *Interlude* reminds us of the more trivial nature of these later performances, from which, however, most of the popular ideas about Morality plays have usually been derived [1].

The 'Enterlude of Hycke-scorner,' which, as printed by Wynkyn de Worde, may be reckoned as one of the earliest specimens of the new Moralities, is in many respects a good example of its class. It opens with a colloquy between *Pity* and *Contemplation*, who are soon joined by *Perseverance*. They lament together over the wickedness of the times, and their place is then taken by *Freewill* and *Imagination*, who recount to each other the pranks they have been playing in

---

[1] An example of this confusion is to be found in the prominence assigned in all accounts of the *Morality* to the character of the *Vice*, to whom allusion is made by Ben Jonson in his *Staple of News*, ii. 1, and *The Devil is an Ass*, i. 1, and by other Elizabethan writers. In the *Morality* proper the Vice has no part, but when the desire was felt for some humourous relief in the didactic interludes, a character probably dressed in the traditional garb of the domestic Fool was introduced and attained great popularity. The etymology of the name is doubtful, for in Heywood's *Play of the Wether* (1534), one of the earliest instances in which the Vice is specifically mentioned by name, he plays the part of *Mery Report*, who is a jester pure and simple, without any connection with any of the deadly sins. So in *Jack Juggler*, *Jack* himself is called the Vice, and in *Godly Queen Hester* (1561) the name is given to a jester called *Hardy Dardy*. In other plays, however, the part of the Vice is assigned to characters such as *Sin, Fraud, Inclination, Ambition,* &c., and the list given in the *Devil is an Ass* (Fraud or Covetousness, or lady Vanity, or old Iniquity), confirms the theory that the obvious etymology is the true one.

very unseemly language. To them enters *Hickscorner*, a traveller, who soon proves himself a worthy comrade. He comes to blows, however, with *Imagination*, and *Pity* returns to help keep the peace. The three knaves, indignant at his intervention, bind him and go their ways. *Pity* is released by *Perseverance* and *Contemplation*, and goes in quest of his adversaries. Meanwhile *Freewill* has been imprisoned in Newgate for 'conveying' a cup, but has been delivered by *Imagination*. He is now confronted by *Perseverance* and *Contemplation*, who effect his conversion by their arguments. *Imagination* again appears on the scene, at first only to scoff, but in a little while he too is converted, and in this edifying manner the play ends. *Hickscorner*, it will be noted, after whom the interlude is named, disappears altogether unnoticed, and there is no single dramatic touch in the whole production. The play, however, must have enjoyed a fairly long life, for the author of an *Interlude of Youth*, printed by Waley, probably in the reign of Mary, took it as his model, and incorporated whole sentences from it into his own work. With *Hickscorner* and *Youth* may be classified 'an enterlude,' printed both by Vele and by William Copland, 'called Lusty Juuentus, lyuely describing the frailtie of youth: of natur prone to vyce: by grace and good counsayll traynable to vertue.' This very dull play, only relieved by two rather good songs, was the work of a vehemently Protestant author. The characters are—a *Messenger*, *Lusty Juuentus*, *Good Counsaill*, *Knowledge*, *Sathan the deuyll*, *Hypocrisie*, *Felowship*, *Abhominable Lyuyng*, *God's Merciful Promises*, and their names sufficiently indicate the general course of the plot. *Juventus* is nourished in the strictest principles of the Reformation, until by direction of *Satan*, *Hypocrisy*, under the name of *Friendship*, leads him first into heresy and from heresy into unclean living, from which he is finally rescued by his former friends *Good Counsaill* and *Knowledge*.

Although the moral plays mentioned above seem to modern readers dull and very unsuitable for performance in the pauses of a feast they and their like enjoyed a long popularity. The chief attempts to supply something different which have come down to us are all connected with a single circle, that of Sir Thomas More, the centrality of More and the intimacy of the connexion having been brought out in a series of papers published during the six years (1917–23) by Dr. A. W. Reed, giving the results of researches which have enlarged knowledge and cleared up difficulties at a dozen different points [1].

We get a kind of overture to this limited revolt in the morality of *Mankind*, the latest in date of the three *Macro Plays* discussed in our last section. In the light-hearted introduction which, at the bidding of Dr. Furnivall, I contributed to the Early English Text Society's edition in 1904, I suggested 'about 1475' as the date of *Mankind*. In an excellent paper on the play (*Some notes on* Mankind. *Modern Philology*, xiv. 45–58, 101, 121) Mr. W. K. Smart gave reasons for believing that it was written for performance on Shrove Tuesday, 26 February 1471. He also identified as local magnates in Cambridgeshire and Norfolk a number of persons named in the play as to be asked, or not to be asked, to give money to the performers, and Mr. Reed (in ignorance of Mr. Smart's paper) has lately found out more about them. When I wrote my introduction in 1904, I deduced from the play that the four (or three) men and three lads who played it were strolling players, and that the performance was given in the yard of an inn. It now seems to me more likely that the players were amateurs, possibly amateurs with the impecuniosity of youth, and that the play

---

[1] John Heywood and his friends. *The Library*, 3rd series, vol. viii, July and September 1917.

The Canon of John Heywood's Plays. *The Library*, 3rd series, vol. ix, January and April 1918.

John Rastell's Plays. *The Library*, 3rd series, vol. x, January 1919.

John Rastell, printer, lawyer, venturer, dramatist, and controversialist. *Transactions of the Bibliographical Society*, vol. xv, 1920. (Read to the Society, 19 November 1917.)

The Beginnings of the English Secular and Romantic Drama. A paper read before the Shakespeare Association, 29 February 1920. Published by Humphrey Milford, 1922.

The Editor of the English Works of Sir Thomas More. (William Rastell). *The Library*, 4th series, vol. iv, June 1923.

The matter of all these in a revised form is now available in Dr. Reed's *The Early Tudor Drama*. (Methuen, 1926.)

was written and acted by a group of friends, who gave their
entertainment the form of a *Morality* because it was the lightest
form they knew, but who resented being obliged to preach when
they only wished to amuse. The theme of the play is the
usual contest for the tutelage of the man-in-the-street, here
called *Mankynde*, the opposing parties being *Mercy* on the one
hand and on the other two major combatants *Myscheff* and
Tutivillus (who we might think of as the vice and the devil only
they are never on the stage together, and may have been performed by the same actor) and their three satellites, *Nought*,
New-gyse, and *Now-a-days*, probably played by lads. The
character of *Mercy* is occasionally taken seriously, but he is
deliberately made to talk ' Englysch Laten ' of which the
satellites make fun, even to the point of giving him a ribald
sentence and bidding him :

> Now opyn yowur sachell with Laten wordis
> And sey me this in clerycall manere.

Also when *Mankynde* is under the influence of *Mercy* he is made
ridiculous by being given polysyllables of the same sort. On
the other hand, though *Myscheff* and the rest are unspeakably
ribald, they not only have a wholesome objection to Latin
English, but are more mischievous than wicked, even *Tutivillus*,
as to whom the spectators are told that they must pay hand-
somely ' yf ye wyll se hys abhomynabull presens,' is not above
such a simple trick as hiding a board at the place where *Mankind*, with patently self-conscious virtue (' to eschew ydullnes,
I do yt myn own selffe '), is about to dig. We thus find ourselves
confronted with a group who could not take the Morality seriously,
and it is interesting to find that one of the local magnates
mentioned by the satellites when they are thinking from whom
contributions may be levied is ' master Alyngton of Botysam,'
the Allingtons of Bottisham in Cambridgeshire being, Mr. Reed
tells me, close family friends of the Mores.

If our overture seems some way off we get nearer to More in
Medwall's *Fulgens and Lucres*. Of this the only surviving copy
(save two leaves at the British Museum) was sold for £3,400 in
a sale of early plays belonging to Lord Mostyn in March 1919,
and acquired by Mr. Henry E. Huntington for his library at

San Gabriel, California [1]. From the two leaves at the Museum
the play had already been identified by Robert Proctor as
printed by John Rastell (More's brother-in-law), and by Professor Creizenach as based on the *De Vera Nobilitate* of Bonus
Accursius, or Bonaccorso, of Pistoia, who died in 1429. Just
before the sale in 1919 Mr. Reed found the immediate source of
the play in an English version of this translated by John Tiptoft,
Earl of Worcester, from the French rendering by Jean Mielot,
secretary of Philip of Burgundy. The French rendering had
been printed by Colard Mansion, Caxton's associate, at Bruges,
and the English was printed by Caxton himself in 1481 at the
end of the Earl of Worcester's translations of Cicero's *De Amicitia*
and *De Senectute*. The title of Rastell's edition of the play
reads :

❡ Here is cõteyned a godely interlude of Fulgens / Cenatoure of
Rome. Lucres his doughter. Gayus / flaminius & Publi*us* Corneli*us*
of the disputacyon of / noblenes, & is deuyded in two pa*r*tyes to be
played at / ii. tymes. Cõpyled by mayster Henry medwall, late /
chapelayne to yᵉ ryght reuerent fader in god Johan / Morton cardynall
& Archebysshop of Cau*n*terbury.

And it ends with the colophon : ❡ Emprinted at london by
Johan rastell dwellynge on the south syde of paulys chyrche by
syde paulys cheyne. Now it was in Morton's household that
Thomas More grew up, and according to his son-in-law William
Roper would ' sodenly sometymes slip in among the players, and
never studyinge for the matter, make a parte of his own there
presently among them, which made the onlookers more sport
than all the players beside.' Thomas Medwall himself seems to
have been a clerk in minor orders and public notary, who died
soon after 1501; that John Rastell printed this play of his,
probably about 1518, and John's son, William, subsequently
printed *Nature*, his other extant interlude, suggests that Medwall was an important person in the eyes of More's friends, and
even that More may have taken one of two parts in *Fulgens*,
specially adapted for improvisations.

[1] With great public spirit Mr. Huntington the next year published
a facsimile of the play : *Fulgens and Lucres*, by Henry Medwall. With
an introductory note by Seymour de Ricci. In 1926 Drs. F. S. Boas
and A. W. Reed edited an annotated text for the Clarendon Press.

In dramatizing a prose treatise on true nobility Medwall made
two innovations. He revived as a dramatic 'disputacyon' the
old 'débat' in which a poet propounded a problem leaving the
solution to be discussed by his audience, and substituted this
for the unflinching 'predycacyon' of the Moralities; also he
introduced his low comedy simply to amuse, without passing any
unreal judgement on it, as a yielding to sin. The question as to
what makes a gentleman is often touched on by Chaucer, and
in *Fulgens* it is threshed out in the contest between Publius
Cornelius, a rich and sport-loving descendant of the Scipios,
and Gaius Flaminius, a man of less wealth and less noble descent,
but a student and active lover of his country, for the hand of
Lucres, the daughter of Fulgens, who leaves the decision in her
hands. In the original the question as to which is the nobler
is left to the Senate; here it is decided by Lucres in favour of
Flaminius, but with much care that the question shall still be
open for discussion. The low comedy is supplied by two lads in
the audience (only distinguished as A and B), who thrust themselves into the play by each offering his services to one of the
lovers. As an underplot, the lads make love to Lucres's maid,
who trusses them up as fighting cocks with a staff under their
arms to fight for her favour, and in the end, while they are thus
tied up, belabours them both for their impudence. The lovers
talk in Chaucer's seven-line stanzas, the lads in short lines
which Mr. Reed calls doggerel. The play never rises very high ;
the low comedy is distinctly low comedy ; but in the absence of
preaching and of the dishonest trick of dragging in humour to
amuse while pretending to condemn it, we have the beginning
of a secular drama, and the Roman setting of the play touches
it with the breath of the Renaissance.

Medwall's other interlude *Nature* opens with rather a fine
speech from Nature, but for the most part is on much more
conventional lines than *Fulgens*. It exhibits man as tempted by
the seven deadly sins and exhorted by their seven virtuous
counterparts, and need not be specially described. It may be
noted that an interlude of *The Fyndyng of Troth*, assigned to
Medwall, and supposed to have been acted before Henry VIII,
appears to have been solely a figment of Payne Collier's.

John Rastell, who married More's sister Elizabeth, is Mr. Reed's great discovery. In his paper read to the Bibliographical Society in November 1917, he illumines each of the five aspects (printer, lawyer, venturer, dramatist, and controversialist) under which he portrays him by the aid of original research, and builds a picture of a man of whom he justly says that ' while he is not one of the great figures of his time, yet there are few that illustrate more completely the eager restlessness, the variety and tragic ironies of the sixteenth century.' In this paper Mr. Reed vindicated Bale's ascription of the *Interlude of the Four Elements* to Rastell, under the title *Natura Naturata*, or the created Nature, who in the play discourses of earth, water, air, and fire, and then hands over *Humanity* to *Studious Desire* for further instruction. *Studious Desire* calls in the aid of *Experience*, and as part of a discourse on cosmography *Experience* tells how

> within this xx yere
> Westward be founde new landes
> That we neuer harde tell of before this
> By wrytynge nor other meanys
> Yet many now haue ben there.

A subsequent passage[1] shows that the twenty years must be dated from the voyage of Amerigo Vespucci in 1497, which gives 1517 as the date of the play, and Mr. Reed proceeded to show from the record of a lawsuit in the Court of Requests that in that year, having been granted Letters of Recommendation by the King to go for a journey ' ad longinquas mundi partes ', Rastell had started in the ' Barbara, of Greenwich,' for the New Found Lands, and been turned back by a mutiny of his crew at Waterford.

Experience continues to discourse :

> And that contrey is so large of rome
> Muche larger than all cristendome . . .
> But what commodytes be within
> No man can tell nor well Imagin
> But yet not longe ago
> Some men of this contrey went
> By the Kinges noble consent
> It for to serche to that entent

> [1] But this new lands found lately
> Been called America, because only
> Americus did first them find.

And coude not be brought therto
But they that wer the venturers
Haue cause to curse their maryners
Fals of promys and dissemblers
That falsly them betrayed
Which wolde take no paine to saile farther
Than their owne lyst and pleasure
Wherfore that voyage and dyuers other
Suche Kaytyffes haue destroyed

Experience is John Rastell telling his own story, and we can guess that if it was acted at his own house in Hertfordshire, not far from More's, the play, which in earlier editions I have described as 'unflinchingly didactic,' must have derived fire and life for its audience from the writer's personality. It is an indication of its importance that the title of this play is illustrated in the more striking of the two devices which Rastell used, as a printer, now reproduced in this edition facing page 97. At the top of the design is the Almighty, and on a scroll the word of creation *Fiat*; at the foot is a semicircle of which the innermost section shows a landscape (Earth), the second a river (Water), the third pillow-like shapes which their recurrence in the upper part of the picture, where beams of light shine through them, shows to be clouds (symbolizing Air), the fourth tongues of flame (Fire). In the centre the sun, moon, and stars represent Rastell's abiding interest in astronomy. The merman and mermaid whose tails are in the river, while they seem to be sitting on the flames, must refer to the Mermaid, the sign of the house in which Rastell was living in 1520. That the Four Elements were chosen as a main feature of his device enhances the importance of the interlude in any consideration of his career.

Two other plays of long disputed authorship, *Gentleness and Nobility* and the fragment from the Spanish *Calisto and Melibea*, have been decisively assigned to Rastell by Mr. Reed, by the close parallels found in them to the *Four Elements* and Rastell's prose writings. Rastell was a thinker and enthusiast, convinced that all things should be tested by 'natural reason and good philosophy,' and when we have been taught to recognize his touch it is unmistakable.

In *Calisto and Melibea* Rastell, who (despite the fact that he erected a stage for plays in his garden) seems to have had no great interest in the drama except as a medium for conveying his ideas, saved himself some trouble by carving a piece out of a huge Spanish tragi-comedy and gave it a moral ending of his own by visiting the heroine's father with a horrible dream, the recital of which reduces her to repentance. The best of the three plays we can now attribute to him, *Gentleness and Nobility*, is fairly described on its title-page as

A dyaloge betwen the Marchant the Knyght and / the plowman dysputyng who is a verey Gentylman / & who is a Noble man and how men shuld come / to auctoryte. Compiled in maner of an enterlude / with divers toys & gestis addyd therto to make / mery pastyme and disport.

It is divided into two parts, doubtless separated by refreshments, the Plowman bethinking himself that he must go off to 'by a halporth of gresse the spokes of my cart therwith to dresse,' but despite the promise of 'toys and gestis' it is sheer 'disputation' and justifies itself by the goodness of this.

Shorn of the claim put forward on his behalf to the authorship of *Gentleness and Nobility* John Heywood, who married Rastell's daughter Joan and seems to have been strongly under More's influence, is left in possession of two triplets of plays, the first mainly argumentative, the second, to which his title is not quite so secure, purely amusing. The argumentative triplet comprises the imperfectly dramatic Dialogue of *Witty and Witless* (or *Wit and Folly*), first printed by the Percy Society, the tedious *Play of Love*, and the singularly bright and pleasing *Play of the Wether*. Until Dr Alois Brandl came to its rescue in 1898 the *Play of Love* had never provoked an editor. Its characters— *Loving not Loved, Loved not Loving, Both Loving and Loved, Neither Loved nor Loving*, &c.—are such mere puppets, that the story is hopelessly confusing to follow. It is a disputation as to the comparative intensities of the happiness and misery to be won from love, interrupted by one long and none too pleasant narrative, and not greatly enlivened by its solitary incident in which *Neither Loved nor Loving* pretends to have set *Loved not Loving* on fire. Its chief merit lies in such an occasional happiness as the complaint of the woman *Loved not Loving* concerning the too pertinacious suit of her admirer :

> For it doth lyke me evyn lyke as one
> Shold offer me servyse most humbly
> With an axe in his hande, contynually
> Besechyng me gentylly that this might be sped,
> To graunt hym my good wyll to stryke off my hed.

The *Play of the Wether* is much better than this, and, with some excisions or slight alterations, would be an excellent play for a Christmas performance by boys and girls. In this 'new and very mery interlude of all maner wethers,' *Jupiter* deputes *Mery Report* (called, quite unfairly, the *Vice*) to hear and recount to him all the different prayers that the various characters put forward for different kinds of weather. *Mery Report's* account of his experiences gives so excellent a summary that I still append in a note[1] his speech, which was first printed here in 1890 before the play had found an editor, and have little doubt that its length will be excused.

[1] *Merry Report*—

> Now such an other sorte as here hath bene
> In all the dayes of my lyfe I haue not sene,
> No sewters now but women, knauys, and boys,
> And all theyr sewtys are in fansyes and toys.
> Yf that there come no wyser after thys cry
> I wyll to the god and make an ende quyckely.
> Oyes, yf that any knaue here
> Be wyllynge to appere
> For wether fowle or clere,
> Come in before thys flocke,
> And be he hole or syckly
> Come shew hys mynde quyckly.
>
> .   .   .   .
>
> All thys tyme I perceyue is spent in wast,
> To wayte for mo sewters, I se non make hast.
> Wherfore I wyll shew the god all thys procys,
> And be delyuered of my symple offys.
> Now, lorde, accordynge to your comaundement,
> Attendyng sewters I haue ben dylygent,
> And, at begynnyng as your wyll was I sholde,
> I come now at ende to shewe what eche man wolde.
> The fyrst sewter before your selfe dyd appere,
> A gentylman desyrynge wether clere,
> Clowdy, nor mysty, nor no wynde to blow,
> For hurt in hys huntynge; and then, as ye know,

The marchaunt sewde for all of that kynde
For wether clere and mesurable wynde,
As they maye best bere theyr saylys to make spede;
And streyght after thys there came to me in dede
An other man who namyd hym selfe a ranger,
And sayd all of hys crafte be farre brought in daunger
For lacke of lyvynge, whyche chefely ys wynde fall,
But he playnely sayth there bloweth no wynde at al,
Wherfore he desyreth, for encrease of theyr fleesys,
Extreme rage of wynde trees to tere in peces.
Then came a water myller, and he cryed out
For water, and sayde the wynde was so stout
The rayne could not fall; wherfore he made request
For plenty of rayne to set the wynde at rest,
And then, syr, there came a wynde myller in,
Who sayde for the rayne he could no wynde wyn,
The water he wysht to be banysht all,
Besechynge your grace of wynde contynuall.
Then came ther another that wolde banysh all this,
A goodly dame, an ydyll thynge iwys;
Wynde, rayne, nor froste, nor sonshyne wold she haue,
But fayre close wether her beautye to save.
Then came there a nother that lyueth by laundry,
Who muste haue wether hot and clere here clothys to dry.
Then came there a boy, for froste and snow contynuall,
Snow to make snowballys and frost for his pytfale,
For whyche, god wote, he seweth full gredely.
Your fyrst man wold haue wether clere and not wyndy;
The seconde, the same saue cooles to blow meanly;
The thyrd desyred stormes and wynde most ext[re]mely;
The fourth, all in water and wolde haue no wynde;
The fyft no water, but all wynde to grynde;
The syxst wold haue non of all these nor no bright son;
The seuenth extremely the hote son wold haue wonne;
The eyght and the last for frost and snow he prayd.
Byr lady we shall take shame I am afrayd!
Who marketh in what maner this sort is led
May thynke yt impossyble all to be sped.
This nomber is smale, there lacketh twayne of ten,
And yet, by the masse, amonge ten thousand men
No one thynge could stand more wyde from the other,
Not one of theyr sewtes agreeth wyth an other.
I promyse you here is a shrewed pece of warke.

Heywood's plays of *Love* and the *Wether* were printed as his by his brother-in-law, William Rastell. Of the triad of farces attributed to him, two were printed by W. Rastell, but without attribution of authorship, while the third, *The Foure PP.*, is not known in a Rastell edition, but is said to be 'made by John Heewood' on the title-page of one by William Middleton, who printed from 1541 to 1547. It is also ascribed to Heywood (as are *Love* and the *Wether*) by Bale. In this play, which has some of the characteristics of the argumentative group, a *Palmer*, a *Pardoner*, and a *Potecary*, with a *Pedlar* to act as judge, contend for pre-eminence, with skill in lying as its final test, and the arbiter's verdict is in favour of the *Palmer*, who has declared that in all his travels he has never seen one woman out of patience. Granting, as seems reasonable, that Middleton's attribution was right, it seems to carry with it by links of style the two unadulterated farces, *A Play between John the husband, Tyb the wife, and Sir John the priest*, which takes a hen-pecked husband for its subject, and owes something to a French original, and *A merry Play between the Pardoner and the Frere, the curate and neybour Pratte*, in which a Pardoner and a Friar simultaneously come to a church to preach (and collect alms) and put up a good fight against the parish priest, who with the help of the local constable tries forcibly to eject them. These two plays would represent a quite natural development from *The Foure PP.*, and yet stand by themselves as more purely dramatic than any previous English work. It is noteworthy that William Rastell does not assign them to Heywood, as he assigns the *Love* and the *Wether*, and that Bale also is silent as to them. On the other hand, Bale states that Thomas More wrote 'comoediae iuveniles,' and in the forefront of his great edition of More's English works William Rastell printed 'A mery iest how a sergeant would learne to playe the frere. Written by Maister Thomas More in hys youth.' This may have arisen out of an actual event, and narrates how a 'sergeant' being charged to arrest for debt a young spendthrift who was sedulously staying at home (as against arrest for debt an Englishman's house was already 'his castle'), in order to get access to his victim, arrayed himself in a friar's frock, and persuaded a servant to show him to the debtor's room, whereupon

there ensued just such a rough and tumble fight as that between
the Parson and the Friar in the play. The story begins:

> Wyse men alway Affyrme and say That best is for a man :
> Diligently For to apply The busines that he can,
> And in no wyse To enterpryse An other faculte
> For that that wyll And can no skyll Is neuer like to thee [1],

the sergeant's assumption of the rôle of a friar being adduced as
a proof of this. Mr. Reed would clearly be pleased if he could
prove that the two farces were written by More himself, but he
is content to regard them as Heywood's written under More's
influence, and perhaps such a mixt authorship is the best solution.
If they were written by More, as he wrote *The Sergeant and the
Frere*, William Rastell, who must have known their authorship,
might well have printed these also among More's works as he
printed that, unless indeed we are to say that in the reign of
Philip and Mary (the *English works* were published in 1557)
plays to the discredit of friars and priests would not have been
approved.

Taking these eleven plays, the two of Medwall's, Rastell's
three (he also wrote a pageant of *Love and Riches* which has not
survived), and these six which are assigned to Heywood, as
a group, there is a really homogeneous development in them,
and More, who may have acted in *Fulgens and Lucres* and
inspired *Johan Johan* and *The Pardoner and the Frere*, is surely,
as Mr. Reed contends, the central figure which unites them.
The group certainly stands by itself, though we may perhaps
think that the unknown author [2] of *Thersites*, the bright little
Oxford farce adapted from a Latin dialogue of Ravisius Textor,
a French professor at Paris, was encouraged by it to give
a humorous setting to his lesson against unseemly boasting.
Again, we find Rastell's interest in learning continued in the
Wyt and Science of John Redford, written probably towards the
end of the reign of Henry VIII, and first printed in the *Shakespeare Society's Publications* for 1848. Though itself so long in
obtaining the honours of print, Redford's play served as a model
to the anonymous author of 'a new and pleasant enterlude,
intituled the *Marriage of Witte and Science*,' licensed in 1569-
70 to its printer, Thomas Marshe. This is a really amusing

---

[1] prosper. [2] Identified in 1926 as Nic. Udall. See p. 214.

e

play, very brightly and trippingly written, with scarcely a bad
line in it. It was probably composed by a schoolmaster for
performance by his boys, and traces the mishaps of *Wit* in his
endeavour to win the hand of his lady *Science*, the daughter of
Reason and *Experience*. The play is regularly divided into acts
and scenes, and in this and other respects is so widely removed
from the earlier didactic interludes, as hardly to come within the
scope of the present volume. In the same way the *Nice Wanton*
and the *Disobedient Child*, the latter by Thomas Ingelend, both
probably written during the reign of Elizabeth, have passed too
far into the region of comedy to be treated here, though their
inculcation of the necessity of discipline in youth entitles them
to be ranked with the didactic interludes.

As already noted the moral plays of a more old-fashioned
kind continued to be written all through the first half of the
sixteenth century. Skelton's *Magnificence*, which Mr. R. L.
Ramsay in his edition for the Early English Text Society dates
as early as between 14 September 1515 and 13 August 1516[1], is
on the older lines, and a specimen from it is only included here
because of its author's general reputation and connexion with
the court. Though learned and painstaking and with some fine
passages, it is a dull and lifeless performance, which Skelton's
fame as a satirist has caused to be somewhat overrated.

The last play from which extracts are given in the present
volume is the *King John* of Bishop Bale. Bale was not only a
Protestant controversialist, but an antiquary, and it is characteristic of him that in his *God's Promises* and *Johan Baptystes*,
he should have endeavoured to infuse fresh life into the Miracle
play by adapting it to strictly Protestant teaching. In his *King
John* he again endeavours to unite new and old, by welding the
didacticism and personifications of the moral interlude with the
history of an English king. The play apparently remained in
MS. until printed by Mr. Collier in 1838, and there is no reason
to imagine that it in any way influenced the rise of the English
historical drama, which did not take place until more than a

---

[1] On the score of a gybe (lines 279–82) as to largesse being 'little
used' in France since the death of 'Kynge Lewes of Fraunce,' the
reference being to the quarrel between Henry and Francis I (as to
the dowry of his English widow), which began to mend after the Peace of
Noyon.

quarter of a century after its first composition[1]. It is thus as a curious development of the didactic interlude, and not as the forerunner of Shakespeare's chronicle-histories, that *King John* finds a place in the present volume.

§ 8.

The last performance of the York Miracle plays took place in 1579, when Shakespeare had attained his Roman majority. The Newcastle plays lasted ten years longer, by which time his career as a dramatist had begun. The Chester plays were acted till the end of the century and last copied in 1607, when Shakespeare's work was already drawing towards its close. Even later than this we hear of a Passion Play acted before Gondomar, the Spanish ambassador, but as to this allowance must be made for foreign influence, and we may regard the Miracle play as finally dying with the death of Elizabeth. In its prolonged old age it had overlapped the noblest period of the English drama, but its direct influence had long passed away[2], and the reminiscence of the *Harrowing of Hell* in the Porter's speech in *Macbeth*, is perhaps the most notable trace which it has left on the drama of the Shakespearian age. But the Miracle plays had fostered a love of acting in almost every county in England. They had prepared the ground from which the Shakespearian harvest was to spring in all its glorious abundance, and in this indirect manner their influence had been potent for good.

The history of the Morality, in its later development as the didactic interlude, is somewhat different. During the first half of the reign of Elizabeth plays with many of the characteristic features of the later Moralities enjoyed much popularity. Such were the *Triall of Treasure* (printed 1567), *Like Will to Like* (printed 1568), *All for Money* (printed 1578), *The Three Ladies of London* (printed 1584), and *The Three Lords and Three Ladies of London* (printed as late as 1590). The increasing

[1] The play seems to have been revised after the accession of Elizabeth, but was probably written in the reign of Edward VI.

[2] The influence of the old play of St. George of Cappadocia is remotely traceable in the Christmas mummings still acted in a few out-of-the-way villages in different parts of England.

FROM ANTOINE VÉRARD'S 'THERENCE EN FRANÇOYS.'

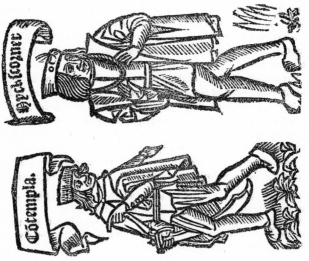

FROM WYNKYN DE WORDE'S 'HYCKSCORNER.'

individuality of the characterization in these plays was doubtless in part only a natural development, but in part also it was due to the influence of the comedies and tragedies founded on classical and Italian models. But though the didactic Interlude learnt something from these splendid rivals, it could not better the instruction, and its latent promise of a domestic drama of purely English growth was never fulfilled. For better or for worse, however, the transformed Morality at this period takes its place as one of the threads which went to make up the wondrous web of the Elizabethan drama, and as such passes out of the scope of the present volume. Here it must suffice us to have attempted to follow the dramatic element in English literature, from a date nearly coincident with the birth of Chaucer, to the time when Shakespeare was old enough to play a boy's part in some moral interlude in praise of learning at the Grammar school of Stratford-on-Avon.

§ 9.

For the idea of adding to the 1904 edition of this little book a few illustrations, mostly more quaint than beautiful, I am indebted to an American critic, who took me rather severely to task for regretting that we had no authentic representations of the costumes, &c., in these early plays. The regret, unfortunately, was only too well founded, for the curious cuts which are found on the title-pages (or the backs of them) of *Hyck-scorner* and one or two other plays printed about 1520 were copies of French or Low Country woodcuts, and therefore cannot be taken as evidence of the dresses of English players. The commonest of them, of which I give two examples taken from Wynkyn de Worde's *Hyckscorner*, are copied, one in reverse, from a French edition of Terence published by Antoine Vérard at Paris about 1500, and I give here reproductions of the originals from which they are taken. The little figure of Every-man on the title page of John Skot's edition of that play, which by the kindness of Mrs. Christie-Miller is reproduced opposite page 77, is also copied from the French Terence, and the grotesque figure of Death, which accompanies it, from Guy Marchant's edition of the *Compost des Bergers* of 1500. I was long under the belief that the title cut (here reproduced) of 'The pleasant and stately morall of the Three Lordes and Three Ladies of London', printed by R. Ihones in 1590, was made for some lost edition of a play printed some twenty years earlier, and really represented, from the rear of the actors, the performance of a Morality in a private hall, the elderly wand-bearer taking the part of a Doctor or Expositor. As a fact it

From 'The Three Lordes and Three Ladies of London,' 1590.

was made for *The Travayled Pylgrime* of Stephen Batman or Bateman (1569) and is ultimately derived from the fifteenth century illustrations to the *Chevalier Délibéré* of Olivier de la Marche. Thus no more can be claimed for it than that in 1590 Ihones thought it would serve to decorate a play, and we are still without any English woodcut directly illustrating an early performance.

To find pictures for the Miracle Plays it has been necessary to cross the Channel and obtain what little light we can from French sources. The picture of Noah's Ark is taken from Vérard's edition of the *Mystère du Vieil Testament,* printed about 1500; those of the Shepherds, of the Fall of Lucifer, and of Justice, Mercy and Truth, from editions of the *Hours of the Blessed Virgin,* printed at Paris between 1490 and 1510. The excuse for borrowing from these is twofold. In the first place, these delightfully illustrated prayer-books were largely printed in Paris for the English market, there being numerous editions for our English ' Use of Sarum '; secondly, the names written on the labels in the picture of the Shepherds which forms our frontispiece— Gobin le gay, le beau Roger, Aloris, Alison, &c.— are those which they and their wives frequently bear in the contemporary French plays, and the Shepherds are bringing with them the rustic gifts mentioned also in our English cycles.

Dr. Reed's discovery of the relevance of one of Rastell's devices to his play of the *Four Elements* (see p. lx) has given us a new picture.

To illustrate *Thersites* we show a combat with a snail from Guy Marchant's *Kalendrier des Bergers* of 1500. An edition of the Kalendar of Shepherds was printed in English (of a sort) at Paris for exportation, so that here again we are not wholly on foreign ground. Moreover *Thersites,* as has been recently shown, is based on one of the Latin Dialogues of J. Ravisius Textor (Jean Texier), educated at and subsequently one of the professors of the Collège de Navarre. Now Guy Marchant's shop was just behind the College, and it is quite possible that it was from seeing this snail-picture on Marchant's counter that the Professor was inspired to write this particular Dialogue. The combat of the man-at-arms and the snail was a venerable medieval joke, especially levelled against the Lombards, to whom a reference will be found in the poem which accompanies the picture in the *Kalendrier* and which is here reproduced.

Lastly, we give from the first edition of Foxe's *Book of Martyrs* (John Day, 1563) a reduced reproduction of a very curious full-page woodcut of the death of King John according to the same version as that followed by Bale in his play. The preliminary absolution, the offer to the King of the poisoned wassail-bowl, the death of the monk and the promised mass being sung for his soul are all here shown in accordance with Bale's dialogue and it is perhaps not wholly fanciful to connect the appearance of this large picture in the *Book of Martyrs* with the revival of the play in the reign of Elizabeth.

Inicium ſancti euāgelii ſcōm ioħānem. Gloria.
In principio erat Verbū ¢ Verbum erat apud
deū. ¢ deus erat Verbū. Hoc erat in principio
apud deū. Dia p ipſum facta ſūt et ſine ipſo
factum eſt nichil. Quod factum eſt in ipſo Vita erat

FROM HEURES A LUSAIGE DE ROME

PARIS, J. DUPRÉ, 1489

ENGLISH MIRACLE PLAYS, &c.

York Plays.

THE BARKERS.

THE CREATION AND THE FALL OF LUCIFER.

[SCENE I. *Heaven.*]

[DEUS.] *Ego sum Alpha et O. vita, via, Veritas, primus et nouissimus.*

1. I am gracyus and grete, god withoutyn begynnyng,
   I am maker unmade, all mighte es in me,
 I am lyfe and way unto welth-wynnyng,
   I am formaste and fyrste, als I byd sall it be.
 My blyssyng o ble sall be blendyng,   5
   And heldand fro harme to be hydande,
   My body in blys ay abydande
 Une[n]dande withoutyn any endyng.

2. Sen I am maker unmade, and moste es of mighte,
   And ay sall be endeles, and noghte es but I,   10
 Unto my dygnyte dere sall diewly be dyghte
   A place full of plente to my plesing at ply,
 And therewith als wyll I have wroght
   Many dyvers doynges be-dene,
   Whilke warke sall mekely contene,   15
 And all sall be made even of noght.

B

3. But onely the worthely warke of my wyll
  In my sprete sall enspyre the mighte of me,
And in the fyrste, faythely, my thoghts to full-fyll,
  Baynely in my blyssyng I byd at here be   20
A blys al-beledande abowte me;
  In the whilke blys I byde at be here
  Nyen ordres of aungels full clere,
In lovyng ay lastande at lowte me.

 Tunc cantant angeli: Te deum laudamus, te dominum
      confitemur.

4. Here undernethe me nowe a nexile I neven, 25
  Whilke Ile sall be erthe now, all be at ones
Erthe haly and helle, this hegheste be heven,
  And that welth sall welde sall won in this wones.
Thys graunte I yowe mynysters myne,
  To-whils yhe ar stabill in thoghte;   30
  And also to thaime that ar noghte
Be put to my presone at pyne.   *[To Lucifer.*

5. Of all the mightes I have made moste nexte after me,
  I make the als master and merour of my mighte,
I beelde the here baynely in blys for to be, 35
  I name the for Lucifer, als berar of lyghte.
No thyng here sall the be derand
  In this blys sall be yhour beeldyng,
  And have al welth in youre weledyng,
Ay whils yhe ar buxomly berande.   40

Tunc cantant Angeli, Sanctus sanctus sanctus, dominus deus
      sabaoth.

6. PRIMUS ANGELUS SERAPHYN.

 A! mercyfull maker, full mekill es thi mighte,
  That all this warke at a worde worthely has wroghte
 Ay loved be that lufly lorde of his lighte,
  That us thus mighty has made, that nowe was righte
   noghte;

In blys for to byde in hys blyssyng   45
   Ay lastande, in luf lat us lowte hym,
   At beelde us thus baynely abowte hym,
Of myrthe nevermore to have myssyng.

7. Primus Angelus deficiens Lucifere.

All the myrth that es made es markide in me,
   The bemes of my brighthode ar byrnande so bryghte,
And I so semely in syghte my selfe now I se,   51
   For lyke a lorde am I lefte to lende in this lighte,
More fayrear be far than my feres,
   In me is no poynte that may payre,
   I fele me fetys and fayre,   55
My power es passande my peres.

8. Ang. Cherabyn.

Lord! wyth a lastande luf we love the allone,
   Thou mightefull maker that markid us and made us,
And wroghte us thus worthely to wone in this wone,
   Ther never felyng of fylth may full us nor fade us,
All blys es here beeldande a-boute us,   61
   To-whyls we are stabyll in thoughte
   In the worschipp of hym that us wroghte
Of dere never thar us more dowte us.

9. Prim. ang. defic.

O what! I am fetys and fayre and fygured full fytt!
   The forme of all fayrehede apon me es feste,   66
All welth in my weelde es, I wete be my wytte,
   The bemes of my brighthede are bygged with the
      beste.
My schewyng es schemerande and schynande,
   So bygly to blys am I broghte,   70
   Me nedes for to noy me righte noghte,
Here sall never payne me be pynande.

10. ANG. SERAPHYN.

With all the wytt at we welde we wyrschip thi wyll,
　　Thu gloryus god that es grunde of all grace,
Ay with stedefaste steven lat us stande styll,　　75
　　Lorde! to be fede with the fode of thi fayre face.
In lyfe that es lely ay lastande,
　　Thi dale, lorde, es ay daynetethly delande,
　　And who so that fode may be felande
To se thi fayre face es noght fastande.　　80

11. PRIM. ANG. DEFEC. LUCIFER.

Owe! certes! what I am worthely wroghte with wyr-
　　　　shyp, i-wys!
　　For in a glorius gle my gleteryng it glemes,
I am so mightyly made my mirth may noghte mys,
　　Ay sall I byde in this blys thorowe brightnes of
　　　　bemes.
Me nedes noghte of noy for to neven,　　85
　　All welth in my welde have I weledande,
　　Abowne *y*hit sall I be beeldand,
On heghte in the hyeste of hewven.

12. Ther sall I set my selfe, full semely to seyghte,
　　To ressayve my reverence thorowe right o renowne,
I sall be lyke unto hym that es hyeste on heghte; 91
　　Owe! what I am derworth and defte.—Owe! dewes!
　　　　all goes downe!
My mighte and my mayne es all marrande,
　　Helpe! felawes, in faythe I am fallande.
SEC. ANGEL. DEFEC.
　　Fra heven are we heledande on all hande,　　95
To wo are we weendande, I warande.

[SCENE II. *Hell.*]

13. LUCIFER DEIABOLUS IN INFERNO.

Owte owte ! harrowe ! helples, slyke hote at es here,
This es a dongon of dole that I am to dyghte,
Whare es my kynde be-come, so cumly and clere,
Nowe am I laytheste, allas ! that are was lighte.
My bryghtnes es blakkeste and blo nowe ;   101
My bale es ay betande and brynande,
That gares ane go gowlande and gyrnande.
Owte ! ay walaway ! I well even in wo nowe !

14. SECUNDUS DIABOLUS.

Owte ! owte ! I go wode for wo, my wytte es all wente
nowe   105
All oure fode es but filth, we fynde us beforn,
We that ware beelded in blys in bale are we brent
nowe,
Owte ! on the Lucifer, lurdan ! oure lyghte has thu
lorne.
Thi dedes to this dole nowe has dyghte us,
To spille us thu was oure spedar,   110
For thou was oure lyghte and oure ledar,
The hegheste of heven hade thu hyght us.

15. LUCIFER IN INFERNO.

Walaway ! wa es me now, nowe es it war thane it was.
Unthryvandely threpe *y*he, I sayde but a thoghte.
SECUND. DIAB.   We ! lurdane, thu lost us.
LUC. IN INF.   *Y*he ly, owte ! allas !
I wyste noghte this wo sculde be wroghte.   116
Owte on *y*how ! lurdans, *y*he smore me in smoke.
SECUND. DIAB.   This wo has thu wroughte us.
LUC. IN INF.   *Y*he ly, *y*he ly !
SECUND. DIAB.   Thou lyes, and that sall thu by.
We ! lurdans, have at *y*owe, lat loke.   120

[SCENE III. *Heaven.*]

16. ANGELUS CHERUBYN.

A! lorde, lovid be thi name that us this lighte lente,
    Sen Lucifer oure ledar es lighted so lawe,
For hys unbuxumnes in bale to be brente.
    Thi rightwysnes [redes] to rewarde on rowe
Ilke warke eftyr [it] is wroghte.   125
    Thorowe grace of thi mercyfull myghte
    The cause I se itt in syghte,
Wharefore to bale he es broghte.

17. DEUS. Those foles for thaire fayre-hede in fantasyes
    fell,
    And hade mayne of mighte that marked tham and
        made tham,   130
For-thi efter thaire warkes were, in wo sall thai well,
    For sum ar fallen into fylthe that evermore sall fade
        tham,
And never sall have grace for to gyrth tham.
    So passande of power tham thoght tham,
    Thai wolde noght me worschip that wroghte tham,
For-thi sall my wreth ever go with tham.   136

18. Ande all that me wyrschippe sall wone here, i-wys,
    For-thi more forthe of my worke wyrke nowe I will.
Syn than ther mighte es for-marryde that mente all
    o-mys,
    Even to myne awne fygure this blys to fulfyll, 140
Mankynde of moulde will I make;
    But fyrste wille I fourme, hym before,
    All thyng that sall hym restore,
To whilke that his talents will take.

19. Ande in my fyrste makyng to mustyr my mighte, 145
    Sen erthe is vayne and voyde, and myrknes emel,
I byd in my blyssyng *y*he aungels gyf lyghte
    To the erthe, for it faded when the fendes fell.

In hell sall never myrknes be myssande,
   The myrknes thus name I for nighte,   150
   The day that call I this lyghte.
My after-warkes sall thai be wyssande;

20. Ande now in my blyssyng I twyne tham in two,
   The nighte even fro the day, so that thai mete never,
But ather in a kynde courese thaire gates for to go.
   Bothe the nighte and the day, does dewly *y*hour
      deyver,   156
To all I sall wirke be *y*he wysshyng.
   This day warke es done ilke a dele,
   And all this warke lykes me ryght wele,
And baynely I gyf it my blyssyng.   160

Explicit.

Chester Plays.

I. NOAH'S FLOOD.

THE WATTER LEADERS AND THE DRAWERS OF DEE PLAYE.

GOD. I, God, that all this worlde hath wroughte,
    Heaven and eairth, and all of naughte,
    I see my people in deede and thoughte
      Are sette fowle in synne;
    My ghoste shall not linge in mone.   5
    That through fleshe-likinge is my fonne,
    But tell sixe skore yeaires be comen and gone,
      To loke if they will blynne.
    Man that I made I will destroye,
    Beaste, worme and fowle to flye;   10
    For one eairth they doe me nye,
      The folke that are theirone;
    It harmes me so hurtfullye,
    The malice that doth nowe multiplye,
    That sore yt greives me hartelye   15
      That ever I made mon.
    Therefore, Noye, my servante free,
    That rightious man arte, as I see,
    A shippe sone thou shall make thee,
      Of treeyes drye and lighte;   20
    Littill chamberes therin thou make,
    And byndinge slyche also thou take,
    Within and without thou ne slake
      To anoynte yt through all thy mighte.

Three hundreth cubettes it shall be longe,   25
And fiftie brode, to make yt stronge ;
Of heighte fiftie the meete thou fonge,
    Thus messuer thou it aboute.
One wyndowe worcke through thy wytte,
A cubitte of lengthe and breade make itt,   30
Upon the syde a dore shall sit
    For to come in and oute.
Eattinge places thou make alsoe,
Three rowfed chamberes on a roe :
For with watter I thinke to slowe   35
    Man that I can make ;
Destroyed all the worlde shalbe,
Save thou, thy wiffe, and children three,
And ther wiffes also with thee
    Shall saved be for thy sake.   40

Noye. O, Lorde, I thanke thee lowde and still,
That to me arte in suche will,
And spares me and my howse to spill,
    As I nowe southly fynde.
Thy byddinge, Lorde, I shall fulfill,   45
And never more thee greve nor grill,
That such grace hath sente me till
    Amonght all mankinde.
Have done, you men and wemen all,
Hye you, leste this watter fall,   50
To worche this shippe, chamber and hall,
    As God hath bedden us doe.

Sem. Father, I am all readye bowne ;
An axe I have, by my crowne !
As sharpe as anye in all this towne,   55
    For to goe therto.

Cam. I have a hacchatt wounder keeyne,
To bitte well, as maye be seene,

A better grownden, as I wene,
   Is not in all this towne.   60

JAFFETTE. And I can make well a pynne,
   And with this hamer knocke it in :
   Goe wee worcke boute more dynne,
     And I am readye bowne.

NOYES WIFFE. And we shall bringe tymber too,   65
   For we mone nothinge elles doe ;
   Wemen be weeke to underfoe
     Any greate travill.

SEMES WIFFE. Hear is a good hacckinge-stoccke,
   One this you maye hewe and knocke ;   70
   Shall none be idle in this floccke ;
     Ney nowe maye noe man fayle.

CAMMES WIFFE. And I will goe gaither slyche,
   The shippe for to caulke and pyche,
   Anoynte yt muste be every stiche,   75
     Borde, tree, and pynne.

JEFFETTES WYFFE. And I will gaither chippes heare
   To make a fier for you in feare,
   And for to dighte youer dynner,
     Againste your cominge in.   80

Then Noye begineth to builde the Arcke, and speaketh Noye :

NOYE. Now in the name of God, I will begyne
   To make the shippe that we shall in,
   That we maye be readye for to swyme
     At the cominge of the fludde :
   Thes bordes heare I pynne togeither,   85
   To beare us saffe from the weither,
   That we maye rowe both heither and theither,
     And saffe be from the fludde.

Of this treey will I make the maste,
Tyed with cabbelles that will laste,   90
With a saile yarde for iche blaste,
 And iche thinge in their kinde :
With toppe-castill, and boe spritte,
With cordes and roppes, I hold all meete
To sayle fourth at the nexte weete,   95
 This shippe is att an ende.
Wyffe, in this vessel we shall be kepte :
My children and thou, I woulde in ye lepte.

Noyes Wiffe. In fayth, Noye, I hade as leffe thou slepte !
 For all thy frynishe fare,   100
I will not doe after thy reade.

Noye. Good wyffe, doe nowe as I thee bydde.

Noyes Wiffe. Be Christe ! not or I see more neede,
 Though thou stande all the daye and stare.

Noye. Lorde, that wemen be crabbed aye,   105
And non are meke, I dare well saye,
This is well seene by me to daye,
 In witnesse of you ichone.
Goodwiffe, lett be all this beare,
That thou maiste in this place heare ;   110
For all the wene that thou arte maister,
 And so thou arte, by Sante John !

Then Noye with all his familie shall make a signe as though
the wroughte upon the shippe with divers instrumentes
and after that God shall speak to Noye, sayinge :

God. Noye, take thou thy meanye,
And in the shippe hie that you be,
For non soe righteous man to me   115
 Is nowe one earth livinge ;

Of cleane beastes with thee thou take,
Seven and seven, or then thou slake,
He and shee, make to make,
   Belive in that thou bringe.   120
Of beastes uncleane towe and towe,
Male and femalle, boute moe,
Of cleane fowles seven alsoe,
   The he and shee togeither;
Off fowles uncleane twene and noe more,   125
As I of beastes sayde before;
That man be saved through my lore,
   Againste I sende this weither.
Of all meates that mone be eatten,
Into the shippe loke there be getten;   130
For that maye be noe waye forgetten,
   And doe all this bydene,
To sustayne man and beaste therin,
Tell the watter cease and blynne.
This worlde ys filled full of synne,   135
   And that is nowe well seene
Seven dayes be yette cominge,
You shall have space them in to bringe;
After that it is my likinge,
   Mankinde for to anoye.   140
Fourtye dayes and fortye nightes
Raine shall fall for ther unrightes,
And that I have made through my mightes,
   Nowe thinke I to destroye.

NOYE. Lorde, to thy byddinge I am bayne,   145
   Seinge noe other grace will gayne,
  Yt will I fulfill fayne,
   For gracious I thee fynde;
  A hundred wyntter and twentye
  This shippe makinge taryed have I,   150

Yf through amendment thy mercye
  Woulde fall to mankinde.
Have donne, you men and wemen alle,
Hye you, leste this watter fall,
That iich beaste were in stalle,   155
  And into the shippe broughte;
Of cleane beastes seven shalbe,
Of uncleane two, this God bade me:
The fludde is nye, you maye well see,
  Therefore tarye you naughte.   160

Then Noye shall goe into the Arcke with all his familye, his
  wife excepte, and the Arcke must be borded round about,
  and one the bordes all the beastes and foules painted.

SEM. Sir, heare are lions, leapardes, in,
  Horses, mares, oxen, and swyne;
Goote and caulfe, sheepe and kine
  Heare sitten thou maye see.

CAM. Camelles, asses, man maye fynde,   165
  Bucke and doo, harte and hinde,
And beastes of all maner kinde
  Here be, as thinketh me.

JAFFETT. Take heare cattes, dogges too,
  Atter and foxe, fullimartes alsoe;   170
Hares hoppinge gaylie can goe,
  Heare have coule for to eate.

NOYES WIFFE. And heare are beares, woulfes sette,
  Apes, oules, marmosette,
Weyscelles, squirelles, and firrette,   175
  Heare the eaten ther meate.

SEMES WIFFE. Heare are beastes in this howse,
  Heare cattes make yt crousse,
Heare a rotten, heare a mousse,
  That standeth nighe togeither.   180

CAMES WIFFE. And heare are fowles lesse and more,
 Hearnes, cranes, and bittor,
 Swannes, peacokes, and them before
  Meate for this weither.

JEFFATTES WIFFE. Heare are cockes, kites, croes, 185
 Rookes, ravens, manye roes,
 Cuckoes, curlues, who ever knowes,
  Iche one in his kinde;
 Heare are doves, digges, drackes,
 Red-shonckes roninge through the lackes, 190
 And ech fowle that leden makes
  In this shippe men maye fynde.

NOYE. Wiffe, come in: why standes thou their?
 Thou arte ever frowarde, I dare well sweare;
 Come in, one Godes halfe! tyme yt were, 195
  For feare leste that we drowne.

NOYES WIFFE. Yea, sir, sette up youer saile,
 And rowe fourth with evill haile,
 For withouten [anye] fayle
  I will not oute of this towne; 200
 But I have my gossippes everyechone,
 One foote further I will not gone:
 The shall not drowne, by Sante John!
  And I may save ther life.
 The loven me full well, by Christe! 205
 But thou lett them into thy cheiste,
 Elles rowe nowe wher thee leiste,
  And gette thee a newe wiffe.

NOYE. Seme, sonne, loe! thy mother is wrawe:
 Forsooth, such another I doe not knowe. 210

SEM. Father, I shall fetch her in, I trowe,
 Withoutten anye fayle.—
 Mother, my father after thee sende,

And byddes thee into yeinder shippe wende.
Loke up and see the wynde,   215
  For we bene readye to sayle.

NOYES WIFFE. Seme, goe againe to hym, I saie;
  I will not come theirin to daye.

NOYE. Come in, wiffe, in twentye devilles waye!
  Or elles stand there without.   220

CAM. Shall we all feche her in?

NOYE. Yea, sonnes, in Christe blessinge and myne!
  I woulde you hied you be-tyme,
    For of this flude I am in doubte.

THE GOOD GOSSIPPE'S SONGE.

The flude comes fleetinges in full faste,   225
  One every syde that spreades full ferre;
For feare of drowninge I am agaste;
  Good gossippes, lett us drawe nere
And lett us drinke or we departe,
  For ofte tymes we have done soe;   230
For att a draughte thou drinkes a quarte,
  And soe will I do or I goe.
Heare is a pottill full of Malmsine, good and stronge;
It will rejoyce bouth harte and tonge;
Though Noye thinke us never so longe,   235
  Heare we will drinke alike.

JEFFATTE. Mother, we praye you all together,
  For we are heare, youer owne childer,
Come into the shippe for feare of the weither,
  For his love that you boughte!   240

NOYES WIFFE. That will not I, for all youer call,
  But I have my gossippes all.

Sem. In faith, mother, yett you shalle,
  Wheither thou wylte or [nought].

Noye. Welckome, wiffe, into this botte.   245

Noyes Wiffe. Have thou that for thy note!

Noye. Ha, ha! marye, this is hotte!
    It is good for to be still.
    Ha! children, me thinkes my botte remeves.
    Our tarryinge heare highlye me greves,   250
    Over the lande the watter spreades;
      God doe as he will.
    A! greate God, that arte so good,
    That worckes not thy will is wood.
    Nowe all this worlde is one a flude,   255
      As I see well in sighte.
    This wyndowe I will shutte anon,
    And into my chamber I will gone,
    Tell this watter, so greate one,
      Be slacked through thy mighte.   260

*Then shall Noye shutte the wyndowe of the Arcke, and for a
  littill space be silent, and afterwards lookinge rounde
  aboute shall saye:*

    [Now* 40 dayes are fullie gone
    Send a raven I will anone
    If ought-were earth, tree or stone,
      Be drye in any place.
    And if this foule come not againe   265*
    It is a signe, soth to sayne,
    That drye it is on hill or playne,
      And God hath done some grace.

Tunc dimittet corvum et capiens columbam in manibus dicat.

    Ah, Lord, wherever this raven be,
    Somewhere is drye, well I see;   270*

    * The following 47 lines occur only in MS. Harl. 2124.

Nature humaine a desprise
Mon commandement dont iay dueil
Par quoy ie commande et si vueil
Que les eaües la terre inundent
Et en tel quantité habondent
Que la terre en soit toute plene
   ¶ Icy commence a aplouuoir

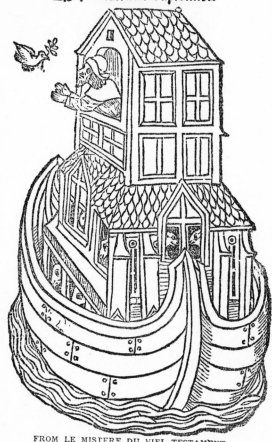

FROM LE MISTERE DU VIEL TESTAMENT

PARIS, A. VÉRARD, C. 1500

But yet a dove, by my lewtye!
After I will sende.
       *   *   *   *   *

Thou wilt turne againe to me,
For of all fowles that may flye
    Thou art most meke and hend.   275*

Tunc emittet columbam et erit in nave alia columba ferens
olivam in ore quam dimittet aliquis ex malo per funem
in manus Noe ; et postea dicat Noe.

Ah lord, blessed be thou aye,
That me hast confort thus to day;
By this sight, I may well saye,
    This flood beginnes to cease.
My sweete dove to me brought hase   280*
A branch of olyve from some place,
This betokeneth God has done us some grace
    And is a signe of peace.
Ah lord honoured most thou be,
All earthe dryes now, I see,   285*
But yet tyll thou comaunde me
    Hence will I not hye.
All this water is awaye
Therfore as sone as I maye
Sacryfice I shall doo in faye   290*
    To thee devoutlye.

DEUS. Noe take thy wife anone,
    And thy children every one,
    Out of the shippe thou shalt gone,
        And they all with thee.   295*
    Beastes and all that can flie
    Out anone they shall hye,
    On earth to grow and multeplye ;
        I wyll that yt soe be.

Noe. Lord I thanke the through thy mighte,   300*
    Thy bydding shall be done in height,
    And as fast as I may dighte,
      I will doe the honoure
    And to thee offer sacrifice,
    Therfore comes in all wise,   305*
    For of these beastes that bene hise
      Offer I will this stower.

Tunc egrediens archam cum tota familia sua accipiet animalia
sua et volucres et offeret ea et mactabit.]

Noye. Lorde God, in magestie,
    That suche grace hath graunted me,
    Wher all was [lorne] salfe to be,
      Theirfore nowe I am boune,
    My wife, my children, and my meanye,   265
    With sacrifice to honour thee
    Of beastes, fowles, as thou maiste see,
      And full devocion.

God. Noye, to me thou arte full able,
    And thy sacrifice acceptable,   270
    For I have founde thee true and stable ;
      On thee nowe muste I myne ;
    Warrye eairth I will noe more
    For mannes synnes that greves me sore,
    For of youth mon full yore   275
      Has bene inclynde to synne.
    You shall nowe growe and multiplye,
    And eairth againe to edifye,
    Ich beaste, and fowle that maye flye,
      Shalbe feared of you ;   280
    And fish in sea that maye fleete
    Shall sustaine you, I thee behett,

To eate of them ye ne lette,
    That cleane bene, you mon knowe;
Theras you have eaten before   285
Grasse and rootes, since you were bore,
Of cleane beastes nowe lesse and more
    I give you leve to eate;
Save bloode and fleshe, bouth in feare,
Of rouge dead carrion that is heare,   290
Eate not of that in noe manere,
    For that aye you shall lete.
Man-slaughter also you shall flee,
For that is not pleasante unto me;
The that sheedeth blood, he or shee,   295
    Oughte-wher amonge mankinde,
That bloode fowle shedde shalbe
And vengeance have, that men shall see;
Therfore beware now all ye,
    You falle not into that synne.   300
A forward, Noye, with thee I make,
And all thy seede, for thy sake,
Of suche vengance for to slake,
    For nowe I have my will;
Heare I behette thee a heste,   305
That man, woman, fowle, ney beste,
With watter, while this worlde shall leste,
    I will noe more spill.
My bowe betweyne you and me
In the firmamente shalbe,   310
By verey tocken that you shall see,
    That suche vengance shall cease,
That man ne woman shall never more
Be wasted with watter, as hath before;
But for synne that greveth me sore,   315
    Therfore this vengance was.
Wher cloudes in the welckine bene,

That ilke bowe shalbe seene,
In tocken that my wrath and teene
    Shall never thus wrocken be.   320
The stringe is torned towardes you,
And towarde me is bente the bowe,
That suche weither shall never shewe,
    And this behighte I thee.
My blessinge, Noye, I geve thee heare,   325
To thee, Noye, my servante deare;
For vengance shall noe more appeare,
    And nowe fare well, my darlinge deare.

*Finis. Deo gratias ! per me, George Bellin. 1592.   Come
Lorde Jesu, come quicklye.*

II. THE SACRIFICE OF ISAAC.

[From the Histories of Lot and Abraham, the fourth of the Chester Plays, acted by the ' Barbers and the Waxe Chaundlers.' The first part of the play is occupied with the meeting of Abraham and Lot, God's covenant with Abraham, and the explanations of these events by the Expositor.]

GOD. Abraham, my servante, Abraham.

ABRAHAM. Loe, Lorde, all readye heare I am. 210

GOD. Take, Isaake, thy sonne by name,
That thou loveste the best of all,
And in sacrifice offer hym to me
Uppon that hyll their besides thee.
Abraham, I will that soe it be, 215
For oughte that maye befalle.

ABRAHAM. My Lorde, to thee is myne intente
Ever to be obediente.
That sonne that thou to me hast sente,
Offer I will to thee, 220
And fulfill thy comaundemente,
With hartie will, as I am kente.
Highe God, Lorde omnipotente,
Thy byddinge done shalbe.
My meanye and my children eichone 225
Lenges at home, bouth all and one,
Save Isaake, my sonne, with me shall gone
To a hill heare besyde.

Heare Abraham, torninge hym to his sonne Isaake, saith :

> Make thee readye, my deare darlinge,
> For we must doe a littill thinge.   230
> This woode doe on thy backe it bringe,
> We maye no longer abyde.
> A sworde and fier that I will take;

> [*Heare Abraham taketh a sworde and fier.*]

> For sacrafice me behoves to make :
> Godes byddinge will I not forsake,   235
> But ever obediente be.

Heare Isaake speaketh to his father, and taketh a burne of stickes and beareth after his father, and saieth :

ISAAKE. Father, I am all readye
> To doe your byddinge moste mekelye,
> And to beare this woode full beane am I,
> As you comaunded me.   240

ABRAHAM. O Isaake, my darlinge deare,
> My blessinge nowe I geve thee heare,
> Take up this faggote with good cheare,
> And on thy backe it bringe.
> And fier with us I will take.   245

ISAAKE. Your byddinge I will not forsake ;
> Father, I will never slake
> To fulfill your byddinge.

> [*Heare they goe bouth to the place to doe sacriffice.*]

ABRAHAM. Now, Isaake sonne, goe we our waie
> To yender mounte, yf that we maye.   250

ISAAKE. My deare father, I will asaye
> To followe you full fayne.

Abraham, beinge mynded to sleye his sonne Isaake, leiftes up his handes, and saith fowlowinge.

ABRAHAM. O ! my harte will breake in three,
> To heare thy wordes I have pittye ;

As thou wylte, Lorde, so muste yt be,   255
     To thee I wilbe bayne.
Laye downe thy faggote, my owne sonne deare.

ISAAKE. All readye, father, loe yt is heare.
     But whye make you sucke heavye cheare?
       Are you anye thinge adreade?   260
     Father, yf yt be your will,
     Wher is the beaste that we shall kill?

ABRAHAM. Therof, sonne, is non upon this hill,
     That I see here in this steade.

Isaake, fearinge leste his ffather woulde slaye him, saith:

ISAAKE. Father, I am full sore [affearde]   265
     To see you beare that drawne [swerde]:
     I hope for all myddel-earde
     You will not slaye your childe.

Abraham comfortes his sonne, and saieth:

ABRAHAM. Dreede thee not, my childe, I reade;
     Our Lorde will sende of his godheade   270
     Some manner of beaste into this [steade],
     Either tame or wilde.

ISAAKE. Father, tell me or I goe
     Wheither I shalbe harmede or noe.

ABRAHAM. Ah! deare God! that me is woe!   275
     Thou breakes my harte in sunder.

ISAAKE. Father, tell me of this case,
     Why you your sorde drawne hase,
     And beares yt nacked in this place,
     Theirof I have greate wonder.   280

ABRAHAM. Isaake, sonne, peace, I praie thee,
     Thou breakes my harte even in three.

ISAAKE. I praye you, father, leane nothinge from me,
     But tell me what you thinke.

ABRAHAM. Ah! Isaake, Isaake, I muste thee kille! 285

ISAAKE. Alas! father, is that your will,
 Your owine childe for to spill
  Upon this hilles brinke?
 Yf I have treasspasede in anye degree,
 With a yarde you maye beate me; 290
 Put up your sorde, yf your wil be,
  For I am but a childe.

ABRAHAM. O, my deare sonne, I am sorye
 To doe to thee this greate anoye:
 Godes commaundmente doe muste I, 295
  His workes are ever full mylde.

ISAAKE. Woulde God my mother were here with me!
 Shee woulde kneele downe upon her knee,
 Prainge you, father, if yt may be,
  For to save my liffe. 300

ABRAHAM. O! comelye creature, but I thee kille,
 I greve my God, and that full ylle;
 I maye not worke againste his will,
  But ever obediente be.
 O! Isaake, sonne, to thee I saie, 305
 God hath commaunded me to daye
 Sacrifice, this is no naye,
  To make of thy bodye.

ISAAKE. Is yt Godes will I shalbe slayne?

ABRAHAM. Yea, sonne, it is not for to leane; 310
 To his byddinge I wilbe bayne,
  And ever to hym pleasinge.
 But that I do this dilfull deede,
 My Lorde will not quite me in my nede.

ISAAKE. Marye, father, God forbydde, 315
  But you doe your offeringe!
 Father, at home your sonnes you shall fynde,
 That you must love by course of kinde:

Be I onste out of your mynde,
    Your sorowe maie sone cease;   320
But yet you muste do Godes byddinge.
Father, tell my mother for no thinge.

Here Abraham wrynges his handes, and saith:

ABRAHAM. For sorowe I maie my handes wringe,
    Thy mother I can not please.
    Ho! Isaake, Isaake, blessed muste thou be!   325
Allmoste my witte I lose for thee;
The blood of thy bodye so free
    I am full lothe to sheede.

*Here Isaake askinge his father blessinge one his knyes, and
            saith:*

ISAAKE. Father, seinge you muste nedes doe soe,
    Let it passe lightlie, and over goe;   330
    Kneelinge on my kneeyes towe,
        Your blessinge on me spreade.
ABRAHAM. My blessinge deere son, give I thee
    And thy mothers with hart free;
    The blessing of the Trinitie   335
        My deare sone, on thee lighte.
ISAAKE. Father, I praye you hyde my eyne
    That I see not the sorde so keyne,
    Your strocke, father, woulde I not seene,
        Leste I againste yt grylle.   340

ABRAHAM. My deare sonne Isaake, speake no more,
    Thy wordes makes my harte full sore.

ISAAKE. O deare father, wherefore! wherefore!
    Seinge I muste nedes be dead,
    Of on thinge I will you praie,   345
    Seithen I muste dye the death to daie,
    As fewe strockes as you well maie,
        When you smyte of my heade.

ABRAHAM. Thy meeknes, childe, makes me affraye;
    My songe maye be wayle-a-waie.   350

ISAAKE. O dere father, doe awaye, do awaye
      Your makeinge so moche mone!
    Nowe, trewlye, father, this talkinge
    Doth but make longe taryeinge.
    I praye you, come and make endinge,   355
      And let me hense be gone.

*Hence Isaake riseth and cometh to his father, and he taketh
hym, and byndeth and laieth hym upon the alter to
sacrifice hym, and saith:*

ABRAHAM. Come heither, my childe, thou arte soe sweete,
    Thou muste be bounde both hande and feete.

ISAAKE. Father, we muste no more meete,
      Be oughte that I maie see;   360
    But doe with me then as you will,
    I muste obaye, and that is skille,
    Godes commaundmente to fulfill,
      For nedes soe must yt be.
    Upon the porpose that you have sette you,   365
    For south, father, I will not let you,
    But ever more to you bowe,
      While that ever I maie.
    Father, greete well my brethren yinge,
    And praye my mother of her blessinge,   370
    I come noe more under her wynge,
      Fare well for ever and aye;
    But father! crye you mercye,
    For all that ever I have trespassed to thee,
    Forgeven, father, that it maye be   375
      Untell domesdaie.

ABRAHAM. My deare sonne, let be thy mones!
    My childe, thou greved me [n]ever ones;

Blessed be thou bodye and bones,
 And I forgeve thee heare!   380
Nowe, my deere sonne, here shalt thou lye,
Unto my worke nowe must I hie;
I hade as leeve my selfe to die,
 As thou, my darlinge deare.

ISAAKE. Father, if you be to me kinde,   385
 Aboute my head a carschaffe bynde,
 And let me lightlie out of your mynde,
  And sone that I were speede.

Here Abraham doth kisse his sonne Isaake, and byndes a
charschaffe aboute his heade.

ABRAHAM. Fare well, my sweete sonne of grace!

Here let Isaake kneele downe and speake.

ISAAKE. I praye you, father, torne downe my face 390
 A litill while, while you have space,
  For I am sore adreade.

ABRAHAM. To doe this deed I am sorye.

ISAAKE. Yea, Lorde, to thee I call and crye,
 Of my soule thou have mercye,   395
  Hartelye I thee praie!

ABRAHAM. Lorde, I woulde fayne worke thy will,
 This yonge innocente that lieth so still
 Full loth were me hym to kille,
  By anye maner a waye.   400

ISAAKE. My deare father, I thee praye,
 Let me take my clothes awaie,
 For sheedinge blude on them to daye
  At my laste endinge.

ABRAHAM. Harte, yf thou wouldeste borste in three, 405
 Thou shalte never master me;

I will no longer let for thee;
 My God I maye not greeve.

ISAAKE. A! mercye, father, why tarye you soe?
 Smyte of my head, and let me goe.   410
 I pray you rydd me of my woe,
  For nowe I take my leve.

ABRAHAM. Ah, sonne! my harte will breake in three,
 To heare thee speake such wordes to me.
 Jesu! on me thou have pittye,   415
  That I have moste in mynde.

ISAAKE. Nowe father, I see that I shall dye:
 Almightie God in magistie!
 My soule I offer unto thee;
  Lorde, to yt be kinde.   420

Here let Abraham take and bynde his sonne Isaake upon the
 alter; let hym make a signe as though he woulde cut of
 his head with his sorde; then let the angell come and
 take the sworde by the end and staie it, sainge:

ANGELLUS. Abraham, my servante dere.

ABRAHAM. Loe, Lorde, I am all readye here!

ANGELLUS. Laye not thy sworde in noe manere
 On Isake, thy deare darlinge;
 And do to hym no anoye.   425
 For thou dredes God, wel wote I,
 That of thy sonne has no mercye,
  To fulfill his byddinge.

SECUNDUS ANGELLUS. And for hys byddinge thou dose aye,
 And spareste nether for feare nor fraye,   430
 To doe thy sonne to death to daie,
  Isake, to thee full deare:
 Therfore, God hathe sent by me, in faye!

A lambe, that is bouth good and gaye,
Into this place as thou se may,   435
   Lo, have hym righte here.

ABRAHAM. Ah! Lorde of heaven, and kinge of blesse,
Thy byddinge shalbe done, i-wysse!
Sacrafice here sente me is,
   And all, Lorde, through thy grace.   440
A horned weither here I see,
Amonge the breyers tyed is he,
To thee offred shall he be
   Anon righte in this place.

Then let Abraham take the lambe and kille hym, and let
God saie:

GOD   Abraham, by my selfe I sweare,   445
   For thou haste bene obediente ever,
And spared not thy sonne to teare,
   To fulfill my byddinge,
Thou shalbe blessed, that pleased me,
Thy seed I shall so multiplie,   450
As starres and sande so manye het I,
   Of thy bodye cominge.
Of enemyes thou shalte have power,
And thy bloode also in feare,
Thou haste bene meke and bonere,   455
   To do as I thee bade;
And of all nacions, leve thou me,
Blessed ever more shall thou be,
Through frute that shall come of thee,
   And saved be through thy seede.   460

EXPOSITOR. Lordinges, th[e] significacioun
   Of this deed of devocion,
And you will, you witten mone,
   Maye torne you to moche good.

This deed you see done here in this place, 465
In example of Jesu done it was,
That for to wynne mankindes grace
    Was sacrifised on the roode.
By Abraham I maie understande
The father of heaven, that can fand 470
With his sonnes bloode to breake that bande,
    That the devill had broughte us to.
By Isaake understande I maie
Jesu, that was obedient aye,
His fathers will to worke alwaie, 475
    And death for to confounde.

Here let the docter knele downe, and saie

Such obedience grante us, O Lorde!
Ever to thy moste holye worde,
That in the same we maie accorde
    As this Abraham was bayne ; 480
And then al togaither shall we
That worthy kinge in heaven see,
And dwell with hym in greate glorye
    For ever and ever, amen.

Here the messinger maketh an ende.

Make rombe, lordinges, and geve us waye, 485
And let Balacke come in and plaie,
And Balame that well can saie,
    To tell you of prophescie.
That Lorde that died on Good Frydaie,
He save you all bouth nighte and daie ! 490
Fare well, my lordinges ; I goe my waie,
    I maye no longer abyde.

Finis. Deo gratias ! per me, Georgi Bellin. 1592.
Come, Lorde Jesu, come quicklye. Anno 1592.

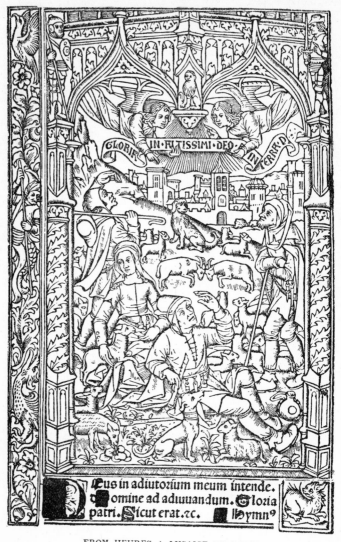

GLORIA · IN · ALTISSIMI · DEO · IN · TERRA · D

Deus in adiutorium meum intende. Domine ad adiuuandum. Gloria patri. Sicut erat. ⁊c. Hymn⁹

FROM HEURES A LUSAIGE DE ROME

PARIS, P. PIGOUCHET FOR S. VOSTRE. 1497

Towneley Plays.

SECUNDA PASTORUM.

[Abridged.]

PRIMUS PASTOR. Lord, what these weders ar cold, and
    I am ylle happyd;
I am nere-hande dold, so long have I nappyd;
My legys thay fold, my fyngers ar chappyd,
It is not as I wold, for I am al lappyd
   In sorow.   5
In stormes and tempest,
Now in the eest, now in the west,
Wo is hym has never rest
   Myd-day nor morow.
Bot we sely shepardes, that walkys on the moore,
In fayth we are nere-handys outt of the doore; 11
No wonder, as it standys, if we be poore,
For the tylthe of oure landys lyys falow as the floore,
   As ye ken.
We ar so hamyd,   15
For-taxed and ramyd,
We ar mayde hand-tamyd,
   Withe thyse gentlery men.
Thus they refe us oure rest, Oure Lady theym wary!
These men that ar lord-fest, thay cause the ploghe
    tary.   20
That men say is for the best we fynde it contrary,
Thus ar husbandys opprest, in pointe to myscary,
   On lyfe.

Thus hold thay us hunder,
Thus thay bryng us in blonder,   25
It were greatte wonder,
    And ever shuld we thryfe.
For may he gett a paynt slefe or a broche now on
        dayes,
Wo is hym that hym grefe, or onys agane says,
Dar no man hym reprefe, what mastry he mays.   30
And yit may no man lefe oone word that he says,
    No letter.
He can make purveance,
With boste and bragance,
And alle is thrughe mantenance   35
    Of men that are gretter.
Ther shalle com a swane as prowde as a po,
He must borow my wane, my ploghe also.
Then I am fulle fane to graunt or he go.
Thus lyf we in payne, anger, and wo,   40
    By nyght and day;
He must have, if he langyd;
If I shuld forgang it,
I were better be hangyd
    Then oones say hym nay.   45
It dos me good, as I walk thus by myn oone
Of this warld for to talk in maner of mone.
To my shepe wylle I stalk and herkyn anone,
Ther abyde on a balk or sytt on a stone
    Full soyne.   50
For I trowe, parde,
Trew men if thay be,
We gett more compane
    Or it be noyne.

[*The second and third shepherd arrive, each with his com-
    plaint.   To cheer themselves they sing a catch, and are*

then joined by Mak *a neighbour of ill repute for thievery.*
After some talk they all betake them to sleep, the shepherds
making Mak *lie down between them so as to keep him*
under guard. Despite this precaution his thoughts are
set on sheepstealing: he rises, while the shepherds sleep,
and says :]

Mak. Now were tyme for a man, that lakkys what he
  wold,   280
 To stalk prevely than unto a fold,
 And neemly to wyrk than, and be not to bold,
 For he myght aby the bargan, if it were told
  At the endyng.
 Now were tyme for to reylle;   285
 Bot he nedes good counselle
 That fayn wold fare weylle,
  And has bot lytylle spendyng.
 Bot abowte you a serkylle, as rownde as a moyn,
 To I have done that I wylle, tylle that it be noyn,
 That ye lyg stone stylle, to that I have doyne, 291
 And I shall say thertylle of good wordes a foyne.
  On hight
 Over youre heydys my hand I lyft,
 Outt go youre een, fordo your syght,   295
 Bot yit I must make better shyft,
  And it be right.
 Lord, what thay slepe harde, that may ye alle here,
 Was I never a shepard, bot now wylle I lere.
 If the flok be skard, yit shalle I nyp nere.   300
 How! drawes hederward: now mendys oure chere
  Fro sorow.
 A fatt shepe I dar say,
 A good flese dar I lay,
 Eft-whyte when I may,   305
  Bot this wille I borow.

[*He steals the sheep and goes home with it.*]

How, Gylle, art thou in? Gett us som lyght.

UXOR EJUS. Who makys sich dyn this tyme of the nyght?
I am sett for to spyn: I hope not I myght
Ryse a penny to wyn: I shrew them on hight. 310
So farys
A huswyff that has bene
To be rasyd thus betwene:
There may no note be sene
For sich smalle charys. 315

MAK. Good wyff, open the hek. Seys thou not what I
bryng?

UXOR. I may thole the dray the snek. A, com in, my
swetyng.

MAK. Yee, thou thar not rek of my long standing.

UXOR. By the nakyd nek art thou lyke for to hyng.

MAK. Do way: 320
I am worthy my mete,
For in a strate can I gett
More then thay that swynke and swette
All the long day.
Thus it felle to my lotte, Gylle, I had sich grace. 325

UXOR. It were a fowlle blot to be hanged for the case.

MAK. I have skapyd, Jelott, oft as hard a glase.

UXOR. Bot so long goys the pott to the water, men says,
At last
Comys it home broken. 330

MAK. Welle knowe I the token,
Bot let it never be spoken;
Bot com and help fast.
I wold he were flayn; I lyst welle ete:
This twelmothe was I not so fayn of oone shepe mete.

UXOR. Com thay or he be slayn, and here the shepe
     blete— 336

MAK. Then myght I be tane: that were a colde swette.
    Go spar
  The gaytt doore.

UXOR.   Yis, Mak,
  For and thay com at thy bak— 340

MAK. Then myght I far, by alle the pak,
    The dewille of the war.

UXOR. A good bowrde have I spied, syn thou can none.
    Here shall we hym hyde, to thay be gone.
    In my credylle abyde. Lett me alone, 345
    And I shalle lyg besyde in chylbed and grone.

MAK. Thou red;
    And I shalle say thou was lyght
    Of a knave childe this nyght.

UXOR. Now welle is me, day bright, 350
    That ever I was bred.
    This is a good gyse and a far cast;
    Yit a woman avyse helpys at the last!
    I wote never who spyse: agane go thou fast.

MAK. Bot I com or thay ryse, els blawes a cold blast. 355
    I wylle go slepe.
    Yit slepys alle this meneye
    And I shall go stalk prevely,
    As if it had never bene I
    That caryed thare shepe. 360

[*Mak resumes his place between the shepherds. They awake
and go to look after their flocks, while Mak returns home.
A sheep is missed, and Mak is suspected. They go to his
house. Bidding them tread softly, he offers them drink:*]

MAK. I wold ye dynyd or ye yode, methynk that ye swette
SECUNDUS PASTOR. Nay, nawther mendys oure mode
    drynke nor mette.

MAK. Why, sir, alys you oght bot goode ?   515

TERCIUS PASTOR. Yee, oure shepe that we gette
    Ar stollyn as thay yode.   Oure los is grette.

MAK. Syrs, drynkys !
    Had I bene thore,
    Some shuld have boght it fulle sore.   520

PRIMUS PASTOR. Mary, som men trowes that ye wore,
    And that us forthynkes.

SECUNDUS PASTOR. Mak, som men trowys that it shuld
    be ye.

TERCIUS PASTOR. Ayther ye or youre spouse ; so say we.

MAK. Now if ye have suspowse to Gille or to me,   525
    Come and rype oure howse, and then may ye se
    Who had hir.
    If I any shepe fott,
    Aythor cow or stott—
    And Gylle, my wyfe, rose nott   530
    Here syn she lade hir.
    As I am true and lele, to God here I pray,
    That this be the fyrst mele that I shalle ete this day.

[*The shepherds search the house, Gyll upbraiding them and
    keeping them away from the cradle.   They find nothing
    and take their leave, rather ashamedly.   As they go a
    thought strikes one of them :*]

PRIMUS PASTOR. Gaf ye the chyld any thyng ?

SECUNDUS PASTOR. I trow not oone farthyng.

TERCIUS PASTOR. Fast agayne wille I flyng,
    Abyde ye me there.   585
    Mak, take it no grefe, if I com to thi barne.
MAK. Nay, thou dos me greatt reprefe, and fowlle has
    thou farne.

TERCIUS PASTOR. The child wille it not grefe, that
    lytylle day starne.
  Mak, with youre leyfe, let me gyf youre barne
    Bot vj pence.   590

MAK. Nay, do way: he slepys.

TERCIUS PASTOR. Me thynk he pepys.

MAK. When he wakyns he wepys.
  I pray you go hence.

TERCIUS PASTOR. Gyf me lefe hym to kys, and lyft up
    the clowtt.   595
  What the dewille is this? he has a long snowte

PRIMUS PASTOR. He is merkyd amys. We wate ille abowte.

SECUNDUS PASTOR. Ille spon weft, i-wis, ay commys foulle
    owte.
  Ay so?
  He is lyke to oure shepe.   600

TERCIUS PASTOR. How, Gyb! May I pepe?

PRIMUS PASTOR. I trow, kynde wille crepe
  Where it may not go.

SECUNDUS PASTOR. This was a qwantt gawde and a far cast.
  It was a hee frawde.

TERCIUS PASTOR.   Yee, sirs, wast.   605
  Lett bren this bawde and bynd hir fast.
  A! fals skawde, hang at the last
    So shalle thou.
  Wylle ye se how thay swedylle
  His foure feytt in the medylle?   610
  Sagh I never in a credylle
    A hornyd lad or now.

MAK. Peasse byd I: what! lett be youre fare;
  I am he that hym gatt, and yond woman hym bare.

PRIMUS PASTOR. What dewille shall he hatt? Mak? lo
    God! Makys ayre!   615

SECUNDUS PASTOR. Lett be alle that. Now God gyf hym
       care,
    I sagh.

UXOR. A pratty child is he
    As syttys on a woman's kne;
    A dyllydowne, perde.   620
       To gar a man laghe.

TERCIUS PASTOR. I know hym by the eere marke: that is
    a good tokyn.

MAK. I telle you, syrs, hark: hys noyse was brokyn.
    Sythen told me a clerk, that he was forspokyn.

PRIMUS PASTOR. This is a false wark. I wold fayn be
       wrokyn.   625
       Gett wepyn.

UXOR. He was takyn with an elfe;
    I saw it myself.
    When the clok stroke twelf
    Was he forshapyn.   630

SECUNDUS PASTOR. Ye two ar welle feft, sam in a stede.

TERCIUS PASTOR. Syn thay manteyn thare theft, let do
       thaym to dede.

MAK. If I trespas eft, gyrd of my heede.
    With you wille I be left.

PRIMUS PASTOR. Syrs, do my reede.   635
       For this trespas,
    We wille nawther ban ne flyte,
    Fyght nor chyte,
    Bot have done as tyte,
       And cast hym in canvas.   [*They toss Mak.*
    Lord, what I am sore, in poynt for to bryst.   640
    In fayth I may no more, therfor wylle I ryst.

SECUNDUS PASTOR. As a shepe of vij skore he weyd in
       my fyst.
    For to slepe ay-whore, me thynk that I lyst.

TERCIUS PASTOR. Now I pray you,
    Lyg downe on this grene.   645

PRIMUS PASTOR. On these thefys yit I mene.

TERCIUS PASTOR. Wherto shuld ye tene
    So, as I say you?

Angelus cantat 'Gloria in Excelsis': postea dicat.

ANGELUS. Ryse, hyrdmen heynd, for now is he borne,
    That shall take fro the feynd that Adam had lorne: 650
    That warloo to sheynd, this nyght is he borne,
    God is made youre freynd: now at this morne
        He behestys,
    At Bedlem go se,
    Ther lygys that fre   655
    In a cryb fulle poorely,
        Betwyx two bestys.

PRIMUS PASTOR. This was a qwant stevyn that ever yit
    I hard.
    It is a marvelle to nevyn thus to be skard.

SECUNDUS PASTOR. Of Godys son of hevyn he spak up
    ward.   660
    Alle the wod on a levyn me thoght that he gard
    Appere.

TERCIUS PASTOR. He spak of a barne
    In Bedlem, I you warne.

PRIMUS PASTOR. That betokyns yond starne;   665
    Let us seke hym there.

SECUNDUS PASTOR. Say, what was his song? hard ye
    not how he crakyd it?
    Thre brefes to a long.

TERCIUS PASTOR.   Yee, mary, he hakt it.
    Was no crochett wrong, nor no thyng that lakt it.

PRIMUS PASTOR. For to syng us emong, right as he
    knakt it, 670
  I can.

SECUNDUS PASTOR. Let se how ye croyne.
  Can ye bark at the mone?

TERCIUS PASTOR. Hold youre tonges, have done.

PRIMUS PASTOR. Hark after, than. 675

SECUNDUS PASTOR. To Bedlem he bad that we shuld gang:
  I am full fard that we tary to lang.

TERCIUS PASTOR. Be mery, and not sad: of myrth is
    oure sang,
  Ever lastyng glad to mede may we fang,
    Withoutt noyse. 680

PRIMUS PASTOR. Hy we theder for-thy;
  If we be wete and wery,
  To that chyld and that lady
    We have it not to lose.

SECUNDUS PASTOR. We fynde by the prophecy—let be
    youre dyn— 685
  Of David and Isay, and mo then I myn;
  Thay prophecyed by clergy, that in a vyrgyn
  Shuld he lyght and ly, to slokyn oure syn
    And slake it,
  Oure kynde from wo; 690
  For Isay sayd so,
  Ecce virgo
    Concipiet a child that is nakyd.

TERCIUS PASTOR. Fulle glad may we be, and abyde
    that day
  That lufly to se, that alle myghtys may. 695
  Lord welle were me, for ones and for ay,
  Might I knele on my kne som word for to say
    To that chylde.

Bot the angelle sayd
In a cryb was he layde ;   700
He was poorly arayd,
    Both mener and mylde.

PRIMUS PASTOR. Patryarkes that has bene, and prophetys
    beforne,
    Thay desyryd to have sene this chylde that is borne.
    Thay ar gone fulle clene, that have thay lorne.   705
    We shalle se hym, I weyn, or it be morne,
      To tokyn.
    When I see hym and fele,
    Then wote I fulle weylle
    It is true as steylle   710
      That prophetes have spokyn,
    To so poore as we ar that he wold appere,
    Fyrst fynd, and declare by his messyngere.

SECUNDUS PASTOR. Go we now, let us fare : the place
    is us nere.

TERCIUS PASTOR. I am redy and yare : go we in fere
    To that bright.   716
    Lord, if thi wylles be,
    We are lewde alle thre,
    Thou grauntt us somkyns gle
      To comforth thi wight. [*They enter the stable.* 720

PRIMUS PASTOR. Haylle, comly and clene : haylle, yong
    child !
    Haylle, maker, as I meyne, of a madyn so mylde.
    Thou has waryd, I weyne, the warlo so wylde,
    The fals gyler of teyn, now goys he begylde.
    Lo, he merys ;   725
    Lo, he laghys, my swetyng,
    A welfare metyng,
    I have holden my hetyng,
      Have a bob of cherys.

SECUNDUS PASTOR. Haylle, sufferan savyoure, for thou
  has us soght: 730
 Haylle, frely foyde and floure, that alle thyng has
  wroght.
 Haylle, fulle of favoure, that made alle of noght!
 Haylle! I kneylle and I cowre. A byrd have I broght
 To my barne.
 Haylle, lytylle tyné mop,   735
 Of oure crede thou art crop:
 I wold drynk on thy cop,
  Lytylle day starne.

TERCIUS PASTOR. Haylle, derlyng dere, fulle of godhede,
 I pray the be nere when that I have nede.   740
 Haylle! swete is thy chere: my hart wold blede
 To se the sytt here in so poore wede,
  With no pennys.
 Haylle! put furthe thy dalle,
 I bryng the bot a balle: 745
 Have and play the with alle.
  And go to the tenys.

MARIA. The fader of heven, God omnypotent,
 That sett alle on seven, his son has he sent.
 My name couthe he neven and lyght or he went. 750
 I conceyved hym fulle even, thrugh myght as he ment;
  And now is he borne.
 He kepe you fro wo:
 I shalle pray him so;
 Telle furth as ye go,   755
  And myn on this morne.

PRIMUS PASTOR. Farewelle, lady, so fare to beholde,
 With thy chylde on thi kne.

SECUNDUS PASTOR.   Bot he lygys fulle cold.
 Lord, welle is me: now we go, thou behold.

Tercius Pastor. For sothe alle redy, it semys to be told
    Fulle oft.   761

Primus Pastor. What grace we have fun.

Secundus Pastor. Com furth, now as we won.

Tertius Pastor. To syng ar we bun:
    Let take on loft.   765

Explicit pagina pastorum.

'Coventry' Plays.

—◆—

XI. THE SALUTATION AND CONCEPTION.

CONTEMPLACIO. Ffowre thowsand sex undryd foure I
    telle,
  Man ffor his offens and ffowle foly,
Hath leyn[1] yeres in the peynes of helle,
  And were wurthy to ly therin endlesly,   4
But thanne xulde perysche your grete mercye.
  Good Lord, have on man pyté,
Have mende of the prayour seyd by Ysaie,
  Lete mercy meke thin hyest magesté.   8

Wolde God thou woldyst breke thin hefne myghtye,
  And com down here into erthe,
And levyn yeres thre and threttye,
  Thyn famyt ffolke with thi fode to fede.   12
To staunche thi thryste lete thi syde blede,
  Ffor erst wole not be mad redempcion.
Cum vesite us in this tyme of nede,
  Of thi careful creatures, Lord, have compassyon!   16

A! woo to us wrecchis that wrecchis be,
  Ffor God hath addyd ssorwe to sorwe;
I prey the, Lorde, thi sowles com se,
  How thei ly and sobbe, both eve and morewe,   20
With thi blyssyd blood ffrom balys[2] hem borwe,
  Thy careful creaturys cryenge in captyvyté,

---

[1] loyn, MS.   [2] babys, MS.

A! tary not, gracyous Lord, tyl it be to-morwe,
  The devyl hath dysceyved hem be his iniquité.   24

A! quod Jeremye, who xal gyff wellys to myn eynes,
  That I may wepe bothe day and nyght,
To se oure bretheryn in so longe peynes?
  Here myschevys amende may thi meche myght!   28
As grett as the se, Lord, was Adamys contryssyon ryght.
  Ffrom oure hed is ffalle the crowne,
Man is comeryd in synne, I crye to thi syght,
  Gracyous Lord! Gracyous Lord! Gracyous Lord, come
    downe!   32

VIRTUTES. Lord! plesyth it thin hi*gh* domynacion,
  On man that thou made to have pyte,
Patryarchys and· prophetys han mad supplycacion,
  Oure offyse is to presente here prayeres to the.   36
Aungelys, archaungelys, we thre
  That ben in the fyrst ierarchie,
Ffor man to thin hy magesté,
  Mercy! mercy! mercy! we crye.   40

The aungel, Lord, thou made so gloryous,
  Whos synne hath mad hym a devyl in helle,
He mevyd man to be so contraryous,
  Man repentyd, and he in his obstynacye doth dwelle.
Hese grete males, good Lord, repelle,   45
  And take man onto thi grace,
Lete thi mercy make hym with aungelys dwelle,
  Of Locyfere to restore the place.   48

PATER. *Propter miseriam inopum, et gemitum pauperum*
               nunc exurgam.

Ffor the wretchydnes of the nedy,
  And the porys lamentacion,
Now xal I ryse that am Almyghty,
  Tyme is come of reconsyliacion,   52

E

My prophetys with prayers have made supplicacion,
    My contryte creaturys crye alle for comforte,
Alle myn aungellys in hefne, withowte cessacion,
    They crye that grace to man myght exorte.   56

VERITAS. Lord, I am thi dowtere, Trewthe,
    Thou wilt se I be not lore,
Thyn unkynde creatures to save were rewthe,
    The offens of man hath grevyd the sore.   60
Whan Adam had synnyd, thou seydest yore,
    That he xulde deye and go to helle,
And now to blysse hym to restore,
    Twey contraryes mow not togedyr dwelle.   64

Thy trewthe, Lord, xal leste withowtyn ende,
    I may in no wyse ffro the go,
That wrecche that was to the so unkende,
    He may not have to meche wo.   68
He dyspysyd the and plesyd thi ffo,
    Thou art his creatour and he is thi creature,
Thou hast lovyd trewthe, it is seyd evyr mo,
    Therfore in peynes lete hym evyrmore endure.   72

MISERICORDIA. O ffadyr of mercye and God of comforte,
    That counselle[st] us in eche trybulacion,
Lete your dowtere Mercy to yow resorte,
    And on man that is myschevyd have compassyon.   76
Hym grevyth fful gretly his transgressyon,
    Alle hefne and erthe crye ffor mercy;
Me semyth ther xuld be non excepcion,
    Ther prayers ben offeryd so specyally.   80

Threwthe sseyth she hath evyr be than,
    I graunt it wel she hath be so,
And thou seyst endlesly that mercy thou hast kept ffor man
    Than mercyabyl lorde, kepe us bothe to,   84
Thu seyst *veritas mea et misericordia mea cum ipso*,
    Suffyr not thi sowlys than in sorwe to slepe,

Legliſe Miſericorde
Juſtice Sapience

FROM HEURES A LUSAIGE DE ROME

PARIS, HARDOUIN, C. 1506

That helle hownde that hatyth the byddyth hym ho!
   Thi love, man, no lengere lete hym kepe.   88

JUSTICIA. Mercy, me merveylyth what *y*ow movyth,
   *Y*e know wel I am *y*our sister Ryghtwysnes,
God is ryghtfful and ryghtffulnes lovyth,
   Man offendyd hym that is endles,   92
Therefore his endles punchement may nevyr sees;
   Also he forsoke his makere that made hym of clay,
And the devyl to his mayster he ches,
   Xulde he be savyd? nay! nay! nay!   96

As wyse as is God he wolde a be,
   This was the abhomynabyl presumpcion,
It is seyd, *y*e know wel this of me,
   That the ryghtwysnes of God hath no diffynicion.   100
Therffore late this be oure conclusyon,
   He that sore synnyd ly stylle in sorwe,
He may nevyr make a seyth be resone,
   Whoo myght thanne thens hym borwe?   104

MISERICORDIA. Syster Ryghtwysnes, ye are to vengeabyl,
   Endles synne God endles may restore,
Above alle hese werkys God is mercyabyl,
   Thow he forsook God be synne, be feyth he forsook
      hym never the more.   108
And thow he presumyd nevyr so sore,
   *Y*e must consyder the frelnes cf mankende,
Lerne, and *y*e lyst, this is Goddys lore,
   The mercy of God is withowtyn ende.   112

PAX. To spare *y*our speches, systeres, it syt;
   It is not onest in vertuys to ben dyscencion,
The pes of God ovyrcomyth alle wytt.
   Thow Trewthe and Ryght sey grett reson,   116
*Y*ett Mercy seyth best to my pleson;
   Ffor yf mannys sowle xulde abyde in helle,

Betwen God and man evyr xulde be dyvysyon,
  And than myght not I Pes dwelle.   120

Therefore me semyth best *y*e thus acorde;
  Than hefne and erthe *y*e xul qweme,
Putt bothe *y*our sentens in oure Lorde,
  And in his hygh wysdam lete hym deme.   124
This is most syttynge me xulde seme,
  And lete se how we ffowre may alle abyde,
That mannys sowle it xulde perysche it wore sweme,
  Or that ony of us ffro othere xulde dyvyde.   128

VERITAS. In trowthe hereto I consente,
  I wole prey oure lorde it may so be.

JUSTICIA. I Ryghtwysnes am wele contente,
  Ffor in hym is very equyté.   132

MISERICORDIA. And I Mercy ffro this counsel wole not fle,
  Tyl wysdam hath seyd I xal ses.

PAX. Here is God now, here is unyté,
  Hefne and erthe is plesyd with Pes.

Mary Magdalen.

Her entyr Syrus, the fader of Mary Maudleyn.

SYRUS. Emperor and kyngges and conquerors kene,
Erlys, and borons, and knytes that byn bold,
Berdes in my bower, so semely to sene,
I commaund yow at onys my hestes to hold.   52
Behold my person, glysteryng in gold,
Semely besyn of all other men :
Cyrus is my name, be cleffys so cold,
I command you all obedyent to beyn ;   56
Wo-so woll nat, in bale I hem bryng,   57
And knett swyche caytyfys in knottes of care.
Thys castell of Maudleyn is at my wylddyng,
With all the contre, bothe lesse and more,   60
And Lord of Jerusalem, who agens me don dare ?
Alle Beteny at my beddyng be ;
I am sett in solas from al syyng sore,
And so xall all my posteryte.
Thus for to leven in rest and ryalte,   65
I have her a sone that is to me ful trew,   66
No comlyar creatur of Goddes creacyon,
To amyabyll douctors, full brygth of ble,
Ful gloryos to my syth an ful of delectacyon.
Lazarus my son, in my respeccyon.   70
Here is Mary, ful fayr and ful of femynyte,
And Martha, ful [of] beute and of delycyte,
Ful of womanly merrorys and of benygnyte,

They have fulfyllyd my hart with consolacyon.   74

*   *   *   *   *   *   *   *

Now Lazarus, my sonne, whech art ther brothyr,   79
The lordshep of Jerusalem I gyff the after my dysses,
And Mary thys castell, alonly, an non othyr ;
And Martha xall have Beteny, I sey exprese :
Thes gyftes I graunt yow withowtyn les,   83
Whyll that I am in good mynd.   84

LAZARUS. Most reverent father ! I thank yow hartely 85
Of yower grett kyndnes shuyd onto me !
Ye have grauntyd swych a lyfelod, worthy
Me to restreyn from all nessesyte.   88
Now, good lord, and hys wyll it be,
Graunt me grace to lyve to thy plesowans,
And a-gens hem so to rewle me
Thatt we may have joye withoutyn weryauns.   92

MARY MAUDLEYN. Thatt God of pes and pryncypall
counsell,   93
More swetter is thi name than hony be kynd !
We thank yow, fathyr, for your gyftes ryall,
Owt of peynes of poverte us to on-bynd ;   96
Thys is a preservatyff from streytnes, we fynd,
From wordly labors to my coumfortyng ;
For thys lyfflod is abyll for the dowtter of a kyng,   99
Thys place of plesauns, the soth to seye.   100

MARTHA. O ye good fathyr of grete degre,   101
Thus to departe with your ryches,
Consederyng ower lowlynes and humylyte,
Us to save from worldly dessetres :
Ye shew us poyntes of grete jentylnes,   105
So mekly to meynteyn us to your grace.
Hey in heven a-wansyd mot yow be
In blysse, to se that lordes face,
Whan ye xal hens passe !

Cyrus. Now I rejoyse with all my mygthtes;   110
To enhanse my chyldryn, it was my delyte :
Now wyn and spycys, ye jentyll knyttes,
On-to thes ladys of jentylnes.

[ll. 114–139. Tiberius Caesar sends orders to Herod to search out
    rebels. ll. 140–228. Herod hears from his 'philosophers' a prophecy
    of Christ's Incarnation and 'rages.' He receives Tiberius' orders
    and sends them on to Pilate. ll. 229–264. Pilate receives the
    orders and declares he will execute them.]

Syrus takyt his deth.

Syrus. A! help! help! I stond in drede   265
Syknes is sett onder my syde!
A! help! deth wyll aquyte me my mede!
A! gret Gode! thou be my gyde;   268
How I am trobyllyd both bak and syde.
Now wythly help me to my bede.
A! this rendyt my rybbys! I xall never goo nor ryde!
The dent of deth is hevyar than led.   272
A! Lord, Lord! what xall I doo this tyde?
A! gracyows God! have ruth on me,
In thys word no lengar to abyde.
I blys yow, my chyldyrn, God mot with us be!   276

Her avoydyt Syrus sodenly, and than [*comyt*] *sayyng, Lazarus.*

Lazarus. Alas, I am sett in grete hevynesse!   277
Ther is no tong my sorow may tell,
So sore I am browth in dystresse ;
In feyntnes I falter, for this fray fell ;   280
Thys dewresse wyl lett me no longar dwelle,
But, God of grace, sone me redresse.
A! how my peynes don me repelle!
Lord, with-stond this duresse!   284

MARY MAGLEYN. The in-wyttissymus God that ever
    xal reyne,   285
Be his help, an sowlys sokor!
To whom it is most nedfull to cumplayn;
He to bryng us owt of ower dolor—   288
He is most mytyest governowr,
From soroyng us to restr[a]yne.   290

MARTHA. A! how I am sett in sorowys sad,
That long my lyf y may nat indeure!
Thes grawous peynes make me ner mad!
Under clower is now my fathyris cure,   294
That sumtyme was here ful mery and glad.
Ower lordes mercy be his mesure,
And defeynd hym from peynes sad!   297

LAZARUS. Now, systyrs, ower fatherys wyll we woll
    exprese :   298
Thys castell is owerys, with all the fee—

MARTHA. As hed and governower, as reson is :
And on this wyse abydyn with yow wyll wee;   301
We wyll natt desevyr, whatt so be-falle.

MARIA. Now, brothyr and systyrs, welcum ye be.
And ther-of specyally I pray yow all.   304

*Her xal entyr the Kyng of the word, then the Kyng of the
    flesch, and then the dylfe, with the seven dedly synnes, a
    bad angyll an an good angyl, thus seyyng the word.*

[THE KING OF THE WORLD.] I am the word, worthyest
    that evyr god wrowth,   305
And also I am the prymatt portatur
Next heveyn, yf the trewth be sowth,—
And that I jugge me to skryptur;—   308
And I am he that lengest xal induer,
And also most of domynacyon;

Yf I be hys foo, woo is abyll to recure?

For the whele of fortune with me hath sett his sentur.　312

　　*　　*　　*　　*　　*　　*　　*　　*

Her xal entyr the Kynge of flesch with slowth, gloteny,
lechery.

I, kyng of flesch, florychyd in my flowers,　334

Of deyntys delycyows I have grett domynacyon,

So ryal a kyng was nevyr borne in bowrys,

Nor hath more delyth ne more delectacyon.

　　*　　*　　*　　*　　*　　*　　*　　*

Here xal entyr the prynse of dylles in a stage, and Helle
ondyrneth that stage, thus seyyng the dylfe.

SATAN. Now I, prynse, pyrked, prykkyd in pryde,　358

Satan ower sovereyn, set with every cyrcumstanse,

For I am a-tyred in my tower to tempt yow this tyde;

As a kyng ryall I sette at my plesauns,　361

With wroth [and] invy at my ryall retynawns;

The boldest in bower I bryng to a-baye;

Mannis sowle to besegyn and bryng to obeysauns,

Ya [with] tyde and tyme I do that I may,　365

For at hem I have dysspyte that he wolde have the joye

That Lycyfer, with many a legyown, lost for ther pryde;

The snares that I xal set wher never set at Troye,

So I thynk to besegyn hem be every waye wyde;　369

I xal getyn hem from grace, wher-so-ever he abyde,

That body and sowle xal com to my hold.

　　　　　Hym for to take,　372

Now my knythtes so stowth,　373

With me ye xall ron in rowte,

My consell to take for a skowte,

Whytly that we wer went for my sake.　376

WRATH. With wrath or wyhylles we xal hyrre wynne.

ENVY. Or with sum sotyllte sett hur in synne.　378

DYLFE. Com of than, let us begynne
To werkyn hur sum wrake. 380

Her xal the deywl go to the word with his compeny.

SATAN. Heyle word, worthyest of a-bowndans! 381
In hast we must a conseyll take;
Ye must aply yow with all your afyauns,
A woman of whorshep ower servant to make.

[ll. 384-469. The World recommends recourse to the Flesh, who sends
   his servant Luxuria (or Lechery) to Mary as she sits mourning her
   father's death. Luxury persuades Mary to amuse herself at Jerusalem.]

*Here takyt Mary hur wey to Ierusalem with Luxsurya, and
   they xal resort to a taverner, thus seyyng the taverner.*

I am a taverner wytty and wyse, 470
That wynys have to sell gret plente.
Of all the taverners I bere the pryse
That be dwellyng withinne the cete; 473
Of wynys I have grete plente,
Both whyte wynne and red that [ys] so cleyr: 475
Here ys wynne of mawt and Malmeseyn,
Clary wynne and claret, and other moo,
Wyn of Gyldyr and of Galles, that made at the grome [?],
Wyn of wyan and vernage, I seye also;
Ther be no better, as ferre as ye can goo. 480

LUXSURYA. Lo, lady, the comfort and the sokower, 481
Go we ner and take a tast,
Thys xal bryng your sprytes to fawor.
Taverner, bryng us of the fynnest thou hast. 484

TAVERNER. Here, lady, is wyn, a repast 485
To man and woman, a good restoratyff;
Ye xall not thynk your mony spent in wast,
From stodyys and hevynes it woll yow relyff. 488

MARY. I-wys ye seye soth, ye grom of blysse;
To me ye be courtes and kynde.   490

Her xal entyr a galaunt thus seyyng.

GALAUNT [CURIOSITY].
Hof, hof, hof, a frysch new galaunt,   491
Ware of thryst, ley that a-doune!
What! wene ye, syrrys, that I were a marchant,
Because that I am new com to town?   494
With sum praty tasppysster wold I fayn rown;

*   *   *   *   *   *   *   *

LUXSURYA. Lady, this man is for yow, as I se can;   507
To sett yow i sporttes and talkyng this tyde.

MARY. Cal hym in, taverner, as ye my love wyll han,
And we xall make ful mery, yf he wolle abyde.   510

[ll. 511–587. Mary departs with the gallant and Satan rejoices over
    her fall. We next see Mary sleeping in an arbour, and then Simon
    the leper preparing for his feast. Then a good angel appears to
    Mary and says:]

GOOD ANGYLL. Woman, woman, why art thou so on-
            stabyll?   588
Ful bytterly thys blysse it wol be bowth;
Why art thou ayens God so veryabyll?
Wy thynkes thou nat God made the of nowth?
In syn and sorow thou art browth,   592
Fleschly lust is to ye full delectabyll;
Salve for thi sowle must be sowth,
And leve thi werkes wayn and veryabyll.   595
Remembyr, woman, for thi pore pryde,   596
How thi sowle xal lyyn in helle fyr!
A! remembyr how sorowful itt is to abyde
Withowtyn eynd in angur and ire!   599
Remember the on mercy, make thi sowle clyr!
I am the gost of goodnesse that so wold ye gydde.

MARY. A! how the speryt of goodnesse hat promtyt
    me this tyde,
And temtyd me with tytyll of trew perfythnesse.
Alas! how betternesse in my hert doth abyde!   604
I am wonddyd with werkes of gret dystresse,   605
A! how pynsynesse potyt me to oppresse,
That I have synnyd on every side.
O lord! wo xall put me from this peynfulnesse?   608
A! woo xall to mercy be my gostly gyde?
I xal porsue the prophett, wherso he be,
For he is the welle of perfyth charyte;   611
Be the oyle of mercy he xal me relyff.
With swete bawmys I wyl seken hym this syth,
And sadly folow his lordshep in eche degre.   614

Here xal entyr the prophet with his desyplys, thus seyyng
Symont leprus.

Now ye be welcom, mastyr, most of magnyfycens,   615
I beseche yow benyngly ye wol be so gracyows
Yf that it be lekyng onto yower hye presens
Thys daye to com dyne at my hows.   618

IESUS. God a mercy, Symontt, that thou wylt me knowe!
I woll entyr thi hows with pes and unyte;   620
I am glad for to rest, ther grace gynnyt grow;
For withinne thi hows xal rest charyte,   622
And the bemys of grace xal byn illumynows.   623
But syth thou wytystsaff a dyner on me,
With pes and grace I entyr thi hows.

SYMOND. I thank yow, master, most benyng and gracyus,
That yow wol of your hye soverente;   627
To me itt is a joye most speceows,
Withinne my hows that I may yow se!
Now syt to the bord, mastyrs alle.   630

Her xal Mary folow alonge, with this lamentacyon.

MARY. O I, cursyd caytyff, that myche wo hath wrowth
Ayens my makar, of mytes most;   632
I have offendyd hym with dede and thowth,
But in his grace is all my trost,   634
Or elles I know well I am but lost,
Body and sowle damdpnyd perpetuall.
Yet, good lord of lorddes, my hope [is] perhenuall, 637
With the to stond in grace and fawour to se,
Thow knowyst my hart and thowt in especyal;
Therfor, good lord, after my hart reward me.   640

Her xal Mary wasche the fett of the prophet with the terres of
hur yys, whypyng hem with hur herre, and than anoynt
hym with a precyus noyttment.

IESUS DICIT. Symond, I thank ye speceally   641
For this grett repast that her hath be;
But Symond, I telle the fectually
I have thynges to seyn to the.   644

   *   *   *   *   *   *   *   *

Symond, behold, this woman in all wyse   665
How she with teres of hyr better wepyng
She wassheth my fete, and doth me servyse,
And anoyntyt hem with onymentes, lowly knelyng,   668
And with her her, fayer and brygth shynnyng,
She wypyth hem agayn with good entent;
But Symont, syth that I entyrd thi hows,   671
To wasshe my fete thou dedyst nat aplye,
Nor to wype my fete thou wer nat so faworus;
Wherfor in thi conscyens thou owttyst nat to replye. 674
But, woman, I sey to the werely,
I forgeyffe the thi wrecchednesse,
And hol in sowle be thou made therby.

[ll. 678–1132. Mary gives thanks : seven devils are cast out of her, and in the next scene we see Satan punishing his angels with blows for their ill-success. The history of the sickness and raising of Lazarus is then enacted, and at l. 924 Part I of the play comes to an end.
Part II begins with a boasting speech of the King of Marcylle ; then we hear the devils crying out because Hell has been harrowed, upon which follows the scene in the garden of Joseph of Arimathea on the morning of Christ's Resurrection.]

Here devoyd all the three Maryys ; and the kynge of Marcyll xall begynne a sacryfyce.

REX MERCYLL. Now, lordes and ladyys of grett a-prise,
A mater to meve yow is in my memoryall,   1134
This day to do a sacryfyce
With multetude of myrth before ower goddes all,   1136
With preors in aspecyall before his presens,
Eche creature with hartt demure.   1138

REGINA. To that lord curteys and keynd,   1139
Mahond, that is so mykyll of myth,
With mynstrelly and myrth in mynd,
Lett us gon ofer in that hye kyngis syth.   1142

Here xal enter an hethen preste and his boye.

PRESBYTER. Now, my clerke, Hawkyn, for love of me
Loke fast myn awter wer arayd ;   1144
Goo, ryng a bell to or thre !
Lythly, chyld, it be natt delayd,   1146
For here xall be a grett solemnyte.
Loke, boy, thou do it with a brayd !   1148

[The boy is impudent, and the priest obeys the stage direction 'bete him.' Enter the King.]

REX DICITT. Now, prystes and clerkys, of this tempyll cler   1178
Yower servyse to sey, lett me se.

PRESBYTER. A, soveryn lord, we shall don ower devyr.
Boy, a boke a-non thou bryng me!   1181
Now, boy, to my awter I wyll me dresse;   1182
On xall my westment and myn aray.

BOY. Now than the lesson I woll expresse,
Lyke as longytt for the servyse of this day :—   1185

Leccyo mahowndys, viri fortissimi sarasenorum.
Glabriosum ad glumandum glumardinorum,
Gormondorum alocorum, stampatinantum cursorum,
Cownthtes fulcatum, congruryandum tersorum
Mursum malgorum, Mararagorum.   1190

　　　*　　*　　*　　*　　*　　*　　*　　*

Howndes and hogges, in hegges and helles,   1198
Snakes and toddes mott be yower belles;
Ragnell and Roffyn, and other, in the wavys,
Grauntt yow grace to dye on the galows.   1201

PRESBYTER. Now, lordes and ladyys, lesse and more,
Knele all don with good devocyon;   1203
Yonge and old, rych and pore,
Do yower oferyng to sentt Mahownde,
And ye xall have grett pardon,   1206
That longyth to this holy place;
And receyve *y*e xall my benesown,
And stond in Mahowndes grace.   1209

REX DICITT. Mahownd, thou art of mytes most,   1210
In my syth a gloryus gost;
Thou comfortyst me both in contre and cost
With thi wesdom and thi wytt;   1213
For truly, lord, in the is my trost.   1214
Good lord, lett natt my sowle be lost!
All my cownsell well thou wotst.
Here in thi presens as I sett,   1217
Thys besawnt of gold, rych and rownd,   1218
I ofer ytt for my lady and me,

F

That thou mayst be ower counfortes in this stownd,
Sweth Mahound, remembyr me.   1221

[ll. 1222–1375. After two scenes representing the receipt of the news
of Christ's Resurrection by Pilate and Tiberius Caesar, the angel
Raphael is sent from heaven to Mary Magdalen.]

ANGELUS. Abasse the noutt, Mary, in this place; 1376
Ower lordes preceptt thou must ful-fyll,
To passe the see in shortt space
On-to the lond of Marcyll.   1379
Kyng and quene converte xall *ye*,
And byn amyttyd as an holy apostylesse;
Alle the lond xall be techyd alonly be the;
Goddes lawys on-to hem ye xall expresse.   1383
Therfor hast yow forth with gladnesse,
Goddes commaundement for to fulfylle.   1385

MARI MAWDLEYN. He that from my person vij dewlles
              mad to fle,   1386
Be vertu of hym alle thyng was wrowth;
To seke thoys pepyll I wol rydy be.
As thou hast commaunddytt, in vertu they xall be browth.
With thi grace, good lord, in deite,   1390
Now to the see I wyll me hy,
Sum sheppyng to asspy.
Now spede me, lord, in eternall glory!
Now be my spede, allmyty trenite!   1394

Here xall entyre a shyp with a mery song.

SHEPMAN. Stryke! skryke! lett fall an ankyr to grownd!
Her is a fayer haven to se!   1396
Connyngly in, loke that ye sownd;
I hope good harbarow have xal wee!   1398
Loke that we have drynke, boy, thou.

[The shipman's boy is as impudent as the priest's, with a like result.]

MAUDLEYN. Master of the shepe, a word with the. 1423

MASTER. All redy, fayer woman, whatt wol *ye* ?

MARY. Of whense is thys shep? tell *ye* me ;
And yf *ye* seyle with-in a whyle. 1426

MASTER. We wol seyle this same day, 1427
Yf the wynd be to ower pay.
This shep that I of sey
Is of the lond of Marcyll. 1430

MARY. Syr, may I natt with yow sayle ? 1431
And *ye* xall have for yower awayle.

MASTER. Of sheppyng the xall natt faylle ;
For us the wynd is good and saffe. 1434
Yond ther is the lond of Torke,
I wher full loth for to lye.

Now xall the shep-men syng.

Of this cors we thar nat a-baffe, 1437
Yender is the lond of Satyllye. 1438
Stryk ! beware of sond !
Cast a led, and in us gyde !
Of Marcyll this is the kyngges lond. 1441
Go a lond, thow fayer woman, this tyde,
To the kyngges place ; yonder may *ye* see.
Sett of, sett of, from lond.

THE BOY. All redy, master, at thyn hand. 1445

Her goth the shep owt of the place.

[Mary Magdalen goes to the King and preaches to him.]

REX. Herke, woman, thow hast many resonnes grett; 1527
I thyngk, on-to my goddes aperteynyng they beth.
But thou make me answer son, I xall the frett,
And cut the tonge owt of thi hed. 1530

MARY. Syr, yf I seyd amys, I woll return agayn. 1531
Leve yower encomberowns of perturbacyon,
And lett me know what yower goddes byn,
And how they may save us from treubelacyon. 1534

REX. Hens to the tempyll that we war, 1535
And ther xall thow se a solom syth.
Com on all, both lesse and more,
Thys day to se my goddes myth. 1538

Here goth the Kynge with all his a-tendaunt to the tempyll.

Loke now, qwatt seyyst thow be this syth? 1539
How plezeaunttly they stond, se thow how!
Lord, I besech thi grett myth,
Speke to this chrisetyn that here sestt thou. 1542
Speke, god lord, speke! se how I do bow!
Herke, thou pryst! qwat menytt all this?
What! speke, good lord! speke! what eylytt the now?
Speke, as thow artt bote of all blysse! 1546

PRYSBYTER. Lord, he woll natt speke whyle chriseten
her is.

MARY. Syr kyng, and it pleze yower gentyllnesse, 1548
Gyff me lycens my prayors to make
On-to my God in heven blysch,
Sum merakyll to shewyn for yower sake.

REX. Pray thi fylle, tyll thi[1] knees ake. 1552

MARY. Dominus, illuminacio mea, quem timebo!
Dominus, protecctor vite mee, a quo trepedabo!

Here xal the mament tremyll and quake.

Now, lord of lordes, to thi blyssyd name sanctificatt,
Most mekely my feyth I recummend. 1556
Pott don the pryd of mamentes violatt!
Lord, to thi lover thi goodnesse descend; 1558

---

[1] then, MS.

Lett natt ther pryd to thi poste pretend,
Wher-as is rehersyd thi hye name Jhesus.
Good lord, my preor I feythfully send ;
Lord, thi rythwysnesse here dyscus ! 1562

*Here xall comme a clowd from heven, and sett the tempyl one
a fyer, and the pryst and the clerk xall synke.*

[The remainder of the play shows the voyage of the King and Queen to
the Holy Land, the wonderful restoration to life of the Queen and
her baby by the aid of Mary Magdalen, the feeding of Mary in the
wilderness by angels, her death, and her ascension.]

The Castell of Perseverance.

HUMANUM GENUS.

        After oure forme faderes' kende
    This nyth I waus of my moder born;
        Fro my moder I walke, I wende,
    Ful feynt and febyl I fare you beforn.
        I am nakyd of lym and lende,   (5)
    As mankynde is schapyn and schorn,
        I not wedyr to gon ne to lende,
    To helpe my-self mydday ny morn,
            For schame I stonde and schende.
    I waus born this nyth in blody ble   (10)
    And nakyd I am as ye may se.
    A! Lord God in trinite,
            Whow mankende is unchende!

        Where-to I waus to this werld browth,
    I ne wot but to woo and wepynge.   (15)
        I am born and have ryth nowth
    To helpe my self in no doynge.
        I s[t]onde¹ and stodye, al ful of thowth;
    Bare and pore is my clothynge,
        A sely crysme my hed hath cawth,   (20)
    That I tok at myn crystenynge;
            Certes I have no more.
    Of erthe I cam, I wot ryth wele,
    And as erthe I stande this sele;

        ¹ sonde, MS.

Of mankende it is gret dele, (25)
    Lord God, I cry thyne ore.

  Two[1] aungels bene a-synyd to me :
The ton techyth me to goode,
  On my ryth syde *y*e may hym se,
He cam fro Criste that deyed on rode. (30)
  A-nother ordeynyd her to be,
That is my foo be fen and flode,
  He is a-bout in every degre
To[2] drawe me to the dewylys wode,
    That in helle ben thycke. (35)
  Swyche to hath every man on lyve,
To rewlyn hym and hys wyttes fyve,
Whanne man doth evyl the ton wolde shryve,
    The tother drawyth to wycke.

  But syn these aungelys be to me falle, (40)
Lord Jhū to *y*ou I bydde a bone,
  That I may folwe, be strete and stalle,
The aungyl that cam fro hevene trone.
  Now lord Jhū, in hevene halle,
Here, whane I make my mone ! (45)
  Coryows Criste, to *y*ou I calle.
As a grysly gost I grucche and grone,
  I wene ryth ful of thowth.
  A ! Lord Jhū, wedyr may I goo ?
  A crysyme I have and no moo ! (50)
  Alas ! men may be wondyr woo
    Whanne thei be fyrst forth browth.

BONUS ANGELUS.
    *Y*a forsothe and that is wel sene,
  Of woful wo man may synge,
    For iche creature helpeth hym self bedene, (55)
  Save only man, at hys comynge,

---

    [1] Ij, MS.   [2] Do, MS.

Nevyr-the-lesse turne the fro tene
And serve Jhū, hevene kynge,
And thou shalt, be grevys grene,
Fare well in all thynge.   (60)
That lord thi lyfe hath lante!
Have hym alway in thi mynde,
That deyed on rode for mankynde,
And serve hym to thi lyfes ende,
And sertes thou schalt not wante.   (65)

MALUS ANGELUS.

Pes aungel, thi wordes are not wyse,
Thou counselyst hym not a-ryth.
He schal hym drawyn to the werdes servyse,
To dwelle with caysere, kynge and knyth,
That in londe be hym non lyche.   (70)
Cum on with me, stylle as ston :
Thou and I to the werd schul goon,
And thanne thou schalt sen a-non
Whow sone thou schalt be ryche.

BONUS ANGELUS.

A ! pes aungel, thou spekyst folye!   (75)
Why schuld he coveyt werldes goode,
Syn Criste in erthe and hys meynye
All in povert here thei stode?
Werldes wele, be strete and stye,
Faylyth and fadyth as fysch in flode,   (80)
But hevene ryche is good and trye,
Ther Criste syttyth, bryth as blode,
Withoutyn any dystresse.
To the world wolde he not flyt,
But forsok it every whytt ;   (85)
Example I fynde in holy wryt,
He wyl bere me wytnesse.

Divicias et paupertatem ne dederis m[ihi] dñe.

MALUS ANGELUS. *Y*a, *y*a, man, leve hym nowth,
 But cum with me be stye and strete.
  Have thou a gobet of the werld cawth, (90)
 Thou schalt fynde it good and swete.
  A fayre lady the schal be tawth,
 That in bowre thi bale schal bete.
  With ryche rentes thou schalt be frawth,
 With sylke sendel to syttyn in sete. (95)
  I rede late bedys be :
 If thou wylt have wel thyn hele,
 And faryn wel at mete and mele,
 With goddes servyse may thou not dele,
  But cum and folwe me. (100)

HUMANUM GENUS. Whom to folwe wetyn I ne may :
 I stonde in stodye and gynne to rave,
  I wolde be ryche in gret aray,
 And fayn I wolde my sowle save.
  As wynde in watyr I wave : (105)
 Thou woldyst to the werld I me toke,
 And he wolde that I it forsoke,
 Now so God me helpe, and the holy boke,
  I not wyche I may have.

MALUS ANGELUS. Cum on, man ! where of hast thou care ?
 Go we to the werld, I rede the, blyve ; (111)
  For ther thou schalt now [1] ryth wel fare,
 In case if thou thynke for to thryve,
  No lord schal be the lyche.
 Take the werld to thine entent, (115)
 And late thi love be ther on lent,
 With gold and sylvyr and ryche rent
  A-none thou schalt be ryche.

[1] mow, MS.

HUMANUM GENUS. Now syn thou hast be-hetyn me so
  I wyl go with the and a-say ;   (120)
   I ne lette for frende ner fo,
  But with the world I wyl go play,
   Certes a lytyl throwe.
  In this world is al my trust
  To lyv[y]n in lykyng and in lust: (**125**)
  Have he and I onys cust,
   We schal not part I trowe.

BONUS ANGELUS. A ! nay, man ! for Cristes blod !
  Cum agayn be strete and style !
   The werld is wyckyd and ful wod, (130)
  And thou schalt levyn but a whyle.
   What coveytyst thou to wynne ?
  Man, thynke on thyn endynge day,
  Whanne thou schalt be closyd under clay,
  And if thou thenke of that a-ray,   (135)
   Certes thou schalt not synne.

   Homo memento finis et in eternũ non peccabis.

MALUS ANGELUS. *Y*a, on thi sowle thou schalt thynke al
   be tyme ;
  Cum forth, man, and take non hede,
   Cum on and thou schalt holdyn hym inne.
  Thi flesch thou schalt foster and fede (140)
   With lofly lyvys fode.
  With the werld thou mayst be bold,
  Tyl thou be sexty wynter hold ;
  Wanne thi nose waxit cold
   Thanne mayst thou drawe to goode. (145)

HUMANUM GENUS. I vow to God, and so I may
  Make mery a ful gret throwe—
   I may levyn many a day,
  I am but yonge, as I trowe.

    For to do that I schulde. (150)
Myth I ryde be sompe and syke,
And be ryche and lord lyke,
Certes, thanne schulde I be fryke
    And a mery man on molde.

MALUS ANGELUS. *Y*ys, be my feyth, thou schalt be a lord,
    And ellys hange me be the hals. (156)
      But thou muste be at myn a-cord,
Other whyle thou muste be fals
    A-monge kythe and kynne.
Now go we forth swythe a-non, (160)
To the werld us must gon,
And bere the manly evere a-mong,
    Whanne thou comyst out or inne.

HUMANUM GENUS. *Y*ys, and ellys have thou my necke
    But I be manly be downe and dyche, (165)
      And thou I be fals I ne recke,
With so that I be lord lyche
    I folowe the as I can.
Thou schalt be my bote of bale,
For were I ryche of holt and hale, (170)
Thanne wolde I *y*eve nevere tale
    Of God ne of good man.

BONUS ANGELUS. I weyle and I wrynge and make mone
This man with woo schal be pylt.
    I sye sore and grysly grone, (175)
For hys folye schal make hym spylt.
    I not weder to gone,

        Pipe up mu[*sic*]

Mankynde hath forsakyn me !
Alas, man, for love of the !
*Y*a, for this gamyn and this gle (180)
    Thou schalt grocchyn and grone.

      *   *   *   *   *   ⁎

MUNDUS. Welcum, syr, semly in syth!
  Thou art welcum to worthy wede,   (185)
   For thou wylt be my servaunt day and nyth,
  With my servyse I schal the foster and fede;
   Thi bak schal be betyn with besawntes bryth;
  Thou schalt have byggynges be bankes brede;
   To thi cors schal knele kayser and knyth,
  Where that thou walke be sty or be strete,
   And ladys lovely on lere.   (190)
  But goddys servyse thou must forsake,
  And holy to the werld the take,
  And thanne a man I schal the make
   That non schal be thi pere.

HUMANUM GENUS. *Y*ys, Werld, and ther-to here myn honde
  To forsake God and hys servyse,   (196)
   To medys thou yeve me howse and londe,
  That I regne rychely at myn emprise.
   So that I fare wel be strete and stronde,
  Whil I dwelle here in werldly wyse,   (200)
   I recke nevere of hevene wonde,
  Nor of Jhŭ, that jentyl justyse!
   Of my sowle I have no rewthe,
  What schulde I recknen of domysday
  So that I be ryche and of gret a-ray?   (205)
  I schal make mery whyl I may,
   And ther-to here my trewthe.

MUNDUS. Now sertes, syr, thou seyst wel!
  I holde the trewe ffro top to the too!
   But thou were ryche it were gret dele, (210)
  And all men that wyl fare soo.

   Tunc ascendat Humanum Genus ad Mundum.

  Cum up, my serwaunt, trow as stele,
  Thou schalt be ryche whereso thou goo,

Men schul servyn the at mele
With mynstralsye, and bemys blo, (215)
   With metes and drynkes trye.
Lust and lykynge schal be thin ese,
Lovely ladys the schal plese,
Who so do the any disese,
     He schal ben hangyd hye. (220)
   Lykynge, be-lyve !
   Late slothe hym swythe
   In robys ryve
     With ryche aray.
   Folye, thou fonde, (225)
   Be strete and stronde
   Serve hym at honde
     Bothe nyth and day.

VOLUPTAS. Trostyly,
   Lord, redy! (230)
   Je vous pry,
     Syr, I say.
   In lyckynge and lust
   He schal rust,
   Tyl dethys dust (235)
     Do hym to clay.

STULTICIA. And I, folye,
   Schal hyen hym hye,
   Tyl sum enmye
     Hym over-goo. (240)
   In worldes wyt,
   That in folye syt,
   I thynke yyt
     Hes sowle to sloo.

     *   *   *   *   *   *

HUMANUM GENUS. Mankynde I am callyd be kynde,
   With cursydnesse in costes knet, (246)

In sowre swettenesse my syth I sende,
With sevene synnys sadde be-set.
   Mekyl myrthe I move in mynde,
With melody [al]¹ my mowth is met,   (250)
   My prowd power schal I not pende
Tyl I be putte in peynys pyt,
      To helle hent fro hens.
   In dale of dole tyl we are downe
   We schul be clad in a gay gowne.   (255)
   I see no man but the use somme
     Of these vij dedly synnys,
     For comonly it is seldom seyne.
Who so no[l]² be lecherous
   Of other man he schal have disdeyne,   (260)
And ben prowde or covetous,
     In synne iche man is founde.
   Ther is pore nor ryche, be londe ne lake,
   That alle vij wyl forsake,
   But with on or other he schal be take   (265)
     And in here bytter bondes bownde.

BONUS ANGELUS. So mekyl the werse, wele a woo,
   That evere good aungyl waus ordeynyd the!
   Thou art rewlyd after the fende, that is thi foo,
And no thynge, certes, aftyr me!   (270)
   Wele away, weder may I goo?
Man doth me bleykyn blody ble,
   Hes swete sowle he wyl now slo,
He schal wepe al hes game and gle
     At on dayes tyme,   (275)
   Ye se wel all, sothly in syth,
   I am a bowte, both day and nyth,
   To brynge hys sowle into blis bryth,
     And hym self wyl it brynge to pyne.

---

¹ at. MS.   ² now, MS.

Malus Angelus. No, good aungyl, thou art not in sesun,
  Ffewe men in the ffeyth they fynde,   (281)
   For thou hast schewyd a ballyd resun,
  Goode syre, cum [get thee me] behynde,
   Trewly man hathe non chesun
  On thi god to grede and grynde,   (285)
   Ffor that schuld cunne Cristis lessoun
  In penaunce hes body he muste bynde,
   And forsake the worldes [mynde][1].
  Men arn loth on the to crye,
   Or don penaunce for here folye;   (290)
  Therfore have I now maystrye
   Wel ny over al mankynde.

Bonus Angelus. Alas, mankynde
  Is bobbyt and blent as the blynde,
  In feyth I fynde   (295)
  To Crist he can nowt be kynde.
  Alas, mankynne
  Is soylyd and saggyd in synne,
  He wyl not blynne
  Tyl body and sowle parte a-twynne.   (300)
  Alas, he is blendyd;
  A-mys man's lyf is i-spendyd,
  With fendes fendyd;
  Mercy, God, that man were a-mendyd!

Confessio. What! man's aungel goode and trewe, (305)
  Why syest thou and sobbyst sore?
   Sertes, sore it schal me rewe,
  If I se the make mornynge more.
   May any bote thi bale brewe,
  Or any thynge thi stat astore?   (310)
   For all felyschepys, olde and newe,
  Why makyst thou grochynge under gore.

---

[1] MS. mende.

With pynynge poyntes pale?
Why waus al this gretynge gunne,
With sore syinge undyr sunne?　　　(315)
Tell me, and I schal, if I cunne,
　　Brewe the bote of bale.

Bonus Angelus. Of byttyr balys thou mayste me bete,
Swete Schryfte, if that thou wylt.
　　For mankynde it is that I grete:　　　(320)
He is in poynt to be spylt.
　　He is set in sevene synnys sete,
And wyl, certes, tyl he be kylt.
　　With me he thynkyth nevere more to mete,
He hath me forsake and I have no gylt!　　(325)
　　　No man wyl hym amende!
　　Therfore, Schryfte, so God me spede,
　　But if thou helpe at this nede,
　　Mankynde getyth nevere other mede
　　　But peyne withowtyn ende.　　　(330)

*　　*　　*　　*　　*　　*

Humanum Genus. A sete of sorwe in me is set,
Sertys, for synne I sye sore,
　　Mone of mercy in me is met,
Ffor werldys myrthe I morne more.
　　In wepynge wo my wele is wet,　　　(335)
Mercy, thou muste myn fatt a-store.
　　Ffro oure lordys lyth thou hast me let,
Sory synne, thou grysly gore.
　　　Owte on the, dedly synne!
　　Synne, thou haste mankynde schent,　　(340)
　　In dedly synne my lyfe is spent;
　　Mercy, God omnipotent,
　　　In youre grace I be-gynne.

Ffor, thou mankynde have don a-mys,
And he wyl falle in repentaunce,　　　(345)

Crist schal hym bryngyn to bowre of blys,
If sorwe of hert lache hym with launce.
　　Lordyngys, ye se wel alle thys—
Mankynde hathe ben in gret bobaunce,
　　I now for-sake the, synne, i-wys,　　　　(350)
And take me holy to penaunce:
　　　　On Crist I crye and calle.
　　A mercy! schryfte! I wyl no more!
Ffor dedly synne myn herte is sore:
　　Stuffe mankynde with thyne store,　　　(355)
　　　　And have hym to thyne halle.

CONFESSIO. Schryffte may no man for-sake:
　　Whanne mankynde cryeth I am redy,
　　　　Whanne sorwe of hert the hathe take
Schryfte prefytyth veryly.　　　　　　　(360)
　　Who-so for synne wyl sorwe make
Crist hym heryth, whanne he wyl crye.
　　Now, man, lete sorwe thyn synne slake[1],
And torne not a-geyn to thi ffolye;
　　　　Ffor that makyth dystaunce,　　　(365)
　　And, if it happe the turne a-geyn to synne,
Ffor Goddes love, lye not longe therinne:
He that dothe alway evyl, and wyl not blynne,
　　That askyth gret venjaunce.

　　　＊　　＊　　＊　　＊　　＊　　＊

HUMANUM GENUS. Now, syr Schryfte, where may I dwelle
　　To kepe me fro synne and woo?　　　(371)
　　　　A comly counseyll ye me spelle,
　　To fende me now fro my foo.
　　　　If these vij synnys here telle
That I am thus fro hem goo,　　　　　(375)
　　The werld, the flesche and the devyl of hell
Schul sekyn my soule for to sloo

[1] MS. slawe.

G

  Into balys bowre.
  Therfore, I prey you, putte me
  Into sum place of surete,   (380)
  That thei may not harmyn me
    With no synnys sowre.

CONFESSIO. To swyche a place I schal the kenne,
  Ther thou mayst dwelle withowtyn dystaunse
    And al wey kepe the fro synne, (385)
  In to the Castell of Perseveraunce.
  If thou wylt to hevene wynne
  And kepe the fro werldyly dystaunce,
    Goo yone castell and kepe the therinne
  Ffor [it] is strenger thanne any in Fraunce; (390)
    To yone castel I the sende.
    That castel is a precyous place,
    Fful of vertu and of grace,
    Who so levyth there hes lyvys space
      No synne schal hym schende. (395)

HUMANUM GENUS. A, Schryfte, blessyd mote thou be!
  This castel is here but at honde;
    Thedyr rathely wyll I tee,
  Sekyr over this sad sonde.
    Good perseveraunce God sende me, (400)
  Whyle I leve here in this londe!
    Ffro fowle fylthe now I fle,
  Fforthe to faryn now I fonde
    To yone precyous port,
    Lord, what man is in mery lyve (405)
    Whanne he is of hes synnys schreve!
    Al my dol adoun is dreve,
      Christe is my counfort.

¶Here begynneth a treatyse how ý hye
fader of heuen sendeth dethe to so-
mon euery creature to come and
gyue a counte of theyr lyues in
this worlde/and is in maner
of a morall playe.

FROM AN EDITION BY JOHN SKOT (C. 1530)

Everyman.

¶. Here begynneth a treatyse how ye hye | fader of heven sendeth dethe
to so|mon every creature to come and | gyve a counte of theyr
lyves in | this worlde, and is in in maner | of a morall playe .✠.
[Woodcut of 'Everyman' and of Death carrying a coffin; between
them at the back stands a cross.]

MESSENGER. I pray you all gyve your audyence
    And here this mater with reverence,
        By fygure a morall playe.
    The somonynge of Everyman called it is,
    That of our lyves and endynge shewes   5
        How transytory we be all daye.
    This matter is wonders precyous,
    But the entent of it is more gracyous
        And swete to bere awaye.
    The story sayth : man, in the begynnynge   10
    Loke well and take good heed to the endynge,
        Be you never so gay,
    Ye thynke synne in the begynnynge full swete,
    Whiche in the ende causeth the soule to wepe,
        Whan the body lyeth in claye.   15
    Here shall you se how Felawshyp, and Iolyte,
    Bothe Strengthe, Pleasure and Beaute,
        Wyll fade from the as floure in maye.
    For ye shall here how our heven kynge
    Calleth Everyman to a general rekenynge.   20
        Gyve audyence and here what he doth saye.

God spekyth :

God. ⁋. I perceyve here in my maieste
How that all creatures be to me unkynde,
Lyvynge without drede in worldly prosperyte ;
Of ghostly syght the people be so blynde,   25
Drowned in synne they know me not for theyr god ;
In worldlye ryches is all theyr mynde.

*   *   *   *   *   *   *

I se, the more that I them forbere,   42
The worse they be fro yere to yere,
All that lyveth appayreth faste,
Therfore I wyll in all the haste   45
Have a rekenynge of every mannes persone.

*   *   *   *   *   *   *

They be so combred with worldly ryches   60
That nedes on them I must do justyce,
On every man lyvynge without fere.
Where arte thou, Deth, thou mighty messengere ?

DETHE.

DETHE. Almighty God, I am here at your wyll,
Your commaundement to fulfylle.   65

God. Go thou to Every man,
And shewe hym in my name
A pylgrymage he must on hym take,
Whiche he in no wyse may escape,
And that he brynge with him a sure rekenynge   70
Without delay or ony taryenge.

DETHE. Lorde I wyll in the worlde go renne over all
And cruelly out serche bothe grete and small.
Every man wyll I beset that lyveth beestly
Out of Goddes lawes and dredeth not foly.   75
He that loveth rychesse I wylle stryke with my darte,
His syght to blynde and fro heven to departe,

Except that almes be his good frende,
In hell for to dwell, worlde without ende.
Loo yonder I se Everyman walkynge,   80
Full lytell he thynketh on my comynge !
His mynde is on flesshely lustes and his treasure,
And grete payne it shall cause hym to endure
Before the lorde, heven kynge.
Everyman, stande styll. Whyder arte thou goynge, 85
Thus gayly ? hast thou thy Maker forgete ?

EVERYMAN.

EVERYMAN. Why asketh thou ?
Woldest thou wete ?

DETHE. Ye, syr, I wyll shewe you :
In grete hast I am sende to the   90
Fro God, out of his mageste.

EVERYMAN. What, sente to me ?

DETHE. Ye, certaynly.
Thoughe thou have forgete hym here,
He thynketh on the in the hevenly spere,   95
As, or we departe, thou shalte knowe.

EVERYMAN. What desyreth God of me ?

DETHE. That shall I shewe the :
A rekenynge he wyll nedes have,
Without ony lenger respyte.   100

EVERYMAN. To gyve a rekenynge longer layser I crave,
This blinde mater troubleth my wytte.

DETHE. On the thou must take a longe journey,
Therfore thy boke of counte with the thou bryng,
For tourne agayne thou can not by no waye ;   105
And loke thou be sure of thy rekenynge,
For before God thou shalte answere and shewe
Thy many badde dedes and good but a fewe,

How thou hast spente thy lyfe, and in what wyse,
Before the chefe lorde of paradyse.   110
Have ado we were in that waye,
For, wete thou well, thou shalte make none attournay.

EVERYMAN. Full unredy I am suche rekenynge to gyve.
I knowe the not. What messenger arte thou?

DETHE. I am Dethe, that no man dredeth.   115
For every man I rest and no man spareth,
For it is Goddes commaundement
That all to me sholde be obedyent.

EVERYMAN.
O deth, thou comest whan I had thee leest in mynde!
In thy power it lyeth me to save,   120
Yet of my good wyl I gyve thee, yf thou wyl be kynde.
Ye, a thousande pounde shalte thou have,
And dyfferre this mater tyll another daye.

DETHE. Everyman, it may not be by no waye.
I set not by golde, sylver, nor rychesse,   125
Ne by pope, emperour, kynge, duke ne prynces,
For, and I wolde receyve gyftes grete,
All the worlde I myght gete;
But my custom is clene contrary.
I gyve the no respyte, come hens and not tary.   130

EVERYMAN. Alas! shall I have no lenger respyte?
I may saye deth gyveth no warnynge!
To thynke on the it maketh my herte seke,
For all unredy is my boke of rekenynge.
But, xii yere and I myght have abydynge,   135
My countynge boke I wolde make so clere,
That my rekenynge I sholde not nede to fere.
Wherfore, deth, I praye the, for Goddes mercy,
Spare me tyll I be provyded of remedy.

DETHE. The avayleth not to crye, wepe and praye.   140
But hast the lyghtly that thou were gone the journaye,

And preve thy frendes, yf thou can.
For, wete thou well, the tyde abydeth no man,
And in the worlde eche lyvynge creature
For Adams synne must dye of nature.   145

EVERYMAN. Dethe, yf I sholde this pylgrymage take,
And my rekenynge suerly make,
Shewe me, for saynt charyte,
Sholde I not come agayne shortly?

DETHE. No, Everyman, and thou be ones there,   150
Thou mayst never more come here,
Trust me veryly.

EVERYMAN. O gracyous God, in the hye sete celestyall,
Have mercy on me in this moost nede.
Shall I have no company fro this vale terestryall   155
Of myne acqueynte, that way me to lede?

DETHE. Ye, yf ony be so hardy
That wolde go with the and bere the company.
Hye the, that thou were gone to Goddes magnyfycence,
Thy rekenynge to gyve before his presence.   160
What, wenest thou thy lyve is gyven the
And thy worldely goodes also?

EVERYMAN. I had wende so veryle.

DETHE. Nay, nay, it was but lende the,
For as sone as thou arte go   165
Another a whyle shall have it and than go¹ ther fro,
Even as thou hast done.
Everyman, thou art made! Thou hast thy wyttes fyve,
And here on erthe wyll not amende thy lyve!
For sodeynly I do come.   170

EVERYMAN. O wretched caytyfe, wheder shall I flee,
That I myght scape this endles sorowe?

---

¹ than thou go, *Ed.* against the sense

Now, gentyll deth, spare me tyll to morowe,
That I may amende me
With good advysement.   175

DETHE. Naye, therto I wyll not consent,
Nor no man wyll I respyte,
But to the herte sodeynly I shall smyte
Without ony advysement.
And now out of thy syght I wyll me hy,   180
Se thou make the redy shortely,
For thou mayst saye this is the daye
That no man lyvynge may scape awaye.

EVERYMAN. Alas I may well wepe with syghes depe,
Now have I no maner of company,   185
To helpe me in my journey and me to kepe,
And also my wrytynge is butt unredy.
How shall I do now for to exscuse me?
I wolde to God I had never be gete!
To my soule a full grete profyte it had be,   190
For now I fere paynes huge and grete!
The tyme passeth, Lorde helpe that all wrought!
For though I mourne it avayleth nought.
The day passeth and is almoost ago,
I wote not well what for to do.   195
To whome were I best my complaynt to make?
What and I to Felawshyp therof spake,
And shewed hym of this sodeyne chaunce?
For in hym is all myne affyaunce;
We have in the worlde so many a daye   200
Be good frendes in sporte and playe.
I se hym yonder certaynely,
I trust that he wyll bere me company,
Therfore to hym wyll I speke to ese my sorowe.
Well mette, good Felawshyp, and good morowe.   205

Felawshyp *speketh.*

FELAWSHYP. Everyman, good morowe by this daye.
　Syr, why lokest thou so pyteously?
　If ony thynge be amysse I praye the me saye,
　　That I may helpe to remedy.

EVERYMAN. Ye, good Felawshyp, ye,　　　　　210
　I am in greate jeoparde.

FELAWSHYP. My true frende, shewe to me your mynde,
　I wyll not forsake the to thy lyves ende,
　In the way of good company.

EVERYMAN. That was well spoken and lovyngly.

FELAWSHYP. Syr, I must nedes knowe your hevynesse.
　I have pyte to se you in ony dystresse.　　217
　If ony have you wronged ye shall revenged be,
　Though I on the grounde be slayne for the,
　Though that I knowe before that I sholde dye.　220

EVERYMAN. Veryly, Felawshyp, gramercy.

FELAWSHYP. Tusshe, by thy thankes I set not a strawe,
　Shewe me your grefe and saye no more.

EVERYMAN. If I my herte sholde to you breke,
　　And than you to tourne your mynde fro me,　225
　And wolde not me comforte whan ye here me speke,
　　Then sholde I ten tymes soryer be.

FELAWSHYP. Syr, I saye as I wyll do in dede.

EVERYMAN. Than be you a good frende at nede,
　I have founde you true herebefore.　　　　230

FELAWSHYP. And so ye shall evermore,
　For, in fayth, and thou go to hell
　　I wyll not forsake the by the waye.

EVERYMAN.
　Ye speke lyke a good frende, I byleve you well,
　　I shall deserve it, and I maye.　　　　235

FELAWSHYP. I speke of no deservynge, by this daye,
   For he that wyll saye and nothynge do
   Is not worthy with good company to go.
   Therfore shewe me the grefe of your mynde
   As to your frende moost lovynge and kynde.   240

EVERYMAN. I shall shewe you how it is:
    Commannded I am to go a journaye,
  A longe waye, harde and daungerous,
    And gyve a strayte counte, without delaye,
  Before the hye Juge Adonay.   245
  Wherfore, I pray you, bere me company,
    As ye have promysed, in this journaye.

FELAWSHYP. That is mater in dede! Promyse is duty,
  But and I sholde take suche vyage on me,
  I knowe it well, it sholde be to my payne;   250
  Also it make[s] me aferde, certayne.
  But let us take counsell here as well as we can,
  For your wordes wolde fere a stronge man.

EVERYMAN. Why, ye sayd, yf I had nede,
  Ye wolde me never forsake, quycke ne deed,   255
  Though it were to hell, truely.

FELAWSHYP. So I sayd certaynely,
  But suche pleasures be set a syde, the sothe to saye,
  And also, yf we toke suche a journaye,
  Whan sholde we come agayne?   260

EVERYMAN. Naye, never agayne, tyll the daye of dome.

FELAWSHYP. In fayth, than wyll not I come there.
   Who hath you these tydynges brought?

EVERYMAN. In dede, deth was with me here.

FELAWSHYP. Now, by God that all hathe bought,   265
  If deth were the messenger,
  For no man that is lyvynge to daye
  I wyll not go that lothe journaye,
  Not for the fader that bygate me.

EVERYMAN. Ye promysed other wyse, parde.   270

FELAWSHYP. I wote well I say so, truely,
    And yet yf thou wylte ete and drynke and make good
        chere
    Or haunt to women the lusty company,
        I wolde not forsake you, whyle the day is clere,
    Trust me veryly.   275

EVERYMAN. Ye, therto ye wolde be redy :
    To go to myrthe, solas and playe
    Your mynde wyll soner apply,
        Than to bere me company in my longe journaye.

FELAWSHIP. Now, in good fayth, I wyll not that waye,
    But and thou wylt murder, or ony man kyll,   281
    In that I wyll helpe the with a good wyll.

EVERYMAN. O that is a symple advyse in dede !
    Gentyll felawe, helpe me in my necessyte ;
    We have loved longe, and now I nede !   285
        And now, gentyll Felawshyp, remember me.

FELAWSHYP. Wheder ye have loved me or no,
    By saynt John I wyll not with the go.

EVERYMAN.
    Yet I pray the, take the labour and do so moche for me,
    To brynge me forwarde, for saynt charyte,   290
    And comforte me tyll I come without the towne.

FELAWSHYP. Nay, and thou wolde gyve me a newe gowne,
    I wyll not a fote with the go ;
    But and thou had taryed I wolde not have lefte the so ;
    And, as now, God spede the in thy journaye,   295
    For from the I wyll departe as fast as I maye.

EVERYMAN.
    Wheder a-waye, felawshyp? wyll thou forsake me?

FELAWSHYP. Ye, by my faye ! To God I betake the.

EVERYMAN.

    Farewell, good Fellawshyp! For the my herte is sore!

    Adewe forever, I shall se the no more.   300

FELAWSHYP.

    In fayth, Everyman, fare well now at the ende,

    For you I wyll remembre that partynge is mournynge.

EVERYMAN. Alacke, shall we thus[1] departe in dede—

    A lady! helpe! without ony more comforte?

    Lo Felawshyp forsaketh me in my moost nede[2].   305

    For helpe in this worlde wheder shall I resorte?

    Felawshyp here before with me wolde mery make,

    And nowe lytell sorowe for me dooth he take.

    It is sayd in prosperyte men frendes may fynde

    Whiche in adversyte be full unkynde.   310

    Nowe whither for socoure shall I flee,

    Syth that Felawshyp hath forsaken me?

    To my kynnes men I wyll truely,

    Prayenge them to helpe in my necessyte.

    I beleve that they wyll do so,   315

    For kynde wyll crepe where it may not go.

        *   *   *   *   *   *

[The 147 lines here omitted are summed up in the following speech.]

EVERYMAN. O to whome shall I make my mone

    For to go with me in that hevy journaye?

    Fyrst Felawshyp sayd he wolde with me gone;   465

    His wordes were very plesaunt and gaye,

    But afterwarde he lefte me alone.

    Than spake I to my kynnesmen all in dyspayre,

    An[d] also they gave me wordes fayre;

    They lacked no fayre spekynge,   470

    But all forsake me in the endynge.

---

[1] *For* thus, *the Ed. reads* this.
[2] From l. 305 we have the help of Pynson's text.

Than wente I to my Goodes, that I loved best,
In hope to have comforte, but there had I leest;
For my Goodes sharpely dyd me tell
That he bryngeth many into hell.   475
Than of my selfe I was ashamed,
And so I am worthy to be blamed.
Thus may I well my selfe hate.
Of whome shall I now conseyll take?
I thinke that I shall never spede   480
Tyll that I go to my Good Dede.
But, alas, she is so weke
That she can nother go nor speke.
Yet will I venter on her now.
My Good Dedes, where be you?   485

GOOD DEDES. Here I lye, colde in the grounde,
Thy synnes hath me sore bounde
That I can nat stere.

EVERYMAN. O Good Dedes, I stande in great [1] fere,
I must you pray of counseyll,   490
For helpe now sholde come ryght well.

GOOD DEDES. Everyman, I have understandynge
    That ye be somoned a counte to make
Before Myssyas, of Jherusalem kynge,   494
    And you do by me the journay with you wyll I take.
EVERYMAN. Therfore I come to you my moone to make.
I praye you that ye wyll go with me.
GOOD DEDES.
I wolde full fayne, but I can nat stand veryly.
EVERYMAN. Why, is there onythynge on you fall?
GOOD DEDES. Ye, syr, I may thanke you of all.   500
If ye had parfytely chered me,
Your boke of counte nowe full redy had be.
Loke, the bokes of your workes and dedes eke

Ase howe they lye here under the fete,
  To your soules hevynes.   505

EVERYMAN. Our Lorde Jesus helpe me,
  For one letter here I can nat se.
GOOD DEDES.
  There is a blynde reckenynge in tyme of dystres.

EVERYMAN. Good dedes, I praye you helpe me in this nede,
  Or elles I am for ever dampned in dede;   510
  Therfore helpe me to make my rekenynge
  Before the Redemer of all thynge,
  That kynge is, and was, and ever shall.
GOOD DEDES. Everyman, I am sory of your fall,
  And fayne wolde I helpe you, and I were able.   515
EVERYMAN.
  Good Dedes, your counseyll I pray you gyve me.
GOOD DEDES. That shall I do veryly,
  Thoughe that on my fete I may nat go.
  I have a syster that shall with you also,
  Called Knowlege, whiche shall with you abyde,   520
  To helpe you to make that dredefull rekenynge.
KNOWLEGE.
  Everyman, I wyll go with the and be thy gyde,
  In thy moost nede to go by thy syde.
EVERYMAN.
  In good condycyon I am now in every thynge,
  And am holy[1] content with this good thynge   525
  Thanked be[2] God my creatoure.

            *   *   *   *   *   *

[EVERYMAN is taken to CONFESSION and does penance for his sins.]

GOOD DEDES. Every man, pylgryme, my specyall frende,
  Blessyd be thou without ende,   630
  For the is preparate the eternall glorye

----

[1] hole, *Skot.*   [2] by, *Skot.*

Ye have me made hole and sounde,
Therfor I wyll byde by the in every stounde.

EVERYMAN.
Welcome, my Good Dedes! Now I here thy voyce
I wepe for very swetenes of love.   635

KNOWLEGE. Be no more sad, but ever rejoyce.
God seeth thy lyvynge in his trone above,
Put on this [1] garment, to thy behove,
Which is wette with your teres,
Or elles before God you may it mysse,   640
Whan ye to your journeys ende come shall.

EVERYMAN. Gentyll Knowlege, what do you yt call?

KNOWLEGE. It is called the garment of sorowe,
Fro payne it wyll you borowe,
Contrycyon it is,   645
That getteth forgyveness,
He pleaseth God passynge well.

GOOD DEDES. Everyman, wyll you ~~were~~ *wear* it for your ~~hele?~~ *heal*

EVERYMAN. Now blessyd be Jesu, Maryes sone,
For nowe have I on true contrycyon,   650
And lette us go now without taryenge.
Good Dedes, have we clere our rekenynge?

GOOD DEDES. Ye, in dede, I have them [2] here.

EVERYMAN. Than I trust we nede not fere.
Now, frendes, let us not parte in twayne.   655

KNOWLEGE [3]. Nay, Everyman, that wyll we nat certayne.

GOOD DEDES. Yet must thou leade [4] with thee
Thre persones of grete myght.

---

[1] *Skot* only, *rest* thy.   [2] *om. Skot.*   [3] The editions all
assign this line and also l. 666 to Kynrede, but surely wrongly, since
Kynrede left the stage at l. 366.   [4] led, *Skot.*

EVERYMAN. Who sholde they be?

GOOD DEDES. Dyscrecyon and Strength they hyght,   660
　And thy Beaute may not abyde behinde.

KNOWLEGE. Also ye must call to mynde
　Your Fyve Wyttes, as for your counseylours.

GOOD DEDES. You must have them redy at all houres.

EVERYMAN. Howe shall I gette them hyder?   665

KNOWLEGE. You must call them all togyder,
　And they wyll here you incontynent.

EVERYMAN. My frendes, come hyder and be present,
　Discrecyon, Strengthe, my Fyve Wyttes and Beaute.

BEAUTE. Here at your wyll we be all redy,   670
　What wyll ye that we shulde do?

GOOD DEDES. That ye wolde with Everyman go,
　And helpe him in his pylgrymage.
　Advyse you, wyll ye with him or not in that vyage?

STRENGTH. We wyll brynge hym all thyder   675
　To his helpe and comforte, ye may byleve me.

DYSCRECYON. So wyll we go with hym all togyder.

*　　*　　*　　*　　*　　*

[EVERYMAN receives the last Sacrament:]

FYVE WITTES. Peas, for yonder I see Everyman come,
　Whiche hath made trewe satysfaccyon.

GOOD DEDES. Me thynke, it is he indede.   770

EVERYMAN. Now Jesu be our[1] alder spede!
　I have receyved the sacrament for my redempcyon,
　And than myne extreme unccyon.
　Blessyd be all they that counseyled me to take it!
　And now frendes, let us go without longer respyte.

[1] your, *Skot.*

I thanke God that ye have taryed so longe. 776
Now set eche of you on this rodde his honde,
And shortely folowe me.
I go before there I wolde be.
God be our[1] gyde! 780

STRENGTHE. Everyman, we will nat fro you go,
    Tyll ye have gone this vyage longe.

DYSCRECYON. I, Dyscrecyon, wyll byde by you also.

KNOWLEGE.
    And though this pylgrymage be never so stronge
I wyll never parte you fro. 785

STRENGTH. Everyman, I will be as sure by the
    As ever I was[2] by Judas Machabe.

EVERYMAN. Alas, I am so faynt I may not stande,
    My lymmes under me doth folde.
Frendes, let us nat tourne agayne to this lande, 790
    Nat for all the worldes golde,
For into this cave must I crepe,
And torne to the erthe, and there slepe[3].

BEAUTE. What in to this grave, alas!

EVERYMAN.
    Ye, there shall we consume, more and lesse! 795

BEAUTE. And what, sholde I smoder here

EVERYMAN. Ye, be my fayth, and never more appere!
    In this worlde lyve no more we shall,
    But in heven before the hyest lorde of all.

BEAUTE. I crosse out all this! adewe by saynt Johan!
    I take my cappe[4] in my lappe, and am gone. 801

EVERYMAN. What, Beaute, whyder wyll ye?

---

[1] your, *Skot.*   [2] dyd, *Skot.*   [3] And tourne to erth and there
to slepe, *Skot.*   Mr. Hazlitt assigns this line and the next but one to
Beauty, and ll. 794, 796 to *Everyman.*   [4] cappe, *Skot* only, *rest* tappe.

BEAUTE. Peas! I am defe, I loke not behynde me,
  Nat and thou woldest gyve me all the golde in thy chest.

EVERYMAN. Alas! wherto may I truste?   805
  Beaute gothe fast awaye fro me.
  She promysed with me to lyve and dye.

STRENGTH. Everyman, I wyll the also forsake and denye,
  Thy game lyketh me nat at all.

EVERYMAN. Why than ye wyll forsake me all!   810
  Swete Strength, tarry a lytel space[1]!

STRENGTH. Nay, syr, by the rode of grace,
  I wyll hye me from the fast,
  Though thou wepe till[2] thy hert brast.

EVERYMAN. Ye wolde ever byde by me, ye sayd.   815

STRENGTH. Ye, I have you ferre ynoughe conveyed.
  Ye be olde ynoughe, I understande,
  Your pylgrymage to take on hand.
  I repent me that I hyder came.

EVERYMAN. Strengthe, you to dysplease I am to blame,
  Yet promyse is dette, this ye well wot[3].   821

STRENGTH. In fayth, as for that[4] I care not!
  Thou arte but a foole to complayne,
  You spende your speche and wast your brayne;
  Go thryst[5] the into the grounde!   825

EVERYMAN. I had wende surer I sholde you have founde,
  But I se well[6] he that trusteth in his strength
  She hym deceyveth[7] at the length,
  For Strength and Beaute forsaketh me,
  Yet they promysed me fayre and lovyngly[8].   830

---

[1] Strength, tary I pray you a lytell space, *Pynson*.   [2] wepe to thy
herte to brast, *Skot*.   [3] Wyll ye breke promyse that is dette (losing
the rime), *Skot*.   [4] as for that, *om. Skot*.   [5] trusse, *Pynson*.
[6] *om. Skot*.   [7] Is greatly disceyved, *Pynson*.   [8] stedfast to be,
Pynson.

DISCRETION. Everyman, I wyll after Strengthe be gone;
    As for me, I wyll leve you alone.

EVERYMAN. Why, Dyscrecyon, wyll ye forsake me?

DYSCRECYON. Ye, in good[1] fayth, I wyll go fro the,
    For whan Strength goth before   835
    I folowe after ever more.

EVERYMAN. Yet I pray the, for love of the Trynyte,
    Loke in my grave ones pyteously.

DYSCRECYON. Nay, so nye wyll I not come!
    Now farewell, fellowes[2], everychone.   840

EVERYMAN. O all thynge fayleth save God alone,
    Beaute, Strengthe and Dyscrecyon;
    For whan Deth bloweth his blast
    They all renne fro me full fast.

FYVE WYTTES. Everyman, my leve now of the I take,
    I wyll folowe the other, for here I the forsake.   846

EVERYMAN. Alas, then may I wayle and wepe,
    For I toke you for my best frende.

FYVE WYTTES. I wyll no lenger the kepe,
    Now farewell, and there an ende.   850

EVERYMAN. O Jesu helpe: all hath forsaken me.

GOOD DEDES. Nay, Everyman, I wyll byde with the,
    I wyll not forsake the in dede,
    Thou shalte fynde me a good frende at nede.

EVERYMAN.
    Gramercy, Good Dedes, now may I true frendes se; 855
    They have forsaken me everychone;
    I loved them better than my Good Dedes alone.
    Knowlege, wyll ye forsake me also?

---

[1] *om. Skot.*   [2] *om. Skot.*

KNOWLEGE. Ye, Everyman, when ye to Deth shall go,
  But not yet for no maner of daunger.   860

EVERYMAN. Gramercy, Knowlege, with all my herte.

KNOWLEGE. Nay, yet I will not from hens departe,
  Tyll I se where ye shall be come.

EVERYMAN. Me thynke, alas, that I must be gone
  To make my rekenynge and my dettes paye,   865
  For I se my tyme is nye spent awaye.
  Take example, all ye that this do here or se,
  How they that I love best do forsake me,
  Excepte my Good Dedes that bydeth truely.

GOOD DEDES. All erthly thynges is but vanyte,   870
  Beaute, Strength and Dyscrecyon do man forsake,
  Folysshe frendes and kynnes men that fayre spake,
  All fleeth save Good Dedes, and that am I.

EVERYMAN. Have mercy on me, God moost myghty,
  And stande by me, thou moder and mayde, holy Mary.

GOOD DEDES. Fere not, I wyll speke for the.   876

EVERYMAN. Here I crye, God mercy.

GOOD DEDES. Shorte our ende and mynyshe our payne,
  Let us go and never come agayne.

EVERYMAN. Into thy handes, lorde, my soule I commende.
  Receyve it, lorde, that it be nat loste!   881
  As thou me boughtest, so me defende,
    And save me fro the fendes boost,
    That I may appere with that blessyd hoost
  That shall be saved at the day of dome.   885
  In manus tuas, of myghtes moost,
  For ever *commendo spiritum meum*.

KNOWLEGE. Nowe hath he suffred that we all shall endure;
   The good dedes shall make all sure.
   Now hath he made endynge,   890
   Me thynketh that I here aungelles synge,
   And make grete joy and melody,
   Where every mannes soule receyved shall be.

THE AUNGELL. Come excellente electe spouse to Jesu!
    Here above thou shalte go,   895
   Bycause of thy synguler vertue.
    Now the soule is taken the body fro
   Thy rekenynge is crystall clere;
   Now shalte thou into the hevenly spere,
   Unto the whiche all ye shall come   900
   That lyveth well before the daye of dome.

DOCTOUR. This morall[1] men may have in mynde:
   Ye herers take it of worth, olde and yonge,
   And forsake Pryde, for he disceyveth you in the ende,
   And remembre Beaute, Five Wyttes, Strength and
      Dyscrecyon,   905
   They all at the last do Everyman forsake,
   Save his Good Dedes there doth he take.
   But beware,—and they be small,
   Before God he hath no helpe at all.
   None excuse may be there for Everyman!   910
   Alas! howe shall he do than?
   For after dethe amendes may no man make,
   For than mercy and pyte doth hym forsake,
   If his rekenynge be not clere when he doth come,
   God wyll saye *Ite maledicti in ignem eternum.*   915
   And he that hath his accounte hole and sounde
   Hye in heven he shall be crounde,
   Unto whiche place God brynge us all thyder
   That we may lyve body and soule togyder!

---

[1] memoryall, *Pynson.*

Therto helpe the Trinyte!
Amen, saye ye, for saynt charyte!

Fɪɴɪs.

⟨ Thus endeth this morall playe of every man
⟨ Imprynted at London in Poules
chyrche yarde by me
Johñ Skot
✠ [1].

---

[1] ⟨. Imprynted at London in Flete Strete | by me Rycharde Pynson | prynter to the kynges moost noble grace.

Johannes · Rastell

Iusticia ꝶ Regat.

JOHN RASTELL'S DEVICES

From his *Tabula libri assisarum et placitorum coronae*

John Rastell's The Four Elements.

THE MESSENGER. Thaboundant grace of the power devyne,
   Whiche doth illumyne the world invyron,
Preserve this audyence and cause them to inclyne
   To charyte, this is my petycyon;
   For by your pacyens and supportacyon   5
A lytyll interlude, late made and preparyd,
Before your presence here shall be declaryd,
Whiche of a few conclusyons is contrivyd,
   And poyntes of phylosophy naturall;
But though the matter be not so well declaryd   10
   As a great clerke coude do, nor so substancyall,
   Yet the auctour hereof requiryth you all,
Though he be ygnorant[1], and can lytyll skyll,
To regarde his only intent and good wyll,
Whiche in his mynde hath oft tymes ponderyd,   15
   What nombre of bokes in our tonge maternall
Of toyes and tryfellys be made and impryntyd,
   And few of them of matter substancyall;
   For though many make bokes, yet unneth ye shall
In our Englyshe tonge fynde any warkes   20
Of connynge, that is regardyd by clerkes.
The Grekes, the Romayns, with many other mo,
   In their moder tonge wrot warkes excellent.
Than yf clerkes in this realme wolde take payn so,

---

[1] yngnorant, *Text*.

Consyderyng that our tonge is now suffycyent   25
    To expoun any hard sentence evydent,
They myght, yf they wolde, in our Englyshe tonge
Wryte workys of gravyté somtyme amonge ;
For dyvers prengnaunt wyttes be in this lande,
    As well of noble men as of meane estate,   30
Whiche nothynge but Englyshe can understande.
    Than yf connynge Laten bokys were translate
    Into Englyshe, wel correct and approbate,
All subtell sciens in Englyshe myght be lernyd,
As well as other people in their owne tonges dyd.   35
But now so it is that in our Englyshe tonge
    Many one there is, that can but rede and wryte,
For his pleasure wyll oft presume amonge
    New bokys to compyle and balates to indyte,
    Some of love or other matter, not worth a myte : 40
Some to opteyn favour wyll flatter and glose,
Some wryte curyous termes nothyng to purpose.
Thus every man after his fantesye
    Wyll wryte his conseyte, be it never so rude,
Be it vertuous, vycyous, wysedome or foly ;   45
Wherfore to my purpose thus I conclude,
    Why shold not than the auctour of this interlude
Utter his owne fantesy and conseyte also,
As well as dyvers other now a dayes do.

[After the Messenger's speech there enter Natura Naturata (created
    Nature), Humanity and Studious Desire. Nature discourses 'of
    the situation, of the four elements, that is to say, the earth, the
    water, the air and fire, and of their qualities and properties, and of
    the generation and corruption of things made of the commixtion of
    them.' Humanity thanks her humbly and is left in the hands of
    Studious Desire for further instruction.]

STUDYOUS DESIRE. Now, Humanyte, call to your memory
    The connynge poyntes that Nature hath declaryd,

And though he have shewed dyvers pointes and many
Of the elementis so wondersly formed,
Yet many other causys there are wolde be lernyd, 330
    As to knowe the generacyon of thynges all
Here in the yerth, how they be ingendryd,
    As herbys, plantys, well-sprynges, ston and metall.

HUMANYTE. Those thynges to knowe for me be full
    expedient,
    But yet in those poyntes which Nature late shewyd me,
My mynde in them as yet is not content, 336
    For I can no maner wyse parceyve nor see,
    Nor prove by reason why the yerth sholde be
In the myddes of the fyrmament hengyng so small,
And the yerth with the water to be rounde withall. 340

STUDYOUS DESIRE. Methynkyth myselfe as to some of
    those pointes
    I coude gyve a suffycyent solucyon ;
For, furst of all, thou must nedys graunt this,
    That the yerth is so depe and botom hath non,
    Or els there is some grose thyng hit stondyth upon,
Or els that it hangyth, thou must nedes consent, 346
Evyn in the myddes of the fyrmament.

HUMANYTE. What than? go forth with thyne argument.

STUDYOUS DESIRE. Than marke well, in the day or in a
    wynters nyght,
    The sone, and mone, and sterris celestyall, 350
In the est furst they do apere to thy syght
    And after in the west they do downe fall,
    And agayne in the morowe, next of all,
Within xxiiij. houres they be come just
To the est pointes again, where thou sawist them furst.
Than yf the erthe shulde be of endles depnes, 356
    Or shulde stande upon any other grose thynge,
It shulde be an impedyment, dowtles,

To the sone, mone and sterris in theyr movynge,
They shulde not so in the est agayne sprynge.
Therfore in reason it semyth moste convenyent   360
The yerth to hange in the myddes of the fyrmament.

HUM. Thyne argument in that poynt doth me confounde,
    That thou hast made, but yet it provytht not ryght
That the yerth by reason shulde be rounde ;
    For though the fyrmament with his sterris bryght 365
    Compas aboute the yerth eche day and nyght,
Yet the yerthe may be playne, peradventure,
Quadrant, triangle, or some other fygure.

STUDYOUS DESYRE. That it cannot be playne I shall well
    prove the,
    Because the sterris that aryse in the oryent   370
Appere more soner to them that there be,
    Than to the other dwellynge in the occident.
    The eclypse is therof a playne experymente,
Of the sone or mone, which, whane it doth fall,
Is never one tyme of the day in placys all ;   375
    Yet the eclyps generally is alwaye
In the hole worlde as one tyme beynge ;
    But whan we that dwell here see it in the mydday,
They in the west partis see it in the mornynge,
And they in the est beholde it in the evenyng ;   380
And why that sholde be so no cause can be found,
But onely by reason that the yerthe is rownde.

HUMANYTE. That reason proveth the yerth at the lest
    One wayes to be rownde I cannot gaynesay,
As for to accompt from the est to the west ;   385
    But yet, not withstondynge all that, it may
    Lese hys rowndenesse by some other waye.

STUDYOUS DESYRE. Na, no dowte yt is rownde everywhere,
Whiche I coulde prove thou shouldest not say nay,
Yf I had therto any tyme and leser ;   390

But I knowe a man callyd Experyens,
  Of dyvers instrumentys is never without,
Cowde prove all these poyntys, and yet by his scyens
  Can tell how many myle the erthe is abowte,
    And many other straunge conclusions no dowte 395
  Hys instrumentys cowde shew them so certayn
  That every rude carter shold them persayve playn.

Hu. Now wolde to God I had that man now here
  For the contembtacyon of my mynde !

Stu. Yf ye wyll, I shall for hym enquere,   400
  And brynge hym heder yf I can hym fynde.

Hu. Then myght I say ye were to me ryght kynde.

Stu. I shall assay, by God that me dere bought,
  For cunnyng is the thynge that wolde be sought.

    *   *   *   *   *   *   *

Sensual Appetyte. Aha ! now god evyn, fole, god evyn !
  It is even the, knave, that I mene.   408
  Hast thou done thy babelyng ?

Stu. Ye, peradventure, what than ?   410

Sen. Than hold downe thy hede lyke a prety man, and
      take my blyssyng.
  Benedicite ! I graunt to the this pardon,
  And gyve the absolucion
  For thy soth saws ; stande up, Jackdaw !
  I beschrew thy faders sone.   415
  Make rome, syrs, and let us be mery,
  With huffa galand, synge tyrll on the bery,
    And let the wyde worlde wynde !
  Synge fryska joly, with hey troly loly,
  For I se wel it is but a foly   420
    For to have a sad mynd :
  For rather than I wolde use suche foly,
  To pray, to study, or be pope-holy

I had as lyf be ded.
By [Jupiter] I tell you trew !   425
I speke as I thynke now, else I beshrew
  Evyn my next felowes hed !
Master Humanyté, syr, be your leve,
I were ryght loth you to greve,
  Though I do hym dyspyse ;   430
For yf ye knewe hym as well as I,
Ye wolde not use his company,
  Nor love hym in no wyse.

Hu. Syr, he looketh lyke an honest man,
  Therfore I merveyll that ye can   435
  This wyse hym deprave.

Sen. Though he loke never so well,
  I promyse you he hath a shrewde smell.

Hu. Why so ? I prey you tell.

Sen. For he saveryth lyke a knave.   440

Stu. Holde your pease, syr, ye mistake me !
  What ! I trowe, that ye wolde make me
  Lyke to one of your kyn.

Sen. Harke, syrs, here ye not how boldly
  He calleth me knave agayne by polycy ?   445
  The devyll pull of his skyn !
I wolde he were hangyd by the throte,
For, by the messe, I love hym not,
  We two can never agre ;
I am content, syr, with you to tary,   450
And I am for you so necessary,
  Ye can not lyve without me.

Hu. Why, syr, I say, what man be ye ?

Sen. I am callyd Sensuall Appetyte,
  All craturs in me delyte   455

I comforte the wyttys fyve,
The tastyng, smellyng, and herynge ;
I refresh the syght and felynge
    To all creaturs alyve.
For whan the body wexith hongry,   460
For lacke of fode, or ellys thursty,
    Than with drynkes pleasaund
I restore hym out of payne,
And oft refresshe nature agayne
    With delycate vyand.   465
With plesaunde sounde of armonye
The herynge alwaye I satysfy,
    I dare this well reporte ;
The smellynge with swete odour,
And the syght with plesaunte fygour   470
    And colours I comforte ;
The felynge, that is so plesaunte,
Of every member, fote or hande,
    What pleasure therin can be
By the towchynge of soft and harde,   475
Of hote or cold, nought in regarde,
    Excepte it come by me.

Hu. Than I cannot see the contrary,
But ye are for me full necessary,
    And ryght convenyent.   480

Stu. Ye, syr, beware, yet, what ye do,
For yf you forsake my companye so,
    Lorde Nature wyll not be contente.
Of hym ye shall never lerne good thyng,
Nother vertu, nor no other connynge,   485
    This dare I well say.

Sen. Mary, avaunt, knave ! I the defye !
Dyde Nature forbyde hym my company ?
What sayst thou therto ? Speke openly.

Hu. As for that I know well nay.   490

Sen. No, by [Jove]! I am ryght sure;
For he knoweth well no creature
Without me can lyve one day.

Hu. Syr, I pray you, be contente,
It is not utterly myne intente   495
Your company to exyle;
But onely to have communycacyon
And a pastyme of recreacyon
With this man for a whyle.

Stu. Well, for your pleasure I wyll departe.   500

Hu. Now go, knave, go! I beshrew thy hart
The devyll sende the forwarde!

Sen. Now, by my trouth, I mervell gretly
That ever ye wolde use the company
So myche of suche a knave;   505
For yf ye do non other thynge,
But ever study and to be musynge,
As he wolde have you, it wyll you brynge
At the last unto your grave!
Ye shulde ever study pryncypall   510
For to comfort your lyfe naturall
With metis and drynkes dilycate,
And other pastymes and pleasures amonge,
Daunsynge, laughynge, or plesaunt songe;
This is mete for your estate.   515

Hu. Because ye sey so, I you promyse
That I have musyd and studyed such wyse,
Me thynketh my wyttes wery;
My nature desyreth some refresshynge,
And also I have ben so longe fastynge,   520
That I am somwhat hongry.

SEN. Well than, wyll ye go with me
    To a taverne, where ye shall se
    Good pastaunce, and at your lyberte
      Have what so ever ye wyll?   525

HU. I am content so for to do,
    Yf that ye wyll not fro me go
      But kepe me company styll.

SEN. Company, quod a? ye, that I shall, poynt devyse,
    And also do you good and trew servyce,   530
      And therto I plyght my trouthe!
    And yf that I ever forsake you,
    I pray God the devyl take you!

HU.   Mary, I thanke you for that othe!

SEN. A myschyfe on it! my tonge, loo,   535
    Wyll tryp somtyme, whatsoever I do,
      But ye wot what I mene well.

HU. Ye, no force! let this matter passe;
    But seydest evin now thou knewyst where was
    A good taverne to make solas?   540
      Where is that? I prey the tell.

SEN. Mary, at the dore evyn hereby;
    Yf we call any thynge on hye,
      The taverner wyll answere.

HU. I prey the, than, call for hym nowe.   545

SEN. Mary, I wyll! How, taverner, how!
    Why doste thou not appere?

Skelton's Magnyfycence.

Magnyfycence | A goodly interlude and a mery | Devysed and made
by | Mayster Skelton, Poet Laureate.

Here FANCY *cometh in.*

MAGN. What tydynges with you, syr, that you loke so
    sad? 1868

FAN. When ye knowe that I knowe, ye wyll not be glad

FOL. What, brother braynsyke, how farest thou? 1870

MAGN. Ye, let be thy japes, and tell me howe
    The case requyreth.

FAN. Alasse, alasse, an hevy metynge!
    I wolde tell you, and yf I myght for wepynge.

FOL. What! is all your myrthe nowe tourned to sorowe?
    Fare well tyll sone, adue tyll to morowe.

Here goth FOLYE *away.*

MAGN. I pray the, Largesse, let be thy sobbynge.

FAN. Alasse, syr, ye are undone with stelyng and robbynge!
    Ye sent us a supervysour for to take hede:
    Take hede of your selfe, for nowe ye have nede. 1880

MAGN. What! hath Sadnesse begyled me so?

FAN. Nay, madnesse hath begyled you and many mo;
    For Lyberte is gone and also Felycyte.

MAGN. Gone? Alasse, ye have undone me!

FAN. Nay, he that ye sent us, Clokyd Colusyon,
 And your payntyd Pleasure, Courtly Abusyon,
 And your demenour with Counterfet Countenaunce,
 And your survayour, Crafty Conveyaunce,
 Or ever we were ware brought us in adversyte
 And had robbyd you quyte from all felycyte.　　1890

MAGN. Why, is this the Largesse that I have usyd?

FAN. Nay, it was your fondnesse that ye have usyd.

MAGN. And is this the credence that I gave to the letter?

FAN. Why, coulde not your wyt serve you no better?

MAGN. Why, who wolde have thought in you suche gyle?

FAN. What? Yes, by the rode, syr, it was I all this whyle
 That you trustyd, and Fansy is my name;
 And Foly, my broder, that made you moche game.

Here cometh in ADVERSYTE.

MAGN. Alas, who[1] is yonder, that grymly lokys?

FAN. Adewe, for I wyll not come in his clokys.　　1900

MAGN. Lorde, so my flesshe trymblyth nowe for drede!

Here MAGNYFYCENCE *is beten downe, and spoylyd from all his
goodys and rayment.*

ADVER. I am Adversyte, that for thy mysdede
 From God am sent to quyte the thy mede,
 Vyle velyarde, thou must not nowe my dynt withstande,
 Thou must not abyde the dynt of my hande:
 Ly there, losell, for all thy pompe and pryde;
 Thy pleasure now with payne and trouble shalbe tryde.
 The stroke of God, Adversyte, I hyght;
 I pluke downe kynge, prynce, lorde and knyght,

---

[1] 'why,' *Text.*

I 2

I rushe at them rughly, and make them ly full lowe,
And in theyr moste truste I make them overthrowe.
Thys losyll was a lorde, and lyvyd at his lust,   1912
And nowe, lyke a lurden, he lyeth in the dust:
He knewe not hymselfe, his harte was so hye;
Now is ther no man that wyll set by hym a flye:
He was wonte to boste, brage and to brace;
Nowe dare he not for shame loke one in the face:
All worldly welth for hym to lytell was;
Nowe hath he ryght nought, naked as an asse.
Somtyme without measure he trusted in golde,   1920
And now without mesure he shall have hunger and
    colde.
Lo, syrs, thus I handell them all
That folowe theyr fansyes in foly to fall:
Man or woman, of what estate they be,
I counsayle them beware of Adversyte.
Of sorowfull servauntes I have many scores:
I vysyte them somtyme with blaynes and with sores;
With botches and carbuckyls in care I them knyt;
With the gowte I make them to grone where they syt;
Some I make lyppers and lazars full horse;   1930
And from that they love best some I devorse;
Some with the marmoll to halte I them make;
And some to cry out of the bone ake;
And some I vysyte with brennynge of fyre;
Of some I wrynge of the necke lyke a wyre;
And some I make in a rope to totter and walter;
And some for to hange themselfe in an halter;
And some I vysyte to batayle, warre and murther,
And make eche man to sle other;
To drowne or to sle themselfe with a knyfe;   1940
And all is for theyr ungracyous lyfe.
Yet somtyme I stryke where is none offence,
Bycause I wolde prove men of theyr pacyence.

But nowe a dayes to stryke I have grete cause,
Lydderyns so lytell set by Goddes lawes.
Faders and moders that be neclygent,
And suffre theyr chyldren to have theyr entent,
To guyde them vertuously that wyll not remembre,
Them, or theyr chyldren, ofte tymes I dysmembre;
Theyr chyldren, bycause that they have no mekenesse;
I vysyte theyr faders and moders with sekenesse; 1951
And yf I se therby that they wyll not amende,
Then myschefe sodaynly I them sende;
For there is nothynge that more dyspleseth God
Than from theyr chyldren to spare the rod
Of correccyon, but let them have theyr wyll;
Some I make lame, and some I do kyll;
And some¹ I stryke with a franesy;
Of some of theyr chyldren I stryke out the eye;
And where the fader by wysdom worshyp hath wonne,
I sende ofte tymes a fole to his sonne.   1961
Wherfore of Adversyte loke ye be ware,
For when I come, comyth sorowe and care:
For I stryke lordys of realmes and landys,
That rule not by mesure that they have in theyr handys,
That sadly rule not theyr howsholde men.
I am Goddys preposytour, I prynt them with a pen;
Because of theyr neglygence and of theyr wanton vagys,
I vysyte them and stryke them with many sore plagys.
To take, syrs, example of that I you tell,   1970
And beware of Adversyte by my counsell,
Take hede of this caytyfe that lyeth here on grounde;
Beholde, howe Fortune of hym hath frounde!
For though we shewe you this in game and play,
Yet it proveth eyrnest, ye may se, every day.
For nowe wyll I from this caytyfe go,
And take myscheffe and vengeaunce of other mo,

¹ syme, *Text.*

That hath deservyd it as well as he.
Howe, where art thou? come hether, Poverte;
Take this caytyfe to thy lore.   1980

Here cometh in POVERTE.

POVER. A, my bonys ake, my lymmys be sore;
Alasse, I have the cyataca full evyll in my hyppe!
Alasse, where is youth that was wont for to skyppe?
I am lowsy, and unlykynge, and full of scurffe,
My colour is tawny, colouryd as a turffe:
I am Poverte, that all men doth hate,
I am baytyd with doggys at every mannys gate;
I am raggyd and rent, as ye may se;
Full fewe but they have envy at me.
Nowe must I this carcasse lyft up: 1990
He dynyd with delyte, with Poverte he must sup.
Ryse up, syr, and welcom unto me.

Hic accedat ad levandum MAGNYFYCENCE *et locabit eum super
locum stratum.*

MAGN. Alasse, where is nowe my golde and fe?
Alasse, I say, where to am I brought?
Alasse, alasse, alasse, I dye for thought!

POVER. Syr, all this wolde have bene thought on before:
He woteth not what welth is that never was sore.

MAGN. Fy, fy, that ever I sholde be brought in this snare!
I wenyd ones never to have knowen of care.

POVER. Lo, suche is this worlde! I fynde it wryt,   2000
In welth to beware, and that is wyt.

MAGN. In welth to beware, yf I had had grace,
Never had I bene brought in this case.

POVER. Nowe, syth it wyll non other be,
All that God sendeth, take it in gre;

For, thoughe you were somtyme a noble estate,
Nowe must you lerne to begge at every mannes gate.

MAGN. Alasse, that ever I sholde be so shamed!
Alasse, that ever I Magnyfycence was named!
Alasse, that ever I was so harde happed,   2010
In mysery and wretchydnesse thus to be lapped!
Alasse, that I coude not myselfe no better gyde!
Alasse, in my cradell that I had not dyde!

POVER. Ye, syr, ye, leve all this rage,
And pray to God your sorowes to asswage:
It is foly to grudge agaynst his vysytacyon.
With harte contryte make your supplycacyon
Unto your Maker, that made both you and me
And, whan it pleaseth God, better may be.

MAGN. Alasse, I wote not what I sholde pray!   2020

POVER. Remembre you better, syr, beware what ye say,
For drede ye dysplease the hygh deyte.
Put your wyll to his wyll, for surely it is he
That may restore you agayne to felycyte,
And brynge you agayne out of adversyte.
Therfore poverte loke pacyently ye take,
And remembre he suffered moche more for your sake,
Howe be it of all synne he was innocent,
And ye have deserved this punysshment.   2029

MAGN. Alasse, with colde my lymmes shall be marde!

POVER. Ye, syr, nowe must ye lerne to lye harde,
That was wonte to lye on fetherbeddes of downe;
Nowe must your fete lye hyer than your crowne:
Where you were wonte to have cawdels for your hede,
Nowe must you monche mamockes and lumpes of
    brede;
And where you had chaunges of ryche aray,
Nowe lap you in a coverlet, full fayne that you may;

And where that ye were pomped with what that ye wolde,
Nowe must ye suffre bothe hunger and colde:
With courtely sylkes[1] ye were wonte to be drawe;   2040
Nowe must ye lerne to lye on the strawe;
Your skynne that was wrapped in shertes of Raynes,
Nowe must ye be storm ybeten with showres and raynes;
Your hede that was wonte to be happed moost drowpy
        and drowsy,
Now shal ye be scabbed, scurvy and lowsy.

MAGN. Fye on this worlde, full of trechery,
That ever noblenesse sholde lyve thus wretchydly!

POVER. Syr, remembre the tourne of Fortunes whele,
That wantonly can wynke, and wynche with her hele.
Nowe she wyll laughe; forthwith she will frowne;   2050
Sodenly set up, and sodenly pluckyd downe:
She dawnsyth varyaunce with mutabylyte;
Nowe all in welth, forthwith in poverte:
In her promyse there is no sykernesse;
All her delyte is set in doublenesse.

MAGN. Alas, of Fortune I may well complayne!

POVER. Ye, syr, yesterday wyll not be callyd agayne:
But yet, syr, nowe in this case,
Take it mekely, and thanke God of his grace;
For nowe go I wyll begge for you some mete;   2060
It is foly agaynst God for to plete;
I wyll walke nowe with my beggers baggys,
And happe you the whyles with these homly raggys.

Discedendo[2] dicat ista verba.

A, howe my lymmys be lyther and lame!
Better it is to begge than to be hangyd with shame,
Yet many had lever hangyd to be,

---

[1] With curteyns of sylke, *Cambridge copy*.   [2] Difidendo, *Text*

Then for to begge theyr mete for charyte :
They thynke it no shame to robbe and stele,
Yet were they better to begge a great dele ;
For by robbynge they rynne to *in manus tuas* quecke,
But beggynge is better medecyne for the necke :   2071
Ye, mary, is it ; ye, so mote I goo :
A Lorde God, howe the gowte wryngeth me by the too !

Ӊeywood's the Pardoner and the Frere.

A mery playe betwene the pardoner and the frere the curate and neybour Pratte.

THE FRERE. *Deus hic*, the Holy Trynyte,
  Preserve all that nowe here be!
  Dere bretherne, yf ye wyll consyder
  The cause why I am come hyder,
  Ye wolde be glad to knowe my intent.   5
  For I com not hyther for monye nor for rent,
  I com not hyther for meate nor for meale,
  But I com hyther for your soules heale,
  I com not hyther to poll nor to shave,
  I com not hyther to begge nor to crave,   10
  I com not hyther to glose nor to flatter,
  I com not hyther to bable nor to clatter,
  I com not hyther to fable nor to lye,
  But I com hyther you[r]e soules to edyfye!
  For we freres are bounde the people to teche,   15
  The gospell of Chryst openly to preche,
  As dyd the appostels, by Chryst theyr mayster sent
  To turne the people and make them to repent.
  But syth the appostels fro heven wolde not come,
  We freres now must occupy theyr rome.   20
  We freres are bounde to serche mennes conscyens,
  We may not care for grotes nor for pens,

We freres have professed wylfull poverte,
No peny in our purse have may we,
Knyfe nor staffe may we none cary,   25
Excepte we shulde from the gospell vary.
For worldly adversyte may we be in no sorowe,
We may not care to day for our meate to-morowe;
Bare fote and bare legged must we go also,
We may not care for frost nor snowe;   30
We may have no maner care, ne thynke,
Nother for our meate nor for our drynke,
But let our thoughtes fro suche thynges be as free
As be the byrdes that in the ayre flee;
For why our lorde, clyped swete Jesus,   35
In the gospell speketh to us thus:
Through all the worlde go ye, sayth he,
And to every creature speke ye of me,
And shew of my doctryne and connynge;
And that they may be glad of your comynge,   40
Yf that you enter in any hous any where,
Loke that ye salute them and byd my peas be there;
And yf that house be worthy and electe,
Thylke peace there than shall take effecte;
And yf that hous be cursyd or parvert,   45
Thylke peace than shall to your selfe revert;
And furthermore yf any suche there be,
Which do deny for to receyve ye,
And do dyspyse your doctryne and your lore,
At suche a house tary ye no more,   50
And from your shoes scrape away the dust,
To theyr reprefe, and I, bothe trew and just,
Shall vengeaunce take of theyr synfull dede.
Wherfore, my frendes, to this text take ye hede,
Beware how ye despyse the pore freres,   55
Which ar in this worlde Crystes mynysters;
But do them with an harty chere receyve,

Leste they happen your houses for to leve,
And than God wyll take vengeaunce in his yre.
Wherfore I now, that am a pore frere,   60
Dyd enquere w[h]ere any people were,
Which were dysposyd the worde of God to here;
And, as I cam hether, one dyd me tell
That in this towne ryght good folke dyd dwell,
Which to here the word of God wolde be glad;   65
And as sone as I therof knolege had,
I hyder hyed me as fast as I myght,
Entendyd by the grace of God almyght,
And by your pacyens and supportacyon,
Here to make a symple colacyon.   70
Wherfore I requyre all ye in this prese[nce]
For to abyde and gyve dew audyence.
But, fyrst of all,
Now here I shall
    To God my prayer make,   75
To gyve ye grace
All in thys place
    His doctryne for to take.

And than kneleth downe the frere sayenge his prayers and in
*   the meane whyle entreth the pardoner with all his relyques*
*   to declare what eche of them ben and the hole power and*
*   vertu thereof.*

THE PARDONER. God and saynt Leonarde sende ye all
        his grace,
    As many as ben assembled in this place!   80
    Good devoute people that here do assemble,
    I pray [God][1] that ye may all well resemble
    The ymage after whiche you are wrought,
    And that ye save that Chryst in you bought

    [1] Good, *Text.*

Devoute Chrysten people, ye shall all wytte   85
That I am comen hyther ye to vysytte,
Wherfore let us pray thus or I begynne;
Our savyoure preserve ye all from synne,
And enable ye to receyve this blessed pardon,
Whiche is the greatest under the son,   90
Graunted by the pope in his bulles under lede,
Whiche pardon ye shall fynde whan ye are dede,
That offereth outher grotes or els pens
To these holy relyques whiche, or I go hens,
I shall here shewe in open audyence,   95
Exortynge ye all to do to them reverence.
But first ye shall knowe well that I com fro Rome,—
Lo here my bulles, all and some,
Our lyege lorde[s] seale, here on my patent,
I bere with me my body to warant,   100
That no man be so bolde, be he preest or clarke,
Me to dysturbe of Chrystes holy warke,
Nor have no dysdayne, nor yet scorne,
Of these holy relyques which sayntes have worne.
Fyrst here I shewe ye of a holy Jewes shepe   105
A bone, (I pray you take good kepe
To my wordes and marke them well,)
Yf any of your bestes belyes do swell,
Dyppe[1] this bone in the water that he dothe take
Into his body, and the swellyinge shall slake.   110

*   *   *   *   *   *   *

Here is a mytten eke, as ye may se,   128
He that his hande wyll put in this myttayn,
He shall have encrease of his grayn,   130
That he hath sowne, be it wete or otys,
So that he offer pens or els grotes.
And another holy relyke eke here se ye may,

[1] Dyype, *Text.*

The blessed arme of swete saynt Sondaye,
And who so ever is blessyd with this ryght hande
Can not spede amysse by se nor by lande,   136
And if he offereth eke with good devocyon
He shall not fayle to come to hyghe promocyon.

* * * * * * *

Here is another relyke, eke a precyous one,   153
Of All Helowes the blessyd jawbone,
Which relyke without any fayle   155
Agaynst poyson chefely dothe prevayle;
For whom so ever it toucheth, without dout
All maner venym from hym shall issue out,
So that it shall hurt no maner wyghte.
Lo of this relyke the great power and myghte,   160
Which preservyth from poyson every man.
Lo of saynt Myghell eke the brayn pan,
Which for the hed ake is a preservatyfe
To every man or beste that beryth lyfe,
And further it shall stande hym in better stede,   165
For his hede shall never ake 'whan that he is dede,
For he shall fele no maner grefe nor payn,
Though with a sworde one cleve it than atwayn,
But be as one that lay in a dede slepe;
Wherfore to these relykes now com crouche and crepe,
But loke that ye offerynge to them make,   171
Or els can ye no maner profyte take.
But one thynge, ye women all, I warant you,
Yf any wyght be in this place now
That hath done syn so horryble that she   175
Dare not for shame thereof shryven be,

* * * * * *

Suche folke shall have no power, nor no grace,   179
To offer to my relykes in this place!   180
And who so fyndeth herselfe out of suche blame
Com hyther to me on Crystes holy name;

And bycause ye
Shall unto me
  Gyve credence at the full ;   185
Myn auctoryte
Now shall ye se,
  Lo here! the popes bull.

Now shall the frere begyn his sermon and evyn at the same
   tyme the pardoner begynneth also to shew and speke of his
   bullys and auctorytes com from Rome.

THE FRERE. *Date et dabitur vobis :*
  Good devout people this place of scrypture
PARDONER. Worshypfull maysters, ye shall understand 190
F. Is to you that have no litterature,
P. That pope Leo the **x**. hath graunted with his hand,
F. Is to say in our Englysshe tonge,
P. And by his bulles confyrmed under lede,
F. As departe your goodes the poore folke amonge, 195
P. To all maner people bothe quycke and dede,
F. And God shall than gyve unto you agayne.
P. Ten thousande yeres and as many lentes of pardon,
F. This in the gospell so is wryten playne,
P. Whan they are dede theyr soules for to guardon, 200
F. Therfore gyve your almes in the largest wyse.
P. That wyll with theyr peny or almes dede
F. Kepe not your goodes : fye, fye on covetyse !
P. Put to theyr handes to the good spede
F. That synne with God is most abhomynable,   **205**
P. Of the holy chapell of swete saynt Leonarde,
F. And is eke the synne that is most dampnable
P. Whiche late by fyre was destroyed and marde.
F. In scrypture eke ; but I say, syrs, how—

P. Ay by the mas, one can not here   310

F. What a bablynge maketh yonder felow!

P. For the bablynge of yonder folysshe frere!

[They resume their respective discourses for a little while, but at length
begin to attack each other.]

F. But, I say, thou pardoner, I byd the holde thy peace!

P. And I say, thou frere, holde thy tonge styl!   252

F. What standest thou there all the day smatterynge?

P. Mary, what standyst thou there all day clatterynge?

FRERE. Mary, felow, I com hyder to prech the word of
    God,   255
    Whyche of no man may be forbode,
    But harde wyth scylence and good entent,
    For why it techeth them evydent
    The very way and path that shall them lede,
    Even to heven gatys, as strayght as any threde;   260
    And he that lettyth the worde of God of audyence
    Standeth accurst in the greate sentence;
    And so art thou for enterruptynge me.

PARDONER. Nay thou art a curst knave, and that shalt
    thou se!
    And all suche that to me make interrupcyon   265
    The pope sendes them excommunycacyon,
    By hys bulles here, redy to be redde,
    By bysshoppes and hys cardynalles confyrmed.
    And eke yf thou dysturbe me any thynge,
    Thou arte also a traytour to the kynge;   270
    For here hath he graunted me, under hys brode seale,
    That no man, yf he love hys hele,
    Sholde me dysturbe or let in any wyse.
    And yf thou dost the kynges commaundement dispise,
    I shall make the be set fast by the fete.   275
    And where thou saydyst that thou arte more mete

Amonge the people here for to preche,
Bycause thou dost them the very way teche
How to come to heven above,
Therin thou lyest, and that shall I prove,　　　280
And by good reason I shall make the bow,
And knowe that I am meter than arte thou.
For thou whan thou hast taught them ones the way,
Thou carest not whether they com there, ye or nay,
But whan that thou hast done all togyder,　　　285
And taught them the way for to com thyther,
Yet all that thou canst ymagyn
Is but to use vertue and abstayne fro syn,
And yf they fall ones than thou canst no more,
Thou canst not gyve them a salve for theyr sore ;　290
But these my letters be clene purgacyon,
All thoug[h]e never so many synnes they have don.
But whan thou hast taught them the way and all,
Yet or they com there they may have many a fall
In the way, or that they com thyther,　　　295
For why the way to heven is very slydder ;
But I wyll teche them after another rate,
For I shall brynge them to heven gate,
And be theyr gydes and conducte all thynges,
And lede them thyther by the purse strynges,　　　300
So that they shall not fall though that they wolde.

FRERE. Holde thy peace, knave, thou art very bolde !
　　Thou pratest in fayth even lyke a pardoner !

PARDONER. Why despysest thou the popes mynyster?
　　Maysters, here I curse hym openly,　　　305
　　And therwith warne all this hole company,
　　By the popes great auctoryte,
　　That ye leve hym and herken unto me ;
　　For tyll he be assoyled his wordes take none effecte,
　　For out of holy chyrche he is now clene rejecte.　310

K

FRERE. My maysters, he dothe but gest and rave:
It forseth not for the wordes of a knave,
But to the worde of God do reverence,
And here me forthe with dewe audyence.

[They again resume their preaching, but after a little while break out
into a fresh quarrel, upon which comes the stage-direction:]

Than the fyght.

FRERE. Lose thy handes away from myn earys!   538

PARD. Than take thou thy handes away from my heres!
Nay, abyde, thou [rascal], I am not downe yet!   540
I trust fyrst to lye the at my fete!
F. Ye, [rascal,] wylt thou scrat and byte?
P. Ye, mary, wyll I, as longe as thou doste smyte!

THE CURATE.

PARSON. Holde your handes! a vengeaunce on ye bothe
two!
That ever ye came hyther to make this ado   545
To polute my chyrche, a myschyefe on you lyght!
I swere to you, by God all-myght,
Ye shall bothe repente, every vayne of your harte,
As sore as ye dyd ever thynge, or ye departe.

FRERE. Mayster parson, I marvayll ye wyll gyve lycence
To this false knave in this audience   551
To publysh his ragman rolles with lyes.
I desyred hym y-wys, more than ones or twyse,
To holde his peas tyll that I had done,
But he wolde here no more than the man in the mone.

PARD. Why sholde I suffre the more than thou me? 556
Mayster parson gave me lycence before the.
And I wolde thou knewyst it! I have relykes here
Other maner stuffe than thou dost bere!

I wyll edefy more with the syght of it   560
Than wyll all the pratynge of holy wryt.
For that, except that the precher hym selfe lyve well,
His predycacyon wyll helpe never a dell,
And I know well that thy lyvynge is nought.

     *   *   *   *   *   *   *

PARSON. No more of this wranglyng in my chyrch!   570
  I shrewe your hartys bothe for this lurche!
  Is ther any blood shed here betwen these knaves?
  Thanked be God, they had no stavys,
  Nor eggetoles[1], for than it had ben wronge!
  Well ye shall synge another songe!   575
  Neybour Prat, com hether I you pray.

PRAT. Why, what is this nyse fraye?

PARSON. I can not tell you. One knave dysdaynes another,
  Wherefore take ye the tone and I shall take the other,
  We shall bestow them there as is most convenyent   580
  For suche a couple. I trow they shall repente
  That ever they met in this chyrche here!
  Neyboure, ye be constable, stande ye nere.
  Take ye that laye knave and let me alone
  With this gentylman. By God and by saynt John   585
  I shall borowe upon presthode[2] somwhat!
  For I may say to the, neybour Prat,
  It is a good dede to punysh such, to the ensample
  Of suche other how that they shall mell
  In lyke facyon as these catyfes do.   590

PRAT. In good fayth, mayster parson, yf ye do so,
  Ye do but well to teche them to be ware.

PARDON. Mayster Prat, I pray ye me to spare;
  For I am sory for that that is done;
  Wherfore I pray ye forgyve me sone   595
  For that I have offendyd within your lybertye,

---

[1] egoteles, *Text.*   [2] prestholde, *Text.*

K 2

And, by my trouthe, syr, ye may trust me,
I wyll never come hether more
Whyle I lyve, and God before.

PRAT. Nay, I am ones charged with the,   600
Wherfore, by saynt John, thou shalt not escape me,
Tyll thou hast scouryd a pare of stokys.

PARSON. Tut, he weneth all is but mockes!
Lay hande on hym, and com ye on, syr frere!
Ye shall of me hardely have your hyre,   605
Ye had none suche this vii yere,
I swere by God and by our Lady dere.

FRERE. Nay, mayster parson, for Goddys passyon,
Intreate not me after that facyon.
For yf ye do it wyll not be for your honesty.   610

PARSON. Honesty or not, but thou shall se
What I shall do by and by.
Make no stroglynge! com forthe soberly!
For it shall not avayle the, I say.

FRERE. Mary, that shall we trye even strayt-way.   615
I defy the, churle preeste, and there be no mo than thou,
I wyll not go with the, I make God a-vow!
We shall se fyrst which is the stronger!
God hath sente me bonys! I do the not fere!

PARSON. Ye, by my fayth, wylt thou be there?   620
Neybour Prat, brynge forthe that knave,
And thou, syr frere, yf thou wylt algatys rave—

FRERE. Nay, chorle, I the defy!
I shall trouble the fyrst,
Thou shalt go to pryson by and by!   625
Let me se now! Do thy worste!

Prat with the pardoner and the parson with the frere.

PARSON. Helpe! helpe! Neybour Prat! Neybour Prat!
In the worship of God, helpe me som what!

PRAT. Nay, deale as thou canst with that elfe,
    For why I have inoughe to do my selfe!   630
    Alas! for payn I am almoste dede,
    The reede blood so ronneth downe aboute my hede,
    Nay, and thou canst, I pray the, helpe me!

PARSON. Nay, by the mas, felowe, it wyll not be!
    I have more tow on my dystaffe than I can well spyn!
    The cursed frere dothe the upper hand wyn!   636

FRERE. Wyll ye leve than, and let us in peace departe?

PARSON and PRAT. Ye, by our Lady, even with all our
    harte!

FRERE and PARD. Than adew, to the devyll, tyll we come
    agayn.

PARSON and PRAT. And a myschefe go with you bothe
    twayne.   640

Imprynted by Wyllyam Rastell the v. day of Apryll
    the yere of our lorde M. CCCCC XXX III.

Cum privilegio.

𝕮𝖍𝖊𝖗𝖘𝖞𝖙𝖊𝖘.

A NEW ENTERLUDE CALLED

THERSYTES.

¶ Thys Enterlude Folowynge Dothe Declare howe that the greatest boesters are not the greatest doers.

¶ THE NAMES OF THE PLAYERS.

THERSITES	*A boster.*
MULCIBER	*A smyth.*
MATER	*A mother.*
MILES	*A knyght.*
TELEMACHUS	*A childe.*

Thersites commeth in fyrste havinge a clubbe uppon his necke.

Have in a ruffler foorth of the Greke lande,
   Called Thersites, if ye wyll me knowe.
Abacke, geve me roume, in my way do ye not stand,
   For if ye do, I wyll soone laye you lowe.
In Homere of my actes ye have red, I trow,   5
Neyther Agamemnon nor Ulysses, I spared to checke,
They coulde not bringe me to be at theyr becke!

Of late frome the sege of Troy I retourned,
   Where all my harnes excepte this clubbe I lost
In an olde house, there it was quyte burned,   10
   Whyle I was preparinge vytayles for the hoste.
I must nedes get me newe, what so ever it cost.

I wyll go seke adventures, for I can not be ydle,
I wyll hamper some of the knaves in a brydle.

It greveth me to heare howe the knaves do bragge, 15
   But by supreme Jupiter, when I am harnessed well,
I shall make the dasters to renne into a bagge
   To hyde them fro me, as from the devyll of hell,
I doubte not but hereafter of me ye shall heare tell,
Howe I have made the knaves for to play cowch quaile.
But nowe to the shop of Mulciber to go I wyll not faile. 21

Mulciber must have a shop made in the place and Thersites
commethe before it, sayinge a-loude.

Mulciber, whom the Poetes doth call the god of fyer,
   Smith unto Jupiter kinge over all,
Come foorth of thy office, I the desyre,   24
   And graunte me my peticion, I aske a thynge but small.
I wyl none of thy lightning, that thou art wont to make
For the goddes supernall, for yre when they do shake,
With whiche they thruste the gyauntes downe to hell,
That were at a convention heaven to bye and sell;
But I woulde have some helpe of Lemnos and Ilva, 30
That of theyr stele, by thy crafte, *condatur mihi galea.*

MULCIBER. What, felowe Thersites, do ye speake Latyn
     nowe?
Nay then, farewell! I make God a vowe
I do not you understande, no Latyn is in my palet.

THERSITES. I say Abyde, good Mulciber! I pray the
     make me a sallet.   35

MULCIBER. Why, Thersites, hast thou anye wytte in thy head?
Woldest thou have a sallet nowe all the herbes are dead?
Besyde that it is not mete for a smyth
To gether herbes, and sallettes to medle with.   39

    *   *   *   *   *   *   *

THERSITES. I meane a sallet with whiche men do fyght,

MULCIBER. It is a small tastinge of a mannes mighte 46
That he shoulde for any matter
Fyght with a fewe herbes in a platter!
No greate laude shoulde folowe that victorye!

THERSITES. [I pray thee,] Mulciber, where is thy wit and
memory?   50
I wolde have a sallet made of stele!

MULCIBER. Whye syr, in youre stomacke longe you shall
it fele.
For stele is harde for to digest.

THERSITES. Mans bones and sydes, hee is worse then a
beest!
I wolde have a sallet to were on my hed,   55
Whiche under my chyn with a thonge red
Buckeled shall be.
Doest thou yet perceyve me?

MULCIBER. Your mynde now I se.
Why, thou pevysshe ladde,   60
Arte thou almost madde,
Or well in thy wytte?
Gette the a wallette!
Wolde thou have a sallette
What woldest thou do with it?   65

THERSITES. I pray the, good Mulciber, make no mo bones,
But let me have a sallet made at ones!

MULCIBER. I must do somewhat for this knave!
What maner of sallet, syr, woulde ye have?

THERSITES. I wold have such a one that nother might
nor mayne   70
Shoulde perse it thorowe, or parte it in twayne;
Whiche nother gonstone, nor sharpe speare,
Shoulde be able other to hurte or teare.

I woulde have it also for to save my heade
Yf Jupiter him selfe woulde have me dead;   75
And if he, in a fume, woulde cast at me his fire,
This sallet I woulde have to kepe me from his yre.

MULCIBER. I perceave youre mynde,
  Ye shall fynde me kynde.
  I wyll for you prepare.   80

And then he goeth in to his shop, and maketh a sallet
for hym : at the laste, he sayth.

Here, Thersites, do this sallet weare,
And on thy head it beare,
And none shall worke the care.

Then Mulciber goeth into his shop, untyll he is called
agayne.

THERSITES. Now woulde I not feare with anye bull to fyghte,
  Or with a raumpinge lyon, nother by daye nor nyghte,
  O what greate strength is in my body so lusty,   86
  Whiche for lacke of exercise is nowe almost rustye !
  Hercules in comparison to me was but a boye
  When the bandogge Cerberus from hell he bare awaye,
  When he kylled the lyons, hydra, and the bere so wylde,
  Compare him to me and he was but a chylde.   91
  Why Sampson, I saye, hast thou no more wytte ?
  Woldest thou be as strong as I ? come suck thy mothers
        tytte !
  Wene you that David, that lyttle elvyshe boye,
  Should with his slinge have take my life awaye ?   95
  Nay ywys, Golyath, for all his fyve stones,
  I woulde have quashed his little boysshe bones
  O howe it woulde do my harte muche good
  To se some of the giauntes before Noes floud !
  I woulde make the knaves to crye creke,   100
  Or elles with my clubbe their braynes I wyll breake !

But Mulciber, yet I have not with the do !
My heade is armed, my necke I woulde have to!
And also my shoulders with some good habergyn
That the devyll, if he shote at me, coulde not enter in.
For I am determined greate battayle to make,   106
Excepte my fumishenes by some meanes may aslake.

MULCIBER. Bokell on this habergyn as fast as thou canne,
And feare for the metinge of nother beast nor manne ;
Yf it were possible for one too shote an oke   110
This habergyn wyll defende thee frome the stroke.
Let them throwe mylstones at the as thick as haile,
Yet the to kyll they shall their purpose faile.
Yf Malverne hylles shoulde on thy shoulders light
They shall not hurt the, nor suppress thy mighte, 115
Yf Bevis of Hampton, Colburne and Guy,
Will the assaye, set not by them a flye,
To be briefe, this habergyn shall the save
Bothe by lande and water. Nowe playe the lusty knave !

Then he goeth in to his shoppe againe.

THERSITES. When I consider my shoulders that so brode
be,   120
When the other partes of my bodye I do beholde,
I verely thinke that none in Chrystente
With me to medele dare be so bolde.
Now have at the lyons on Cotsolde !
I wyll neyther spare for heate nor for colde,   125
Where art thou king Arthur, and the Knightes of the
Rounde Table?
Come, brynge forth your horses out of the stable.
Lo ! with me to mete they be not able !
By the masse, they had rather were a bable !   129
Where arte thou Gawyn the curtesse and Cay the crabed ?
Here be a couple of knightes cowardishe and scabbed !

Appere in thy likenesse Syr Libeus Disconius,
Yf thou wilt have my clubbe lyghte on thy hedibus.
Lo ! ye maye see he beareth not the face
With me to trye a blowe in thys place.   135
Howe syrray, approche Syr Launcelot de Lake !
What renne ye awaie and for feare quake?
Nowe he that did the a knight make
Thought never that thou any battaile shouldest take.
Yf thou wilt not come thy self, some other of thy
        felowes send,   140
To battaile I provoke them, themselfe let them defende.
Lo ! for all the good that ever they se,
They wyll not ones set hande to fight with me.
O good lorde ! howe brode is my brest,
And stronge with all, for hole is my chest !   145
He that should medle with me shall have shrewde rest !
Beholde you my handes, my legges and my feete
Every parte is stronge proportionable and mete.
Thinke you that I am not feared in felde and strete?
Yes, yes, god wote they geve me the wall,   150
Or elles with my clubbe I make them to fall.
Backe knaves ! I saye to them ; then for feare they
        quake
And take me then to the taverne and good chere me
        make.
The proctoure and his men I made to renne their waies,
And some wente to hide them in broken heys.   155
I tell you, [yea, I,]
I set not a [fly]
    By none of them al.
Early and late I wyll walke,
And London stretes stalke,   160
    Spyte of them greate and small.
For I thinke verely,
That none in heaven so hye,

Nor yet in hell so lowe,
Whyle I have this clubbe in my hande,   165
Can be able me to withstande,
    Or me to overthrowe.
But, Mulciber, yet I must the desyre
    To make me briggen yrons for myne armes,
And then I will love the as mine owne syre,   170
    For withoute them I can not be safe frome all harmes.
Those once had, I will not sette a strawe
By all the worlde, for then I wyll by awe
Have all my mynde, or elles, by the holye roode,
I wyll make them thinke the devyll caryeth them to
        the wood.   175
Yf no man wyll with me battayle take,
A vyage to hell quickely I wyll make,
And there I wyll bete the devyll and his dame,
And bringe the soules awaye, I fullye entende the same.
After that in hell I have ruffled so,   180
Streyghte to olde purgatorye wyll I go.
I wyll cleane that so purge rounde aboute,
That we shall nede no pardons to helpe them oute.
Yf I have not fyghte ynoughe this wayes,
I wyll clymbe to heaven and fet awaye Peters kayes,
I wyll kepe them myselfe and let in a great route. 186
What shoulde suche a fysher kepe good felowes out?

MULCIBER. Have here, Thersites, briggen yrons bright,
    And feare thou no man manly to fyghte,
    Thoughe he be stronger then Hercules or Sampson, 190
    Be thou prest and bolde to set him upon.
    Nother Amazon nor Xerxes with their hole rable
    The to assayle shall fynde it profytable.
    I warrante the they wyll fle fro thy face,
    As doth an hare from the dogges in a chase.   195
    Would not thy blacke and rustye grym berde,
    Nowe thou art so armed, make anye man aferde?

Surely if Jupiter dyd see the in this gere,
He woulde renne awaye and hyde hym for feare!
He wold thinke that Typhoeus the gyant were alive 200
And his brother Enceladus, agayn with him to strive!
If that Mars, of battell the god stoute and bold,
In this aray shoulde chaunce the to beholde,
He would yelde up his sworde unto the,
And god of battayle (he would say) thou shouldest be.
Now fare thou wel, go the world through,   206
And seke adventures, thou arte man good ynough.

THERSITES. Mulciber, whyle the starres shal shyne in
        the sky,
And Phaeton's horses with the sonnes charret shall fly,
Whyle the mornynge shall go before none,   210
And cause the darkennesse to vanysshe away soone,
Whyle that the cat shall love well mylke,
And whyle that women shal love to go in sylke,
Whyle beggers have lyce,
And cockneys are nyce,   215
Whyle pardoners can lye,
Marchauntes can by,
And chyldren crye,
Whyle all these laste and more,
Whiche I kepe in store,   220
I do me faythfully bynde,
Thy kyndnes to beare in mynde.
But yet, Mulciber, one thinge I aske more,
Haste thou ever a sworde now in store?
I would have suche a one that would cut stones, 225
And pare a great oke down at ones[1],
That were a sworde, lo, even for the nones.

MULCIBER. Truly I have suche a one in my shoppe
    That wil pare yron, as it were a rope.

---

[1] once, *Text.*

Have, here it is, gyrde it to thy syde.   230
Now fare thou well, Jupiter be thy guyde.

THERSITES. Gramercye, Mulciber, wyth my hole harte.
Geve me thy hande and let us departe.

Mulciber goeth in to hys shoppe againe and Thersites saith
foorth.

Nowe I go hence, and put my selfe in prease.
I wyll seeke adventures, yea and that I wyll not cease,
If there be any present here thys nyghte   236
That wyll take upon them with me to fighte,
Let them come quickly, and the battayle shall be
          pyghte.
Where is Cacus, that knave, not worthe a grote,   239
That was wont to blowe cloudes oute of his throte,
Which stale Hercules kine and hyd them in his cave?
Come hether Cacus, thou lubber and false knave.
I wyll teache all wretches by the to beware,
If thou come hether I trappe the in a snare.
Thou shalt have knocked breade and yll fare.   245
How say you, good godfather, that loke so stale
Ye seeme a man to be borne in the vale,
Dare ye adventure wyth me a stripe or two?
Go, coward, go, hide the, as thou wast wonte to do.
What a sorte of dasterdes have we here   250
None of you to battaile with me dare appeare!
          *   *   *   *   *   *

Well, let all go! whye, wyll none come in,
With me to fyghte that I maye pare his skyn?   265

The mater commeth in.

MATER. What saye you my sonne, wyl ye fyght? God
     it defende!
For what cause to warre do you nowe pretende?

Wyll ye committe to battayles daungerous
Youre lyfe that is to me so precious?

THERSITES. I wyll go! I wyll go! stoppe not my
    waye! 270
Holde me not good mother, I hartely you pray!
If there be any lyons, or other wylde beest,
What wyll not suffer the husbandman in rest,
I wyll go seeche them, and byd them to a feest. 274
They shall abye bytterlye the comminge of suche a gest!
I wyll searche for them bothe in busshe and shrubbe,
And laye on a lode with this lustye clubbe!

MATER. O my swete sonne, I am thy mother,
Wylt thou kyll me and thou hast none other?

THERSITES. No! mother, no! I am not of suche
    iniquitye, 280
That I wyll defyle my handes upon the.
But be contente, mother, for I wyll not rest
Tyll I have foughte with some man or wylde beast.

MATER. Truely, my sonne, yf that ye take thys way,
Thys shall be the conclusion, marke what I shall say!
Other I wyll drowne my selfe for sorowe, 286
And fede fyshes with my body before to morowe,
Or wyth a sharpe swerde, surely I wyll me kyll,
Nowe thou mayst save me, if it be thy wyll.
I wyll also cut my pappes awaye, 290
That gave the sucke so manye a daye,
And so in all the worlde it shall be knowen,
That by my owne sonne I was overthrowen.
Therefore, if my lyfe be to the pleasaunte,
That whiche I desyre, good sonne, do me graunte. 295

THERSITES. Mother, thou spendest thy winde but in
    wast,
The goddes of battayle hyr fury on me hath cast.

I am fullye fyxed battayle for to taste.
O how many to deth I shall dryve in haste !
I wyll ruffle this clubbe aboute my hedde,   300
Or els I pray God I never dye in my bedde !
There shall never a stroke be stroken with my hande
But they shall thynke that Jupiter doth thonder in the land.

MATER. My owne swete sonne, I, knelynge on my knee,
And bothe my handes holdinge up to the,   305
Desyre the to ceasse and no battayle make.
Call to the pacience and better wayes take.

THERSITES. Tushe, mother, I am deafe, I wyll the
    not heare !
No ! no ! yf Jupiter here him selfe nowe were,
And all the goddes, and Juno his wife,   310
And lovinge Minerva, that abhorreth all stryfe,
Yf all these, I saye, would desyre me to be content,
They dyd theyr wynde but in vaine spente.
I wyll have battayle in Wayles or in Kente,
And some of the knaves I wyll all to rent.   315
Where is the valiaunt knighte, Syr Isenbrase ?
Appere, Syr, I praye you, dare ye not shewe your face ?
Where is Robin John and Little Hode ?
Approche hyther quickely, if ye thinke it good.
I wyll teache suche outlawes wyth Chrystes curses   320
How they take hereafter awaye abbottes purses !
Whye, wyll no adventure appeare in thys place ?
Where is Hercules with his greate mase ?
Where is Busyris that fed hys horses,
Full lyke a tyraunte, with dead mens corses ?   325
Come any of you bothe,
And I make an othe,
That yer I eate any breade
I wyll dryve a wayne,
Ye, for neede, twayne,   330

Betwene your bodye and your heade.
[This¹] passeth my braynes!
Wyll none take the paynes
   To trye wyth me a blowe?
O what a fellowe am I, 335
Whome everye man dothe flye,
   That dothe me but once knowe!

  MATER. Sonne all do you feare,
That be present here,
   They wyll not wyth you fyghte. 340
You, as you be worthye,
Have nowe the victorye,
   Wythoute tastynge of youre myghte.
Here is none, I trowe,
That profereth you a blowe, 345
   Man, woman nor chylde.
Do not set your mynde
To fyghte with the wynde,
   Be not so madde nor wylde.

  THERSITES. I saye, aryse, who so ever wyll fighte!
I am to battayle here readye dyghte. 351
Come hyther, other swayne or knyghte,
Let me see who dare presente him to my syghte!
Here with my clubbe readye I stande,
Yf anye wyll come to take them in hand. 355

  MATER. There is no hope left in my brest,
To bring my sonne unto better rest,
He wyll do nothinge at my request,
He regardeth me no more then a best.
I see no remedye, but styll I wyll praye 360
To God, my sonne to gyde in his waye,
That he maye have a prosperous journ[y]ynge,
And to bee save at his returnynge.

¹ Thus, *Ed.*

L

Sonne, God above graunte thys my oration,
That when in battaile thou shalt have concertation   365
With your enemies, other far[r]e or nere,
No wounde in them nor in you may appere,
So that ye nother kyll nor be kylled.

    THERSITES. Mother, thy peticion I praye God be
      fulfylled,
For then no knaves bloude shall be spilled.   370
Felowes, kepe my counsell, by the masse I doo but crake,
I wyll be gentyll enoughe and no busenesse make.
But yet I wyll make her beleve that I am a man!
Thincke you that I wyll fight? no, no, but wyth the can,
Excepte I finde my enemye on thys wyse   375
That he be a slepe or els can not aryse.
Yf his armes and his fete be not fast bounde,
I wyll not profer a stripe, for a thousande pound.
Fare well, mother, and tarrye here no longer,
For after proves of chivalry I do both thyrste and hunger,
I wyll beate the knaves as flatte as a conger.   381

Then the mother goeth in the place which is prepared for her.

What! how long shall I tary? be your hartes in your hose,
Will there none of you in battayl me appose?
Come, prove me! whye stande you so in doubte?
Have you any wylde bloude, that ye would have let oute?
Alacke that a man's strengthe can not be knowen,   386
Because that he lacketh ennemies to be overth[r]owen!

Here a snaile muste appere unto him, and hee muste loke
*   fearefully uppon the snaile, saienge :*

But what a monster do I see nowe
Cominge hetherwarde with an armed browe?
What is it? ah, it is a sowe!   390
No, by [my faith], it is but a grestle,
And on the backe it hath never a brystle.

La femme a hardy couraige
Huy de ce lieu treſozde beſte
qui des Bignes les bourgons māges
Sur arbie et ſur buyſſon

As tout māge iuſques aux brāches
De ma quenoille ſi tu tauances
Je te donray tel horion
quon lentendia dicy a nantes

Les gens darmes
Lymaſſon pour tes grans cornes
Le chaſteau ne lairons daſſaillir
Et ſe pouons te ferons fouyr
De ce beau lieu ou tu repoſes
Oncques lombart ne te mangeat
A telle ſaulce que nous ferons
Si te mettrons en ung grant plat
Au popure noir et aux ongnons
Serre tes cornes ſi te prions
Et nous laiſſe entrer dedans
Autrement nous te aſſaillerons
De noz baſtons qui ſont tranchans

Le lymaſſon
Je ſuys de terrible facon
Et ſi ne ſuys que lymaſſon
Ma maiſon porte ſur mon dos
Et ſi ne ſuis de chair ne dos
Jay deux cornes deſſus ma teſte
Cōme ung beuf queſt groſſe beſte
De ma maiſon ie ſuys arme
Et de mes cornes embaſtonne
Se ces gens darmes la maprochent
Ilz en auront ſur leurs caboches
Mais ie cuide quen bonne foy
quilz trēblent de grant peur de moy

FROM LE COMPOST ET KALENDRIER DES BERGERS

PARIS, GUY MARCHANT, 1500 (REDUCED)

It is not a cow, ah there I fayle,
For then it should have a long tayle.
What the devyll! I was blynde, it is but a snayle! 395
I was never so afrayde in east nor in south,
My harte at the fyrste syght was at my mouth.
Mary, syr, fy! fy! fy! I do sweate for feare!
I thoughte I had craked but to tymely here.
Hens, thou beest, and plucke in thy hornes   400

*   *   *   *   *   *

Haste thou nothynge elles to doo
But come wyth hornes and face me so?
Howe, how my servauntes, get you shelde and spere 405
And let us werye and kyll thys monster here!

Here MILES *cometh in.*

MILES. Is not thys a worthye knyghte,
That wyth a snayle dareth not fight,
Excepte he have hys servauntes ayde?
Is this the chaumpyon that maketh al men afraid?   410
I am a pore souldiour come of late from Calice,
I trust, or I go, to debate some of his malyce,
I wyll tarrye my tyme, till I do see
Betwixt hym and the snayle what the ende wyll be.

THERSITES. Whye ye [rascal] knavys, regard ye not
    my callinge?   415
Whye do ye not come and wyth you weapons brynge?
Why shall this monster so escape kyllinge?
No! that he shal not, and God be wyllinge.

MILES. I promyse you, thys is as worthye a knyghte
As ever shall brede oute of a bottell byte: 420
I thinke he be Dares, of whom Virgyll doth write,
That woulde not let Entellus alone,
But ever provoked and ever called on,

But yet at the last he tooke a fall,
And so within a whyle, I trowe I make the shall.   425

   THERSITES. By [Jupiter], knaves, if I come I wyll you
     fetter!
Regarde ye my callinge and cryinge no better?
Why, [rascals,] I saye, wyll ye not come?
By the masse, the knaves be all from home!
They had better have fette me an errande at Rome!

   MILES. By my trouthe, I thynke that very skante 431
This lubber dare adventure to fighte with an ant!

   THERSITES. Well, seinge my servauntes come to me
     will not,
I must take hede that this monster me spyll not,
I wyll joparde with it a joynte,   435
And, other with my clubbe or my sweardes poynte,
I wyll reche it suche woundes,
As I woulde not have for xl M. poundes.
Plucke in thy hornes, thou unhappy beast,
What, facest thou me? wilte not thou be in reste? 440
Why? wylte not thou thy hornes in holde?
Thinkest thou that I am a cockolde[1]?
[Nay, truly] the monster cometh towarde me styll!
Excepte I fyght manfully, it wyll me surely kyll!

   Then he muste fyghte against the snayle with his club.

   MILES. O Jupiter Lorde! doest thou not see and heare
How he feareth the snayle as it were a bere?   446

   THERSITES. Well, with my clubbe I have had good
     lucke,
Nowe with my sworde have at the a plucke.

   And he must cast his club awaye.

I wyll make the, or I go, for to ducke,
And thou were as tall[2] a man as frier Tucke!   450

     [1] cocklode, *text*.   [2] tale, *text*.

I saye yet agayne thy hornes in drawe,
Or elles I wyll make the to have woundes rawe.
Arte not thou aferde
To have thy bearde
Pared with my swearde? 455

*Here he must fighte then with his sworde against the snayle
and the snayle draweth her hornes in.*

Ah well nowe no more!
Thou mightest have done so before!
I layed at it so sore
That it thoughte it shoulde have be lore.
And it had not drawen in his hornes againe, 460
Surely I woulde the monster have slaine.
But now farewell, I wyll worke the no more payne.
Nowe my fume is paste,
And dothe no longer laste,
That I did to the monster cast. 465
Now in other countreis both farre and neare
Mo dedes of chyvalrye I wyll go inquere.

MILES. Thou nedes not seke any further, for redy I am
here.
I wyll debate anone, I trowe, thy bragginge chere.

THERSITES. Nowe where is any mo that wyll me
assayle? 470
I wyll turne him and tosse him, both toppe and tayle,
Yf he be stronger then Sampson was,
Who with his bare handes kylde lyons apas.

MILES. What nedeth this booste? I am here at hande,
That with the will fighte; kepe the heade and stande!
Surelye for al thy hye wordes I wyll not feare 476
To assaye the a towche tyll some bloude apeare,
I wyll geve the somewhat for the gifte of a new yeare.

And he begynth to fight with him, but Thersites must ren
awaye, and hyde hym behynde hys mother's backe sayinge :

THERSITES. O mother, mother, I praye the me hyde!
Throwe some thinge over me and cover me every syde!

MATER. O my sonne, what thynge eldyth the?   481

THERSITES. Mother, a thousande horsemen do persecute me !

MATER. Marye, sonne then it was time to flye!
I blame the not then, thoughe afrayde thou be.
A deadlye wounde thou mightest there sone catche,   485
One against so manye is no indyfferente matche.

THERSITES. No, mother! but if they had bene but ten
to one,
I woulde not have avoyded, but set them uppon,
But seinge they be so many I ran awaye.
Hyde me, mother, hyde me, I hartely the pray.   490
For if they come hyther and here me fynde
To their horses tayles they wyll me bynde,
And after that fasshyon hall me and kyll me,
And thoughe I were never so bolde and stoute   494
To fyghte againste so manye, I shoulde stande in doubte.

MILES. Thou that doest seke giauntes to conquere,
Come foorth, if thou dare, and in this place appere !
Fy, for shame, doest thou so sone take flighte ?
Come forth and shewe somewhat of thy myghte !

THERSITES. Hyde me, mother, hyde me, and never
worde saye.   500

MILES. Thou olde trotte, seyst thou any man come thys
waye,
Well armed and weaponed and readye to fighte ?

MATER. No forsothe, Maister, there came none in my
sight.

MILES. He dyd avoyde in tyme, for withoute doubtes
I woulde have set on his backe some clowtes. 505
Yf I may take him I wyll make all slowches
To beware by him, that they come not in my clowches.

Then he goeth oute, and the mother saith:

MATER. Come foorth my sonne, youre enemy is gone,
Be not afrayed, for hurte thou canst have none.

Then he loketh aboute if he be gone or not, at the last he sayth:

THERSITES. Ywys thou didest wisely, who so ever thou
be, 510
To tarrye no longer to fighte with me,
For with my clubbe I woulde have broken thy skull,
Yf thou were as bigge as Hercules bull.
Why, thou cowardely knave, no stronger then a ducke
Darest thou trye maystries with me a plucke, 515
Whiche fere nother giauntes nor Jupiters fire bolte,
Nor Beelzebub, the mayster devyll, as ragged as a colte.
I woulde thou wouldest come hyther ones againe,
I thincke thou haddest rather alyve to be flayne.
Come againe and I sweare, by my mothers wombe, 520
I wyll pull the in peeces no more then my thombe,
And thy braines abrode I wyll so scatter
That all knaves shall feare, against me to clatter.

[The play is interrupted here by the incident of the young Telemachus coming to Thersites' mother, to be cured of a disease. When he is gone, Thersites resumes his boasting.]

Then Miles cometh in saynge:

MILES. Wylte thou so in deede?
Hye the, make good spede, 876

I am at hande here prest.
Put awaye tongue shakynge
And this folysshe crakynge,   880
   Let us trye for the best.
Cowardes make speake apase,
   S[t]rypes prove the manne.
Have nowe at thy face!
   Keepe of, if thou canne!   885

And then he muste stryke at hym, and Thersytes muste runne
awaye and leave his clubbe and sworde behynde.

Whye, thou lubber, runnest thou awaye,
   And leavest thy swearde and thy clubbe thee behynde?
Nowe thys is a sure carde, nowe I maye well saye
   That a cowarde crakinge here I dyd fynde.
Maysters, ye maye see by this playe in sighte   890
That great barking dogges do not most byte,
And oft it is sene that the best men in the hoost
Be not suche, that use to bragge moste.
Yf ye wyll avoyde the daunger of confusion,
Printe my wordes in harte and marke this conclusion,
Suche gyftes of God that ye excelle in moste,   896
Use them wyth sobernesse and youre selfe never bost.
Seke the laude of God in all that ye doo,
So shall vertue and honoure come you too.   899
But if you geve youre myndes to the sinne of pryde,·
Vanisshe shall your vertue, youre honoure away wil slide,
For pryde is hated of God above,
And meekenesse sonest obtaineth his love.
To youre rulers and parentes be you obediente,
Never transgressinge their lawefull commaundemente. 905
Be ye merye and joyfull at borde and at bedde,
Imagin no traitourye againste your prince and heade.
Love God and feare him, and after him youre kinge,
Whiche is as victorious as anye is lyvinge.

Praye for his grace, with hartes that dothe not fayne, 910
That longe he may rule us without grefe or paine.
Beseche ye also that God maye save his quene,
Lovely Ladie Jane, and the prince that he hath send
    them betwen
To augment their joy and the comons felicitie.   914
Fare ye wel swete audience, God graunt you al prosperite.

Amen.

¶ Imprinted at London,
by John Tysdale and are to be solde
at hys shop in the upper ende of
Lombard strete in Alhallowes
churche yarde neare
untoo Grace
church.

Bale's King John.

KING JOHN. For non other cawse God hath kyngs constytute
And gevyn them the sword, but forto correct all vyce.
    I have attempted this thyng to execute   1275
Uppon transgressers accordyng unto justyce;
And be-cawse I wyll not be parcyall in myn offyce
For theft and murder to persones spirytuall,
I have ageynst me the pristes and the bysshoppes all.
A lyke dysplesure in my fathers tyme ded fall,   1280
    Forty yeres ago, for ponyshment of a clarke:
No cunsell myght them to reformacyon call,
    In ther openyon they were so stordy and starke,
But ageynst ther prynce to the pope they dyd so barke,
That here in Ynglond in every cyte and towne   1285
Excommunycacyons as thonder-bolts cam downe.
For this ther captayn had a ster apared crowne,
    And dyed upon yt, with-owt the kynges consent.
Than interdiccyons were sent from the popes renowne,
    Whych never left hym tyll he was penytent,   1290
And fully agreed unto the popes apoyntment
In Ynglond to stand with the Chyrches lyberte,
And suffer the pristes to Rome for appeles to flee,
They bownd hym also to helpe Jerusalem cyte
    With ij hundrid men the space of a yere and more, 1295
And thre yere after to maynteyne battell free
    Ageynst the Sarazens whych vext the Spanyards sore.
Synce my fathers tyme I have borne them groge therfore,

Consyderyng the pryde and the capcyose dysdayne,
That they have to kyngs whych oughte over them to
    rayne.   1300

     PRIVAT WELTH *cum in lyke a Cardynall.*
God save you, sur kyng, in your pryncly mageste.

    K. J. Frynd, ye be welcum: what is yowr plesure
    with me?

    P. W. From the holy father, Pope Innocent the thred,
As a massanger I am to yow dyrectyd,
To reforme the peace betwyn Holy Chyrch and yow 1305
And in his behalfe I avertyce yow here now
Of the Chyrchys goods to make full restytucyon,
And to accepte also the popes hely constytucyon
For Stevyn Langton, archebysshop of Canturbery,
And so admytt hym to his state and primacy: 1310
The monkes exilyd ye shall restore agayne
To ther placys and londes, and nothyng of thers retayne.
Owr holy fatheres mynde ys that ye shall agayne restore
All that ye have ravyshyd from Holy Chyrche, with the
    more.

    K. J. I reken yowr father wyll never be so harde,
But he wyll my cawse as well as theres regarde.   1316
I have done nothyng but that I may do well,
And as for ther taxe I have for me the gospell.

    P. W. Tushe, gospell or no, ye must make a recompens.

    K. J. Yowr father is sharpe and very quycke in sentence,
Yf he wayeth the word of God no more than so;   1321
But I shall tell yow in this what Y shall do.
I am well content to receyve the monkes agayne
Upon amendement, but as for Stevyn Langton playne
He shall not cum here, for I know his dysposycyon: 1325
He is moche inclyned to sturdynesse and sedycyon,
There shall no man rewle in the lond where I am kyng
With-owt my consent, for no mannys plesure lyvyng.

Never-the-lesse, yet upon a newe behaver
At the popys request here-after I may hym faver,   1330
And graunt hym to have sum other benyfyce.

   P. W. By thys I perseyve ye bare hym groge and malyce,
Well, thys wyll I say, by-cause ye are so blunte,
A prelate to dyscharge Holy Chyrche was never wont,
But her custome ys to mynyster ponyshment   1335
To kynges and princes beyng dyssobedyent!

   K. J. Avant, pevysh prist : what, dost thow thretten me?
I defye the worst both of thi pope and the.
The power of princys ys gevyn from God above,   1339
And, as sayth Solomon, ther harts the Lord doth move.
God spekyth in ther lyppes whan they geve jugement :
The lawys that they make are by the Lordes appoyntment.
Christ wylled not his the princes to correcte,
But to ther precepptes rether to be subjecte.
The offyce of yow ys not to bere the sword,   1345
But to geve cownsell accordyng to Gods word.
He never tawght his to weare nowther sword ne sallett,
But to preche abrode with-owt staffe, scrypp or walett ;
Yet are ye becum soche myghty lordes this hower,
That ye are able to subdewe all princes power.   1350
I can not perseyve but ye are becum Belles prystes,
Lyvyng by ydolls, yea, the very antychrysts.

   P. W. Ye have sayd yowr mynd, now wyll I say myn also.
Here I cursse yow for the wrongs that ye have do   1354
Unto Holy Churche, with crosse, bocke, bell and candell ;
And by-sydes all thys I must yow other-wyse handell.
Of contumacy the pope hath yow convyt ;
From this day forward your lond stond interdytt.
The bysshope of Norwyche and the bysshope of Wynchester,
Hath full autoryte to spred it in Ynglond here.   1360
The bysshope of Salysbery and the bysshope of Rochester
Shall execute yt in Scotland every where.
The bysshope of Landaffe, seynt Assys, and seynt Davy

In Walles and in Erlond shall publyshe yt openly.
Throwgh-owt all crystyndom the bysshopps shall suspend
All soche as to yow any mayntenance pretend ;   1366
And I cursse all them that geve to yow ther harte,
Dewks, erlls, and lordes so many as take yowr parte:
And I assoyle yowr peple from your obedyence,
That they shall owe yow noyther sewte nor reverence.
By the popys awctoryte I charge them yow to fyght 1371
As with a tyrant agenst Holy Chyrchys ryght ;
And by the popes auctoryte I geve them absolucyon
A pena et culpa, and also clene remyssyon.

SEDYCYON *extra locum.*

Alarum! Alarum! tro ro ro ro ro, tro ro ro ro ro, tro
      ro ro ro ro!   1375
Thomp, thomp, thomp, downe, downe, downe, to go, to
      go, to go!

 K. J. What a noyse is thys that without the dore is
 made ?

 P. W. Suche enniyes are up as wyll yowr realme invade.

 K. J. Ye cowde do no more and ye cam from the
 devyll of hell,

Than ye go abowt here to worke by yowr wyckyd
 cownsell.   1380
Ys this the charyte of that ye call the Churche ?
God graunt Cristen men not after yowr wayes to worche !
I sett not by yowr curssys the shakyng of a rod,
For I know they are of the devyll and not of God.
Yowr curssys we have that we never yet demaundyd, 1385
But we can not have that God hath yow commandyd.

 P. W. What ye mene by that I wold ye shuld opynly
 tell.

 K. J. Why know ye it not ? the prechyng of the gospell.

Take to ye yowr traysh, yowr ryngyng, syngyng, pypyng,
So that we may have the scryptures openyng: 1390
But that we can not have, yt stondyth not with yowr
    avantage.

P. W. Ahe, now I fell yow for this heretycall langage;
I thynke noyther yow nor ony of yowres, iwys,
We wyll so provyd, shall ware the crowne after this.

*   *   *   *   *   *   *

II.

DISSIMULATION. Wassayle, wassayle out of the mylke
    payle,   2065
Wassayle, wassayle, as whyte as my nayle,
Wassayle, wassayle in snowe froste and hayle,
Wassayle, wassayle with partriche and rayle,
Wassayle, wassayle that muche doth avale,
Wassayle, wassayle that never wyll fayle.   2070

K. J. Who is that, Englande? I praye the stepp
    fourth and see.

E. He doth seme a-farre some relygyous man to be.

D. Now Jesus preserve your worthye and excellent grace,
For doubtless there is a very angelyck face.
Now forsoth and God, I woulde thynke my self in heaven,
If I myght remayne with yow but yeares alevyn.   2076
I woulde covete here none other felicyte.

K. J. A lovynge persone thu mayest seme for to be.

D. I am as gentle a worm as ever ye see.

K. J. But what is thy name, good frynde, I praye the
    tell me?   2080

D. Simon of Swynsett my very name is per dee.
I am taken of men for monastycall Devocyon,
And here have I brought yow a marvelouse good pocyon,
For I harde ye saye that ye were very drye.

The Monk bzab of the poyfon, he bzank to the kinge.

A perpetual maffe fung dayipe in Swinftead foz the Monk, that poyfoned the King.

King John pzefented with a

FROM FOXE
Lon

Ego abſoluo te &c.

ⱳonk dⱬinking vnto him.

Here the Monk tempereth his poyſon.

K. J. In dede I wolde gladlye drynke. I praye the
come nye. 2085

D. The dayes of your lyfe never felt ye suche a cuppe,
So good and so holsome, if ye woulde drynke it upp:
It passeth malmesaye, capryck, tyre or ypocras ;
By my fayth I thynke a better drynke never was.

K. J. Begynne, gentle monke: I praye the drynke half
to me. 2090

D. If ye dronke all up, it were the better for ye.
It woulde slake your thirst and also quycken your brayne:
A better drynke is not in Portyngale nor Spayne,
Therfore suppe it of, and make an ende of it quycklye.

K. J. Naye, thu shalte drynke half, there is no remedye.

D. Good luck to ye than ! have at it by and bye ; 2096
Halfe wyll I consume, if there be no remedye.

K. J. God saynt the, good monke, with all my very
harte !

D. I have brought ye half; conveye me that for your
parte. 2099
Where art thu, Sedicyon? by the masse I dye, I dye.
Helpe now at a pynche ! Alas, man, cum away shortlye.

S. Come hyther apace, and gett thee to the farmerye ;
I have provyded for the, by the swete saynt Powle,
Fyve monkes that shall synge contynually for thy sowle,
That, I warande the, thu shalt not come in helle. 2105

D. To sende me to heaven goo rynge the holye belle,
And synge for my sowle a masse of Scala Celi,
That I maye clyme up aloft with Enoch and Heli:
I do not doubte it but I shall be a saynt.
Provyde a gyldar myne image for to paynt. 2110
I dye for the Churche with Thomas of Canterberye :
Ye shall fast my vigyll and upon my daye be merye.

M

No doubt but I shall do myracles in a whyle,
And therefore lete me be shryned in the north yle.

   S. To the than wyll offer both crypple, halte, and
      blynde,   2115
Mad men and mesels, with such as are woo behynde.
                             [*Exeunt.*

   K. J. My bodye me vexeth : I doubt much of a tym-
      panye.

   E. Now, alas, alas ! your grace is betrayed cowardlye.

   K. J. Where became the monke that was here with me
      latelye ?   2119

   E. He is poysened, sir, and lyeth a-dyenge surelye.

   K. J. It can not be so, for he was here even now.

   E. Doubtlesse, sir, it is so true as I have tolde yow :
A false Judas kysse he hath gyven and is gone.
The halte, sore, and lame thys pitiefull case wyll mone.
Never prynce was there that made to poore peoples use 2125
So many masendewes, hospytals and spyttle howses,
As your grace hath done, yet sens the worlde began.

   K. J. Of priestes and of monkes I am counted a wycked
      man,
For that I never buylte churche nor monasterye,
But my pleasure was to helpe suche as were nedye. 2130

   E. The more grace was yours, for at the daye of judg-
      ment
Christe wyll rewarde them whych hath done hys com-
      mandement,
There is no promyse for voluntarye wurkes
No more than there is for sacrifyce of the Turkes.

   K. J. Doubtlesse I do fele muche grevaunce in my
      bodye.   2135

E. As the Lorde wele knoweth, for that I am full sorye.

K. J. There is no malyce to the malyce of the clergye :
Well, the Lorde God of heaven on me and them have
    mercye.
For doynge justyce they have ever hated me.
They caused my lande to be excommunycate,   2140
And me to resygne both crowne and princely dygnyte,
From my obedyence assoylynge every estate ;
And now last of all they have me intoxycate.
I perceyve ryght wele their malyce hath none ende :
I desyre not els but that they maye sone amende,   2145
I have sore hungred and thirsted ryghteousnesse
For the offyce sake that God hath me appoynted,
But now I perceyve that synne and wyckednesse
In thys wretched worlde, lyke as Christe prophecyed,
Have the overhande : in me it is verefyed.   2150
Praye for me, good people, I besych yow hartely,
That the Lorde above on my poore sowle have mercy.
Farwell noble men, with the clergye spirytuall,
Farwell men of lawe, with the whole commynalte.
Your disobedyence I do forgyve yow all,   2155
And desyre God to perdon your iniquyte.
Farwell, swete Englande, now last of all to the :
I am right sorye I coulde do for the no more.
Farwell ones agayne, yea, farwell for evermore.   2159

E. With the leave of God I wyll not leave ye thus,
But styll be with ye tyll he do take yow from us,
And than wyll I kepe your bodye for a memoryall.

K. J. Than plye it, Englande, and provyde for my
    buryall.
A wydowes offyce it is to burye the deade.   2164

E. Alas, swete maistre, ye waye so heavy as leade.
Oh horryble case, that ever so noble a kynge

Shoulde thus be destroyed and lost for ryghteouse doynge,
By a cruell sort of disguysed bloud-souppers,
Unmercyfull murtherers, all dronke in the bloude of
　　　marters!
Report what they wyll in their most furyouse madnesse,
Of thys noble kynge muche was the godlynesse.　　2171
　　　　　　　　　　　　　　　　[Exeunt.

APPENDIX.

I. Mysterium Resurrectionis D. N. Jhesu Christi. From a
MS. of the 13th century in the Library of the City of
Orleans, as printed by Thomas Wright.

II. Ludus super iconia Sancti Nicolai. By Hilarius, a pupil of
Abelard, c. 1125. Text from edition of M. J. J. Cham-
pollion Figeac, entitled: Hilarii Versus et Ludi. Lutetiæ
Parisiorum apud Techner Bibliopolam. (London, William
Pickering) MDCCCXXXVIII. pp. 34-39.

III. The Harrowing of Hell. From a MS. of the reign of
Edward II. Text from edition of Dr. Edward Mall,
entitled: The Harrowing of Hell. Das altenglische Spiel
von Christi Höllenfahrt. Neue Bearbeitung von Dr.
Eduard Mall. *Berlin*, 1871. 8vo.

IV. Extracts from the Brome Play of Abraham and Isaac.
Text from the transcript published by Miss Lucy Toulmin
Smith in *Anglia*, Band VII. Heft 3.

APPENDIX I.

MYSTERIUM
RESURRECTIONIS D. N. JHESU CHRISTI

Ad faciendam similitudinem dominici sepulchri, primum pro-
cedant tres fratres præparati et vestiti in similitudinem
trium Mariarum, pedetentim et quasi tristes alternantes,
hos versus cantent.

PRIMA *earum dicat:*
Heu! pius pastor occidit
Quem culpa nulla infecit!
O res plangenda!

SECUNDA.
Heu! verus pastor obiit,
Qui vitam sanctis contulit!
O mors lugenda!

TERTIA.
Heu! nequam gens Judaica!
Quam dira frendens vesania!
Plebs execranda!

PRIMA.
Cur nece pium impia
Dampnasti Jhesum invida?
O ira nefanda!

SECUNDA.
Quid justus hic promeruit
Quod crucifigi debuit?
O gens dampnanda!

TERTIA.
Heu! quid agemus miseræ
Dulci magistro orbatæ?
Heu! sors lacrimanda!

PRIMA.

Eamus ergo propere,
Quod solum quimus facere,
Mente devota,

SECUNDA.

Condimentis aromatum
Ungamus corpus sanctissimum :
Quo pretiosa

TERTIA.

Nardi vetet commixtio,
Ne putrescat in tumulo
Caro beata.

*Cum autem venerunt in chorum, eant ad monumentum quasi
quærentes, et cantantes omnes simul hunc versum :*
Sed nequimus hoc patere sine adjutorio
Quisnam saxum hoc revolveret ab monumenti ostio ?

*Quibus respondeat Angelus sedens foris, ad caput sepulchri,
vestitus alba deaurata, mitra tectus caput, etsi deinfula-
tus, palmam in sinistra, ramum candelarum plenum
tenens in manu dextra, et dicat moderata et admodum
gravi voce :*

Quem quæritis in sepulchro
O Christicolæ !

MULIERES

Jhesum Nazarenum crucifixum,
O cælicola !

Quibus respondeat ANGELUS :

Quid, christicolæ, viventem quæritis cum mortuis?
Non est hic, sed surrexit, prout dixit discipulis.
Mementote quid jam vobis locutus est in Galilea,
Quod Christum oportebat pati, atque die tertia
Resurgere cum gloria.

MULIERES *conversæ ad populum cantent :*

Ad monumentum Domini venimus
Gementes ; angelum Dei sedentem vidimus
Et dicentem quod surrexit a morte.

Post hæc MARIA MAGDALENE, *relictis duabus aliis, accedat
ad sepulchrum, in quod sæpe aspiciens, dicat :*

Heu dolor! heu! quam dira doloris angustia!
Quod dilecti sum orbata magistri præsentia;
Heu! quis corpus tam dilectum sustulit e tumulo?

Deinde pergat velociter ad illos qui in similitudine Petri et Johannis præstare debent erecti, stansque ante eos quasi tristis, dicat:

Tulerunt Dominum meum,
Et nescio ubi posuerunt eum,
Et monumentum vacuum est inventum,
Et sudarium cum sindone repositum.

Illi autem hoc audientes velociter pergent ad sepulchrum ac si currentes; sed junior, S. Johannes, perveniens stet extra sepulchrum, senior vero, S. Petrus, sequens eum, statim intret, postquam et S. Johannes intret, cum inde exierint, JOHANNES *dicat:*

Miranda sunt quæ vidimus!
An furtim sublatus est dominus?
Cui PETRUS.
Imo, ut prædixit vivus,
Surrexit, credo, Dominus.
JOHANNES.
Sed cur liquit in sepulchro
Sudarium cum linteo?
PETRUS.
Ista quia resurgenti
Non erant necessaria,
Imo resurrectionis
Restant hæc indicia.

Illis autem abeuntibus, accedat MARIA *ad sepulchrum, et prius dicat:*

Heu! dolor! heu! quam dira doloris angustia!
Quod dilecti sum orbata magistri præsentia.
Heu! quis corpus tam dilectum sustulit e tumulo?

Quam alloquantur DUO ANGELI *sedentes infra sepulchrum dicentes:*

Mulier, quid ploras?
MARIA.
Quia tulerunt Dominum meum,
Et nescio ubi posuerunt eum.

ANGELUS.

Noli flere, Maria, resurrexit Dominus.
Alleluia!

MARIA.

Ardens est cor meum desiderio
Videre Dominum meum;
Quæro et non invenio
Ubi posuerunt eum,
Alleluia!

*Interim veniat quidam præparatus in similitudine hortulani,
stansque ad caput sepulchri, dicat:*

Mulier, quid ploras? quem quæris?

MARIA.

Domine, si tu sustulisti eum, dicito michi ubi posuisti eum, et
ego eum tollam.

Et ILLE.

Maria!

Atque procidens ad pedes ejus, MARIA *dicat:*

Rabboni!

At ille subtrahat se, et quasi tactum ejus devitans, dicat:

Noli me tangere, nondum enim ascendi ad Patrem meum et
Patrem vestrum, Dominum meum et dominum vestrum.

Sic discedat Hortulanus, MARIA *vero, conversa ad populum,
dicat:*

Congratulamini michi omnes qui diligitis Dominum, quia
quem quærebam apparuit michi, et dum flerem ad monumentum
vidi Dominum meum.   Alleluia!

Tunc DUO ANGELI *exeant ad ostium sepulchri, ita ut appareant
foris, et dicant:*

Venite et videte locum ubi positus erat Dominus.
Alleluia!
Nolite timere vos:
Vultum tristem jam mutate:
Jhesum vivum nunciate:
Galileam jam adite:
Si placet videre, festinate:
Cito euntes dicite discipulis quod surrexit Dominus.
Alleluia!

Tunc MULIERES *discedentes a sepulchro dicant aa plebem:*
>> Surrexit Dominus de sepulchro,
>> Qui pro nobis pependit in ligno.
>>> Alleluia!

Hoc facto, expandant sindonem, dicentes ad plebem:
>>> Cernite vos, socii, sunt corporis ista beati
>>> Lintea, quæ vacuo jacuere relicta sepulchro.

Postea ponant sindonem super altare, atque revertentes alternent
>> *hos versus:* PRIMA *dicat:*
>>> Resurrexit hodie Deus Deorum.

>>> SECUNDA.
>>> Frustra signas lapidem, plebs Judeorum,

>>> TERTIA.
>>> Jungere jam populo christianorum.

>>> *Item* PRIMA *dicat:*
>>> Resurrexit hodie Rex angelorum.

>>> SECUNDA.
>>> Ducitur de tenebris turba piorum.

>>> TERTIA.
>>> Reseratur aditus regni cælorum.

Interea is qui ante fuit Hortulanus, in similitudinem DOMINI
>> *veniat, dalmaticatus candida dalmatica, candida infula*
>> *infulatus, phylacteria pretiosa in capite, crucem cum*
>> *labaro in dextra, textum auro paratorium in sinistra*
>> *habens, et dicat mulieribus:*

Nolite timere vos, ite, nunciate fratribus meis ut eant in
Galileam, ibi me videbunt sicut prædixi eis.

>>> CHORUS.
>> Alleluia!
>>> Resurrexit hodie Dominus.

>>> *Quo finito, dicant* OMNES *insimul:*
>>> Leo fortis, Christus filius Dei.

>>> *Et* CHORUS *dicat:*
>>> Te Deum laudamus, etc.

>>> *Explicit.*

APPENDIX II.

LUDUS SUPER ICONIA SANCTI NICOLAI.

Ad quem he persone sunt necessarie: persona barbari qui conmisit ei tesaurum; persona iconie; iiii^{or} vel sex latronum; Sancti Nicholai.

In primis BARBARUS, rebus suis congregatis, ad ichoniam veniet, et ei res suas conmendans dicet:

> Nicholae, quidquid possideo,
> Hoc in meo misi teloneo:
> Te custodem rebus adibeo,
>   Serva que sunt ibi.
> Meis, precor, adtende precibus;
> Vide nullus sit locus furibus;
> Preciosis aurum cum vestibus
>   Ego trado tibi.
> Profiscisci foras disposui:
> Te custodem rebus imposui.
> Revertenti redde quæ posui
>   Tua sub tutela.
> Jam sum magis securus solito,
> Te custode rebus inposito;
> Revertenti vide ne merito
>   Mihi sit querela.

Illo autem profecto, fures transeuntes cum viderint hostium apertum et nullum custodem, omnia diripient, BARBARUS vero rediens, non invento tesauro, dicet:

> Gravis sors et dura!
> Hic reliqui plura,
> Sed sub mala cura.
> *Des! quel domage!*
> *Qui pert la sue chose purque n'enrage.*

Hic res plusquam centum
Misi et argentum ;
Sed non est inventum.
Des! quel domage!
Qui pert la sue chose purque n'enrage.
Hic reliqui mea ;
Sed hic non sunt ea.
Est imago rea.
Des! quel domage!
Qui pert la sue chose purque n'enrage.

Deinde accedens ad imaginem, dicet ei :

Mea congregavi,
Tibi commendavi ;
Sed in hoc erravi.
Ha! Nicholax!
Si ne me rent ma chose, tu ol comparras.
Hic res meas misi
Quas tibi conmisi ;
Sed eas amisi.
Ha! Nicholax!
Si ne me rent ma chose, tu ol comparras.

Sumto flagello, dicet :

Ego tibi multum
Inpendebam cultum :
Nun feres inultum.
Hore t' enci
Qu'are me rent ma chose que g'ei mis ci.
Tuum testor deum,
Te, ni reddas meum,
Flagellabo reum.
Hore t' enci
Qu'are me rent ma chose que g'ei mis ci.

Tunc SANCTUS NICHOLAUS, veniens ad latrones, dicet eis :

Miseri, quid facitis ?
Non longua deperditis
Erunt vobis gaudia.
Custos eram positus
Vosque sum intuitus,
Cum portatis omnia.

Flagella sustinui,
Cum ea non potui,
  Ut debebam, reddere:
Verba passus aspera
Cumque verbis verbera;
  Ad vos veni propere.
Reportate perdita.
Erant enim omnia
Sub mea custodia,
Que portasti, posita.
Quod si non feceritis,
Suspensi cras eritis
  Crucis in patibulo.
Vestra namque turpia
Vestra latrocinia
  Nunciabo populo.

Latrones timentes omnia reportabunt. Quibus inventis BARBARUS
    dicet :

Nisi visus fallitur,
  Jo en ai.
Tesaurus hic cernitur.
De si grant merveile en ai.
Rediere perdita,
  Jo en ai.
Nec per mea merita,
De si grant mervegle en ai.
Quam bona custodia
  Jo en ai
Qua redduntur omnia!
De si grant mervegle en ai.

Tunc accedent ad imaginem et suplicans, dicet;

Suplex ad te venio,
  Nicholax,
Nam per te recipio
Tut icei que tu gardas.
Sum profectus peregre,
  Nicholax

Sed recepi integre
Tut ice que tu gardas.
Mens mea convaluit,
Nicholax;
Nichil enim defuit
De tut cei que tu gardas.

Postea aparens ei beatus NICOLAUS, dicet :

Suplicare mihi noli,
Frater ; inmo Deo soli.
Ipse namque factor poli,
Factor maris atque soli,
Restauravit perditum.
Ne sis ultra quod fuisti.
Solum laudes nomen Christi :
Soli Deo credas isti
Per quem tua recepisti.
Mihi nullum meritum.

Cui respondens BARBARUS, dicet :

Hic nulla consultacio,
Nulla erit dilacio,
Quin ab erroris vicio
Jam recedam.
In Christum Dei filium,
Factorem mirabilium,
Ritum linquens gentilium,
Ego credam.
Ipse creavit omnia,
Celum, terram et maria ;
Per quem erroris venia
Mihi detur.
Ipse potens et dominus
Meum delebit facinus,
Cujus regnum ne terminus
Consequetur.

APPENDIX III.

THE HARROWING OF HELL.

Alle herkneþ to me nou,
A strif wille I tellen ou,
Of Jesu and of Satan,
Þo Jesu wes to helle gan
For to fette þenne his   5
And bringen hem to parais;
Þe deuel heuede so michel pouste,
Þat alle mosten to helle te;
Nas non so holi prophete,
Siþþen Adam and Eue þen appel ete,   10
And he were at þis worldes fine,
Þat he ne moste to helle pine;
Ne shulde he neuer þenne come,
Nere Jesu Crist, godes sone;
For þat wes seid to Adam and Eue,   15
Þat were Jesu Crist so leue,
And so wes seid to Abraham,
Þat wes soþfast holi man,
And so wes seid to Dauid, þe king,
Þat wes of Cristes oune ofspring,   20
And to Johan, þe Baptist,
Þat folewede Jesu Crist,
And to Moyses, þe holi wiht,
Þe heuede þe lawe to ȝeme riht,
And to mani oþer holi man,   25
Mo þan ich telle can,
Þat weren alle in more wo,
Þan I can ou telle fro.
Jesu Crist aren hem sore
And seide, he wolde fette hem þore;   30

He lihte of his heȝe tour
On-to seinte Marie bour;
He wes boren for oure nede
In þis world in poure wede,
In þis world he wes ded   35
For to lesen ous fram þe qued.
Þo Jesu heuede shed his blod
For oure sinnes on þe rod,
He nam him þe rihte wei
Unto helle for soþe to sei;   40
Þo he cam þer, þo seide he,
Asse I shal nou telle þe.

DOMINUS. Harde gates haui gon,
Sorewes suffred mani on;
Þritti winter and þridde half ȝer   45
Haui woned in londe her.
Almost is so michel gan,
Siþþen I bicam first man;
Ich haue siþþen þoled and wist
Hot and cold, hunger and þrist: 50
Man haþ don me shame inoh
Wiþ word and dede in here woh;
He nomen me wiþouten sake,
Bounden min honden to mi bake;
He beten me, þat I ran on blode,   55
Demden me to deȝe on rode;
For Adames sinne, ful iwis,
Ich haue þoled al þis.
Adam, þou hauest dere aboht,
Þat þou leuedest me noht;   60
Adam, þou hauest aboht sore
And I nil suffre þat na more;
I shal þe bringe of helle pine
And wiþ þe alle mine.

SATAN. Who is þat ich here þore?   65
Ich him rede speke na more,
For he mai so michel do,
Þat he shal ous come to,

N

For to ben oure fere,
And fonden, hou we pleien here.   70

DOMINUS. [Þou miht wel wite bi mi plei,
Þat mine willi haue awei!]
Wost þou neuer, what ich am?
Almost þe þridde winter is gan,
Þat þou hauest fonded me   75
For to knowe, what I be;
Sinne found þou neuer nan
In me as in oþer man;
And þou shalt wite wel to-dai,
Þat mine willi haue awei,   80
Whan þou bileuest al þin one,
Þanne miht þou grete and grone.

SATAN. Par ma fei! ich holde mine
Alle þo, þat ben her-inne;
Resoun willi telle þe,   85
Þer aȝen miht þou noht be.
Whoso biggeth ani þing,
It is his and his ofspring.
Adam hungri cam me to,
Manrede dide I him me do;   90
For on appel ich ȝaf him,
He is min and al his kin.

DOMINUS. Satanas, it wes min,
Þe appel, þat þou ȝaue him,
Þe appel and þe appel-tre   95
Boþe were maked þourh me.
Hou mihtest þou on ani wise
Of oþer mannes þing make marchandise?
Siþþen he wes boht wiþ min,
Wiþ resoun wil ich hauen him.   100

SATAN. Jesu, wel I knowe þe!
Þat ful sore reweþ me;
Þou art louerd ouer al,
Wo is him, þat þe knowe ne shal!
Heuene and erþe tak to þe,   105
Þe soules in helle lef þou me!

Let me haue þat ich helde,
Þat þou hauest wel mote þou welde!

DOMINUS. Stille be þou, Satanas,
Þe is fallen ambes as!   110
Wendest þou, ich were ded for noht?
For mi deþ is mankin boht!
Þei, þat hauen serued me,
Wiþ me he shulen in heuene be;
Þou shalt ben in more pine,   115
Þan ani, þat þer is her-inne.

SATAN. Ne mai non me werse do,
Þan ich haue had hider-to.
Ich haue had so michel wo,
Þat I ne recche, whider I go;   120
Ȝif þou reuest me of mine,
I shal reue þe of þine;
I shal go fro man to man
And reue þe of mani an.

DOMINUS. God wot! I shal speke þe wiþ   125
And do þe to holde griþ!
So faste shal I binde þe,
Litel shalt þou reue me.
[Were þou among men,
Þou woldest me reuen mani of hem.]   130
Þe smale fendes, þat ben unstronge,
He shulen among men ȝonge,
For to hauen alle hem,
Þat hem ne willen stonden aȝen.
Helle ȝates I come nou to   135
And ich wille, that he undo.
Where is nou þis ȝateward?
Me þinkeþ he is a coward!

JANITOR. Ich haue herd wordes stronge,
Ne dar I her no lengore stonde;   140
Kepe þe ȝates whoso mai,
I lete hem stonde and renne awei.

DOMINUS. Helle ȝates her I felle!
And siþþen wil ich herwe helle.

N 2

Satanas, her I þe binde,   145
Ne shalt þou neuer henne winde,
Her shalt thou ben in bondes ai,
Til þat come domesdai!

ADAM. Welcome, louerd, god of londe,
Godes sone and godes sonde;   150
Welcome, louerd, mote þou be,
Longe haueþ ous þoht after þe!
Louerd, nou þou art comen to ous,
Bring ous of þis loþe hous.
Louerd, wost þou, what ich am?   155
Þou me shope of erþe, Adam;
For I þin heste held noht,
Dere ich haue it her aboht.
Haue merci of ous, godes sone,
Let ous na more her wone;   160
Alle, þat her-inne be,
ȝore hauen ȝerned after þe;
We hopen wel þourh þi coming
Of oure sinnes hauen froring.

EUA. Knou me, louerd, ich am Eue;   165
Ich and Adam þe were so leue,
Þou ȝaue ous to ȝeme parais,
We it ȝemeden asse unwis!
We þin heste dide forleten,
Þo we of þen appel eten;   170
So longe haue we ben her-inne,
Dere haue we bet oure sinne.
Louerd, god, ȝif ous leue,
Adam and me, his wif Eue,
To faren of þis loþe wike   175
To þe blisse of heuene rike!

DOMINUS. Adam, ich haue ȝouen mi lif
For þe and for Eue, þi wif;
Wendest þou, ich were ded for noht?
For mi deþ wes mankin boht.   180

ABRAHAM. Louerd, Crist, ich it am,
Þat þou calledest Abraham;

Þou me seidest, þat of me
Shulde a god childe boren be,
Þat ous shulde bringe of pine,   185
Me and wiþ me alle mine.
Þou art þe child, þou art þe man,
Þat wes boren of Abraham;
Do nou þat þou bihete me,
Bring me to heuene up wiþ þe!   190

DOMINUS. Abraham, ich wot ful wel
What þou seidest, euerich del;
Þat mi suete moder wes
Boren and shaped of þi fles.

DAVID. Louerd, ich am Dauid, þe king,   195
Þat boren wes of þin ofspring;
Do me also þou bihete
Þourh þe lawe of þe prophete;
Nou þou art comen to ous,
Bring ous fram þis dredful hous!   200

DOMINUS. David, þou were boren of mi kin,
For þi godnesse art þou min,
More for þi godnesse,
Þan for ani sibnesse.

JOHANNES. Louerd, Crist, ich am Johan,   205
Þat þe folewede in flum Jordan;
Tuelue moneþ is agon,
Þat I þolede martirdom;
Þou sendest me þe rihte wei
In-to helle for soþe to sei,   210
Þat þou, Crist, godes sone,
Sone shuldest þider come,
For to lesen of helle pine
Alle, þat þou holdest þine.
Nou þou art comen, nou þou do.   215
Þat þou seidest me unto!

DOMINUS. Johan, Johan, ich it wat,
Þat I sende þe þe gat;
Þou shalt se, þat I shal do,
Þat I seide er þe to.   220

MOYSES. Louerd, þou ȝaue me al wiþ skil
 Þe lawe of Sinay upon þe hil;
 Ich am Moyses, þe prophete,
 Ich held þe lawes, þat þou hete,
 Þat men shulde come to bete   225
 Þe sinne, þat Adam þohte suete.

DOMINUS. Moyses, þat ich hihte þe
 In þe olde lawe, þou didest me;
 And alle þe oþer, þat mine ben,
 Shulen to blisse wiþ me ten;   230
 Þei, þat nolden on me leuen,
 Shulen wiþ Satanas bileuen ;
 Þer he shulen wonen ai,
 Til þat come domesdai.

[*Auctor*] God, for his moder loue   235
 Let ous neuer þider come!
 Louerd, for þi michele grace
 Graunte ous in heuene one place ;
 Let ous neuer be forloren
 For no sinne, Crist icoren ;   240
 Ah bring ous out of helle pine,
 Louerd, ous and alle þine ;
 And ȝif ous grace to liue and ende
 In þi seruice and to heuene wende.

                    Amen.

APPENDIX IV.

BROME PLAY OF ABRAHAM AND ISAAC.

ll. 316–435.

THE ANGELL. I am an angell, thou mayist se blythe,   316
    That fro hevyn to the ys senth,
  Our lord thanke the an c. sythe,
    For the kepyng of hys commawment.
  He knowyt thi wyll and also thy harte,   320
    That thou dredyst hym above all thyng,
  And sum of thy hevynes for to departe
    A fayr Ram yynder I gan brynge,
  He standyth teyed, loo! a-mong the breres   324
    Now Abraham, a-mend thy mood,
  For Ysaac, thy yowng son that her ys,
    Thys day schall not sched hys blood;
  Goo, make thy sacryfece with yon Rame.   328
    Now for-wyll blyssyd Abraham,
  For on to hevyn I goo now hom,
    The way ys full gayn.
  Take up thy son soo free.   *[Exit Angel.*   332

ABRAHAM. A! lord I thanke the of thy gret grace,
    Now am I yeyed on dyvers wysse,
  A-rysse up, Ysaac, my dere sunne a-rysse,
    A-rysse up, swete chyld, and cum to me.   336

YSAAC. A! mercy, fader, wy smygth ye not yyt
    A! smygth on, fader, onys with yowr knyffe.

ABRAHAM. Pesse, my swet sir! and take no thowt,
    For our lord of hevyn hath grant thi lyffe   340
  Be hys angell now.
    That thou schalt not dey this day, sunne, truly.

YSAAC. A! fader, full glad than wer I
  I-wys! fader, I sey, i-wys!   344
  Yf thys tale wer trew.

ABRAHAM. An hundyrd tymys, my son fayer of hew,
  For joy thi mowth now wyll I kys.

YSAAC. A! my dere fader, Abraham,   348
  Wyll not God be wroth *th*at we do thus?

ABRAHAM. Noo, noo! harly my swyt son,
  For *y*yn same Rame he hath us sent
  Hether down to us.
  *Y*yn best schall dey here in thi sted. 352
  In the worthschup of owr lord a-lon.
  Goo fet hym hethyr, my chyld, in ded.

YSAAC. Fader, I wyll goo hent hym be the hed, 356
  And bryng *y*on best with me a-non.
  A! scheppe, scheppe! blyssyd mot thou be,
  That ever thow were sent down heder,
  Thow schall thys day dey for me, 360
  In the worchup of the holy Trynyte.
  Now cum fast and goo we to-geder,
    To my fader of hevyn.
  Thow thou be never so jentyll and good 364
  *Y*yt had I lever thow schedyst thi blood,
    I-wysse, scheppe, than I.
  Loo! fader, I have browt here full smerte
    Thys jentyll scheppe, 368
  And hym to *y*ou I *g*yffe
    But lord God, I thanke the with all my hart
  For I am glad that I schall leve,
    And kys onys my dere moder. 372

ABRAHAM. Now be rygth myry, my swete chyld,
  For thys qwyke best that ys so myld,
    Here I schall present before all other.

YSAAC. And I wyll fast begynne to blowe 376
  Thys fyer schall brene a full good spyd;
  But, fader, wyll I stowppe downe lowe,
  *Y*e wyll not kyll me with *y*owr sword, I trowe?

ABRAHAM. Noo, harly, swet son have no dred, 380
  My mornyng ys past,

YSAAC. Ya! but I woold that sword wer in a glad,
  For i-wys, fader, yt make me full yll a-gast.

[Here Abraham mad hys offryng, knelyng and seyyng thus:

ABRAHAM. Now lord God of hevyn in Trynyte, 384
  Allmyty god omnipotent,
  My offeryng I make in the worchope of the,
  And with thys qweke best I the present.
  Lord reseyve thow myn intent. 388
   As art god and grownd of our grace.

DEUS. Abraham, Abraham, wyll mot thow sped,
  And Ysaac, thi yowng son the by,
  Truly, Abraham, for thys dede, 392
  I schall multyplye yowres botheres sede
  As thyke as sterres be in the skye,
   Bothe more and lesse;
  And as thyke as gravell in the see, 396
  So thyke multyplyed your sede schall be,
  Thys grant I yow for yowr goodnesse.
  Off yow schall cume frowte gret,
  And ever be in blysse with owt yynd, 400
  For ye drede me as God a-lon,
  And kepe my commawmentes everyschon.
  My blyssyng I geffe, wer so ever ye goo.

ABRAHAM. Loo, Ysaac, my son, how thynke ye, 404
  Be thys warke that we have wrogth,
  Full glad and blythe we may be
   Agens the wyll of God that we grucched nott,
   Upon thys fayer hetth. 408

YSAAC. A! fader, I thanke our lord every dell,
  That my wyt servyd me so wyll,
   For to drede God more than my detth.

ABRAHAM. Why! dere-wordy son, wer thow a-dred? 412
  Hardely, chyld, tell me thy lore.

YSAAC. *Y*a, be my feyth, fader, now hath I red,
 I wos never soo afrayd before,
  As I have byn at *y*yn hyll.   416
 But be my feyth, fader, I swere
 I wyll never more cume there
  But yt be a-*g*ens my wyll.

ABRAHAM. *Y*a, cum on with me, my owyn swet sonn, 420
 And hom-ward fast now let us goon.

YSAAC. Be my feyth, fader, ther-to I grant,
 I had never so good wyll to gon hom,
  And to speke with my dere moder. 424

ABRAHAM. A! lord of hevyn, I thanke the,
 For now may I led hom with me
 Ysaac, my *y*ownge sonn so fre,
  The gentyllest chyld above all other. 428
  Thys may I wyll a-voee.
 Now goo we forthe, my blyssyd sonn.

YSAAC. I grant, fader, and let us gon,
 For be my trowthe wer I at home, 432
 I wold never gon owt under that forme.
 I prey God *g*effe us grace ever mo,
 And all thow that we be holdyng to.

NOTES.

—◦✦◦—

YORK PLAY.

SUBJECT.—The Creation of the Universe and the Fall of Lucifer form the subject of a play, or part of a play, in each of the four great cycles. The versions followed by the different authors and by the writer of the *Cursor Mundi* exhibit only trifling differences, the chief of which are recorded in the notes. The York Play on this subject may certainly claim pre-eminence over its rivals. It is full of dramatic vigour, and is pervaded by a certain homely grandeur of style, which contrasts very effectively with the baldness of the Coventry playwright or the turgidity of the Chester.

DIALECT.—The dialect in which the York Plays were written was the Northumbrian, but the language of the plays as they have come down to us is strongly affected by the influence of a Midland scribe. Note, however, the Northern *a* for *o* in *formaste, ane, awne*, etc., the Northern form of the second person singular in *thu has, thou lyes, thou was*, the plural in *s* after the substantival subject,

Thi dedes to this dole nowe *has* dyghte us (l. 109),

and again the imperative plural in *es* (the pronoun being absent),

Bothe the nighte and the day, does dewly *y*hour deyver.

Note also the present participles in *and, ande*, and the Northern forms *als, whilke, slyke, gyf, sall*, etc.

METRE.—The metre of this play, like that of the fortieth and forty-fifth, consists of eight-line stanzas, of which the first quatrain rimes abab with four beats to the line, the second quatrain cddc, with three beats. Each line is alliterative on three stressed syllables at least.

TEXT.—The text of this play is taken from the editio princeps with the following title:

'York Plays. The Plays performed by the Crafts or Mysteries of York on the day of Corpus Christi in the 14th, 15th and 16th centuries, Now first printed from the unique manuscript in the Library of Lord Ashburnham. Edited with introduction and glossary by Lucy Toulmin Smith. *Oxford, at the Clarendon Press*, 1885.'

Ego sum Alpha et O., &c. This is compounded of two texts: Rev. xxii. 13, 'I am Alpha and Omega, the beginning and the ending,' and John xiv. 6, 'I am the way, the truth, and the life.' Other cycles quote only from the Revelation.

5. *My blyssyng o ble sall be blendyng, &c.*: it has been suggested that 'ble' here stands absolutely for 'beauty'; if not, we can hardly reject Mr. Joseph Hall's transposition 'O blyssing my ble,' etc. It seems agreed that 'blendyng' means 'a blend' and not 'a blinding.'

15. *mekely*, Mr. Greg suggests 'metely': *contene*, continue.

17. *But onely the worthely warke, &c.*: i.e. but my might shall inspire in my spirit only the worthy work of my will.

23. *Nyen ordres of aungels.* The nine orders are thus summed up in the corresponding Chester play—

> Lord, through thy mighte thou haste us wroughte
> Nine orderes heare, that we maye see
> Cherubyn and Seraphyn through thy grace,
> Thrones and domenaciones in blesse to be.
> With principates that order brighte
> And potestates in blissful lighte,
> Alsoe vertutes through thy greate mighte,
> Angell, also arckeangele.

The *Cursor Mundi* says

> Of angels wald he served be
> That suld of ordres haf thris thre,
> He ches til him that lauerd hend
> The men suld mak the ordre tend.

Cotton MS., 429–432.

But in the Towneley Play the tenth order was originally composed of the Angels who afterwards forfeited their place, for the *Primus demon* in reproaching Lucifer says—

> Thou has maide IX, there was X.

So also in *Cædmon*.

25. *A nexile:* 'an exile, *s.* aisle, from Lat. axilla, a detached part of the structure of the world; here seems to be confounded with *isle.*' (Note in Miss Smith's Glossary, *York Plays,* p. 546.)

28. *And that welth sall welde, &c.:* i. e. and [they] that shall enjoy well-being shall dwell in these habitations.

32. *Be put:* i. e. that they be put.

49. *Markide:* i. e. is made conspicuous.

71. *Me nedes:* i. e. I have no need to trouble myself in any way.

92. *Owe! dewes! all goes downe:* Lucifer's self-gratulation is here cut short by his fall from heaven. In the *Cursor Mundi* and in the Towneley and Chester Plays his sin is represented as more heinous than that of mere boasting.

Thus in the *Cursor* we read—

> 'Sette,' he said, 'mi sete I sal
> Gain him that heist es of all:
> In the north side it sal be sette,
> O me servis sal he non gette,
> Qui suld I him servis yeild?
> Al sal be at myn auen weild.'

> *Cotton MS.,* 457–462.

And in the Plays Lucifer seats himself in God's throne.

106. *All oure fode es but filth, we fynde us beforn:* i. e. all the food we find before us is but filth.

124, 25. *Thi rightwysnes, &c.:* I supply [redes] and [it] as suggested by Dr. Kölbing, and adopt his punctuation.

134. *Tham thoght tham:* 'Thai thoght tham' would mean 'they thought themselves,' and 'tham thoght thai weren,' 'it seemed to them they were.' but 'tham thoght tham' is loose grammar.

142. *Before:* i. e. in point of time.

CHESTER PLAYS.

I. NOAH'S FLOOD.

SUBJECT.—The Building of the Ark, the entrance into it of Noah and his Wife, and the Flood, were among the most popular subjects in the Miracle Cycles. In addition to the York, Towneley, Coventry, and Chester plays, a Newcastle play acted by the Shipwrights' Gild is still preserved, and is printed in Brand's History of Newcastle, vol. ii. In the *Miller's Tale* of Chaucer, where a clerk persuades a foolish carpenter to pass the night in a basket slung from a window in preparation for a second flood, there are naturally many allusions to Noah. See especially lines 348–357.

> ' Hastow nat herd how saved was Noe,
> Whan that our Lord had warned him biforn
> That al the world with watir schulde be lorn ? '
> ' Yis,' quod this carpenter, ' ful yore ago.'
> ' Hastow nought herd,' quod Nicholas, ' also
> The sorwe of Noë with his felaschipe,
> That he hadde or he gat his wyf to schipe ?
> Him hadde wel lever, I dar wel undertake,
> At thilke tyme, than alle his wetheres blake,
> That sche hadde hadde a schip hirself alone.'

The Flood is treated at great length in the alliterative poem on Noah and in the *Cursor Mundi* (ll. 1625–2000), but there is no allusion there to the obstinacy of Noah's wife.

METRE.—Stanzas of eight lines, for the most part riming aaab cccb, but occasionally aaab aaab. The fourth and eighth lines have only three beats, the rest four. There is much use of alliteration.

TEXT.—The Chester Plays have come down to us in five manuscripts, all transcribed within fifteen years, and all late. The earliest, written in 1591 by ' Edward Gregorie, a scholar of Bunbury,' is now in the possession of the Duke of Devonshire, by whose kindness the present editor has had the use of it for this edition. The next two transcripts were made by George Bellin in 1592 and 1600 respectively. These are both in the British Museum, MS. Add. 10,305 and Harl. 2013. The fourth copy is in the Bodleian (MS. 175); it was written by William

Bedford in 1604. The fifth and last, dated 1607, was the work of James Miller, and this also is in the British Museum (Harl. 2124). As to the relations of the five MSS. all that can be said here is that the transcripts of 1592 (here called B) and 1607 (E) show, especially in this play, most striking differences, and that the Devonshire MS. (A) is a link between them, though nearer to B than to E. Harl. 2013 and Bod. 175 belong to the same group as B and are of no great importance. For the present edition I have followed Wright's Shakespeare Society edition (1843), and take my text from B; but with important corrections from A and E, and a long passage for which E is our sole authority. In 1892 the E. E. T. S. issued the first half of the late Dr. Deimling's critical edition, the text of which is based on E.

1. *I, God, that all this worlde hath wrought:* 'hath' for 'have' through the interposition of the word 'God.'

4. *Are sette fowle in synne:* C reads 'Are fowle sotted.'

5. *My ghoste shall not linge in mone . . . but tell, &c.:* my spirit shall only (not . . . but) continue in man for six score years. Cp. Gen. vi. 3.

8. *They:* here and in ll. 11, 201, 204, written *the* in B.

10. *Fowle to flye:* gerundial infinitive, cp. ll. 57, 58, a hacchette wounder keyne to bitte well.

11. *They doe me nye, The Folke, &c.:* 'for on earth they, the folk that are thereon, do me wrong.' This seems better than to omit (with Wright) the comma after 'nye,' when we must render: 'for they cause me to harm the folk that are thereon.'

15. *Hartelye.* A and E read 'inwardlie,' but see Gen. vi. 6.

17. *My servante free:* 'free,' i. e. noble.

19. The directions here given are paraphrased from Gen. vi. 14-16: 'Make thee an ark of gopher wood (treeyes dry and light, l. 20); rooms (littill chambers, l. 21) shalt thou make in the ark, and shalt pitch it within and without with pitch (ll. 22-24). And this is the fashion which thou shalt make it of: the length of the ark shall be three hundred cubits, the breadth of it fifty cubits, and the height of it thirty cubits (ll. 25-28). A window shalt thou make to the ark, and in a cubit shalt thou finish it above (ll. 29-30); and the door of the ark shalt thou set in the side thereof (ll. 31-32); with lower, second and third stories (three rowfed chamberes on a roe, l. 34) shalt thou make it.'

21. *Thou make :* imperative.

27. *The meete thou fonge :* take thou the measure. 'Meete' is the reading of MS. A, for 'nexte' of B, and 'melt' of E. The height as given in Genesis is thirty cubits, not fifty (E) or sixty (A).

31. *A dore shall sit :* i. e. shall be placed. This is the reading of E and rimes with 'wytte' and 'itt.' A and B both read 'sutte,' the northern spelling of 'shutte.'

34. *Three rowfed chamberes on a roe.* These do not answer to the 'rooms' of Gen. vi. 14, but to the 'lower, second and third stories' of verse 16. 'Rowfed' is the reading of E, and shows 'ronette' of A and D to be a mistake for 'rovette,' a northern spelling of the same word. C reads 'round,' and gives us also 'on a roe' instead of the senseless 'one or two' of the other MSS.

35. *Slowe :* i. e. slay, is the reading of E and superior to 'flowe' (? = flood) of the other manuscripts.

40. *Saved be for thy sake :* another reading from E instead of the senseless 'shall fall before thy face,' which loses the rime with 'make' in l. 36.

42. *To me arte in such will :* art so minded towards me.

43. *house,* B 'howseholde.'

50. *Hye you, leste this watter fall.* E reads 'Helpe for aughte that may befall.'

75. *Every stiche :* i. e. every stick. B 'with stiche.'

93. *Toppe-castill :* a ledging surrounding the masthead.

94. *With cordes and roppes, I hold all meete,* E ; the other MSS. read : 'Bouth cordes and roppes I have all meete.'

115. *For non soe righteous man to me :* (to me, i.e. in my sight) A and E. 'For non soe righte, nor non to me,' B.

113–124. Cp. Gen. vii. 1–3.

125–133. Cp. Gen. vi. 19–21.

125. *more,* B 'moe.'

131. *Forgetten,* B 'forgotten.'

137–144. Cp. Gen. vii. 4.

145. *bayne,* B 'beane.'

151. *Yf through amendment, &c. :* i.e. to see if—an explanation of his slowness. The 'hundred wynter and twentye' of line 149 are a repetition of the 'six skore yeaires' of line 7, both being taken from Genesis vi. 3. But according to Genesis v. 32 Noah was apparently over five hundred before the Ark was

begun, and according to Genesis vii. 6 only six hundred when it was finished. The writer reckons by the 'long hundred.'

152. *unto,* B 'to.'

155. *That iich beaste were in stalle:* a wish; cf. Ch². 388, 'And sone that I were speede.'

170. *Fullimartes :* i. e. polecats, A ; 'fulmart,' E. 'Fillie, mare also,' B, which clashes with 'horses, mares,' &c. of l. 162.

187. *Cuckoes, curlues, &c.* For 'cuckoes' we have in B 'Duckes,' but our reading is supported both by its alliteration and by the occurrence in l. 189 of 'digges, drackes.'

Who ever knowes. Perhaps we should only regard this as a loose way of saying 'for anyone who knows to see,' or 'as any one knows;' but lines 189–191 may be taken as explanatory of 'iche one in his kinde,' and the construction be completed by line 192.

206. *But,* 'unless'; *elles,* redundant.

207. *Nowe.* A and E unite in reading Noe in preference to this ('Els rowe forth Noe whether the liste'). B *thy* for *thee.*

220. *There without:* substituted, to save rime and sense, on the authority of A and E, for the 'their all daye' of B.

225. *Fleetinge :* i. e. floating, AE ; 'flitting,' B.

226. *Spreades full ferre* (B 'farre'). The transcriber of E, or his authority, not recognising that the metre of the *Gossippes Song* is different from that of the rest of the play, has altered these words to 'it breadeth (broadens) in haste,' in order to preserve the triple rime with 'faste' and 'agaste.' Again in line 228 he reads : 'Good gossip, let me come in.'

233. *Heare is a pottill, &c.* This and the three following lines are omitted by E. It will be noted that they are metrically an excrescence.

238. *Childer :* retained by A only ; other MSS. 'children.'

244. *nought,* B 'note.'

246. *Have thou that for thy note!* We are to understand that Shem has carried his mother by force into the boat, and that she is replying to her husband's sarcastic welcome with a blow. The reading 'note' (use) makes good sense, and contains a possible pun : it is supported by A and B. But there is much to be said for the 'mote' (argument, speech) which is found in E.

249. *Remeves :* i.e. removes, moves away, AE. 'Renewes' of B is plainly a scribes error.

257. *Shutte,* AB ; steake, E.

259. *So greate one,* AE ; so greate wone, B.

[261*–398*.] The following forty-eight lines are given only by E. As they closely follow the Bible narrative [Gen. viii. 6 sqq.], and supply what in the other texts is an obvious lacuna, while the *naïveté* of the stage directions is an additional argument for their genuineness, I have no hesitation in printing them.

275*. Stage direction: 'Then shall he let loose a dove and there shall be in the ship another dove bearing an olive in her mouth, which some one shall let down [the verb should plainly be *demittet*] by a string into the hands of Noah.'

299*. *Soe be,* text 'be soe.'

305*. *Comes in all wise.* 'Comes,' the northern imperative plural; cp. does Y. 156. 'All wise': by all means.

263. *Wher all was [lorne] salfe to be.* I have ventured thus to emend, despite the agreement of the MSS. in favour of 'borne.' For 'salfe,' A ; safe, E ; MS. B reads 'false.'

268. *And full devocion :* so AB, but in E the line appears as 'I offer here right sone.'

270. *Thy,* AE ; to my, B.

276. *Has,* AE ; halfe, B.

278. *And,* AE ; on, B.

292. *Lete,* B leave.

293. *Flee,* B fleye.

296. *Mankinde :* the rime in l. 300 shows that the original reading was probably 'mankynne.'

305–7. *Heste, beste, leste,* B heiste, beste, last.

311. *Verey,* AE ; every, B.

313, 4. *That man ne woman,* AE; in B the line limps haltingly as, 'man shall never more.' To make up for this the next line is much too long, 'Be wasted with watter, as he hath been before.' I follow A in omitting 'he' and 'bene,' elliptical expressions being common in these plays. E reads: 'as is before.'

318. *Ilke,* AE ; same, B.

II. THE SACRIFICE OF ISAAC.

SUBJECT.—Five other English miracle-plays on this subject have been handed down to us. Of these the least interesting is that of the Coventry series, in which Isaac bows at once to his fate, and the story is told as baldly as possible. Better than this, but still with the omission of much of the small incident and by-play of our text, is the short Towneley version. In the York Play the charm of the story is marred by the unhappy freak of making Isaac thirty years of age, apparently that in this also he should be a type of Christ. In a Dublin play (15th century), printed by J. P. Collier in 1836 from a manuscript in Trinity College, Dublin, the distinguishing features are the introduction of Rebecca and the longer speeches assigned to Deus. The fifth version is that first printed by Miss Toulmin Smith in *Anglia*, Band vii. pp. 323–337, from a 15th century MS. found at Brome in Suffolk. This play has especial interest for us, not only on account of its intrinsic merit, but from the strong resemblance of its lines 164–314 to the corresponding 134 lines in the Chester version. This resemblance, sometimes of phrase, sometimes only of meaning, is interrupted by occasional passages in the Brome MS., which have no equivalents in the Chester. Apparently both editors worked upon a common original, but the Chester poet compressed the more freely, and in so doing greatly heightened the effect of the dialogue. But he shewed poor taste in omitting the charming scene between the Father and the Son after their agony is over, and I give this in full in an Appendix. It is possible, however, that the Chester Play has come down to us mutilated. It was plainly at one time a separate play, and when amalgamated with that of *Abraham and Lot* may well have been cut down for greater convenience of performance.

230. *Doe a littill thinge:* i. e. 'go about a little piece of business,' but the phrase seems to have had some liturgical associations; cp. Chaucer's *Knightes Tale*, 1435, of Emily's sacrifice to Diana—

> Two fyres on the auter gan sche beete,
> And dide hire thinges, as men may biholde;

and in the same way, 'said his thinges' is used for 'said his prayers.'

265. [Affearde] . . . [swerde]. Following Wright, I thus emend 'afrayde'. . . 'sworde' of the MSS.

268. *You will not slaye your childe.* The fine scene which follows, perhaps the most pathetic in our older literature, was doubtless suggested to the dramatist by the consideration that

Isaac, as a type of Christ, must have been a willing sacrifice.
The author of the *Cursor Mundi* had no such inspiration.

> 'Sir,' he said, 'quer sal we take
> The beist of sacrifice to make,
> Sin we wit us now broght has nan.'
> He said, 'drightin sal send us an.'
> Wit this he stod the child nerhand
> And dernlike [privily] he drou the brand
> That the child was not parceveid
> Ar the suerd him hade deceveid.
> > *Cotton MS.,* 3165–72.

271. [Steade]; fyelde, A; feilde, B; stydd, E.

281. *I praie thee . . . even in three.* Here A and E give us
the true reading for B's unmetrical

> Isaake, sonne, peace I thee praie
> Thou breakes my harte in sunder.

299. *If it maye be:* after 'she woulde kneele downe' the
regular construction here requires 'might,' which is actually the
reading of E. But the present tense is full of dramatic vividness.

300. Dr. Kölbing points out that a half stanza has here been
lost, and that we may supply three lines of it from the Brome MS.
178–80 :

> And sythyn that my moder ys not here
> I pray yow, fader, schonge yowr chere,
> And kyll me not with yowyr knyffe.

314. *Will not quite me in my nede,* B; quite me my meede,
AE; the latter reading is perhaps slightly the better. Neither
takes a very high view of Abraham's motive.

319. *Onste.* Wright misread this as 'ouste,' a word probably
not in use at this time. A and E read 'once.'

333. *My blessinge, &c.* These four lines are printed from
A and E. In B (followed by Wright) they do not appear.

335. *The blessing of the Trinitie.* Allusion to the Holy
Trinity are frequent in plays on Old Testament subjects.

336. *Grylle* should rime with *lighte.* Perhaps we should read
gryghte, murmur (from *grucchen*).

369. [*Yinge*]; yonge, MSS.

378. *Thou greved me [n]ever ones*: Dr. Kölbing's emendation from Brome MS. 270 ('In all thy lyffe thou grevyd me
neuer onys') ; thou greves me ever ones, B; thou greeves me
every ones, A; thou greved me but ones, E.

388. *And sone that I were speede:* a wish, cp. C. L. 155.

391. *A litill while, while you have space.* B omits the first 'while,' rather to the improvement of the sense. But the word is more likely to have dropped out in B than to have been repeated in A and E, and is needed for the sake of the metre.

397. *I woulde fayne . . . Full loth were me:* the subtle indication by the tenses that Abraham's resolution is faltering is worth noting.

411. *I praye you rydd me.* This reading (from A), though less forcible than the 'I praye God rydd me' of E, is supported by the Brome MS. The disputed word is omitted altogether in B.

435. *Into this place as thou se may.* Only given in E. Not a good line, but needed for the metre.

446. *ever:* pronounced as 'e'er.'

447. *To teare,* AB ; E weakly reads 'so deare.'

454. *And thy bloode,* AE ; and of thy bloode, B ; but the reference is plainly to Gen. xxii. 17, 'and thy seed shall possess the gate of his enemies.'

456. *To do,* AE ; And do, B.

457. *And of all nacions, &c.* I leave the text of this and the three following lines as it stands in B because it makes good sense, without any emendation, viz. that Abraham is to be blessed of all nations and himself to be saved by his descendant, Christ. But the text followed is plainly Gen. xxii. 18 : 'And in thy seed shall all the nations of the earth be blessed.' Now in l. 458 AE omit *thou,* in l. 459 they read *The* for *Through,* and in the l. 460 omit *be.*

> And of all nations, leve thou me,
> Blessed evermore shall be
> The fruite that shall come of thee,
> And saved through thy seede.

The stanza is thus much closer to Gen. xxii. 18, but contains a most awkward change of construction in the last line.

466. *In example,* AE ; An example, B.

473. *Understande I maie,* AE ; I maie understande, B.

476. *And death for to confounde,* AB ; his death to underfonge, E. Neither reading, it will be observed, supplies a rime to l. 472.

477. *Suche obedience, &c.* The remaining stanzas are not given in E.

485. *Make rombe, lordinges, &c.* Spoken by the herald of the next play, probably on horseback.

TOWNELEY PLAY.

SECUNDA PASTORUM.

SUBJECT.—We have in all six plays treating of the Adoration of the Holy Child by the Shepherds ; two in the Towneley Cycle. which must have been used as alternatives ; one each in those of York, Chester and Coventry ; and a single play acted by the Shearmen and Taylors of Coventry, probably a part of the lost Cycle of the Trade Gilds of that town. The Shepherds of the Coventry (East-Midland ?) Cycle are distinguished from their fellows by their superior learning, by their dulness and their abstinence from gifts. In the other plays the Shepherds are all genuine rustics, rough in their talk and manners, but full of real devotion. They talk of their sheep, eat their poor meals, wrestle (as in the Chester Play) with their lad and are ignominiously beaten, try to imitate the angels' song, and then betake them to Bethlehem, there to offer their humble gifts. All these features appear in the Towneley Play, but inwoven with them is a genuine farce, which makes it of a great importance in the history of the development of the English drama.

DIALECT.—In the main that of the West Riding of Yorkshire.

METRE.—A very vivacious stanza of thirteen, with two and three accents to a line, riming abababababcdddc. This metre runs through five of the Towneley Plays and appears in four others. Couplets, alternates, and other metres appear in the rest of the plays. There is much alliteration.

TEXT.— The MS. of the Towneley Plays (till lately owned by Major Edw. Coates) was originally copied and collated in 1836 for the Surtees Society. The extracts here given are taken from the Early English Text Society's edition (1897).

11. *Nere-hands outt of the doore :* nearly homeless.

13. *Lyys falow :* i.e. because they could not afford to cultivate them.

20. *Lord-fest*, 'strong in lordliness,' Morley; perhaps rather 'attached to a lord' (the opposite of lordless), cp. shamefast, wordfast.

28. *May he gett a paynt slefe, &c.:* i.e. a sleeve with the badge of some great man on it.

32. *He can make purveance.* Purveyance was the right of purchasing provisions and necessaries for the royal household at an arbitrary price in preference to any other buyer. The first of forty statutes against it was made by Canute, but the right was not finally surrendered till 1660. On a smaller scale it would be practised by every feudal lord.

289. *Bot abowte you a serkylle.* Mak (a character who is probably adapted from the favourite comic character, the conjurer and buffoon Maugis of the Romance of the Four Sons of Aymon), like a rustic magician, draws an imaginary circle round the Shepherds, in which they are to sleep until his theft is done and his protestations of innocence ready prepared.

294. *Over your heydys, &c. :* by way of a charm.

309. *I hope not I myght ryse a penny to wyn :* I have no expectation of making anything by getting up.

314. *There may no note be sene, &c. :* such small jobs prevent my having any work to show.

317. *A, com in, my swetyng :* she recognizes her husband.

341. *Then myght I far, by alle the pak, &c. :* then might I fare much the worse at the hands of all the pack. The reading *far, by* instead of *by, for* of text (*far* in Surtees ed. is corrected in errata to *for*) was suggested by Dr. Skeat and (independently) by Dr. Logeman.

598. *We wate ill abowte :* we are waiting about to no purpose. Primus Pastor has not yet discovered Mak's trick.

602. *Kynde wille crepe, &c.* A proverb ; cp. Everyman, l. 315.

614. *I am he that hym gatt.* Mak now pretends that the sheep is a changeling put in place of his child.

634. *With you wille I be left :* I will stand by your judgment.

639. *And cast hym in canvas :* i. e. they toss Mak in a blanket.

642. *A shepe of vii skore :* i. e. of seven score pounds.

655. *Ther lyges that fre.* For the use of 'free' as a substantive (=noble fellow), cp. York Play of the Entry into Jerusalem, l. 183—

> And than we will go mete that free ;

also 'To that bright' in l. 716 of the present play. In the York Play of the *Shepherds*, the Holy Child is called 'that frely foode.'

667. *How he crakyd it :* 'crakyd,' sang out loud (M. E. craken, to cry out : cp. 'corn-crake'), occurs in the York Play, where one of the Shepherds, after imitating the angels' song, says—

> I have so craked in my throte
> That my lippes are nere drye.

671. *I can :* so Pastor Primus in the York Play, says—

> I can synge itt alls wele as hee
> And on a-saie itt sall be sone
>   proved or we passe.
> Yf we will helpe, halde on! late see,
>   for thus it was.

And the Shepherds all sing together. In the Chester Play, on the other hand, Pastor Primus modestly remarks,

> He hade a moche better voyce than I have,
> As in heaven all other have so.

685. *By the prophecy of David and Isay.* In the *Processus Prophetarum* in the Towneley Plays the prophets who appear are Moses, David, the Sibyl and Daniel, but the play has some signs of being imperfect. In the Coventry Play no less than twenty-seven prophets are made to bear their witness.

692. *Ecce virgo, &c. :* Isaiah vii. 14 (in the Vulgate : 'Ecce virgo concipiet et pariet filium, et vocabitur nomen ejus Emmanuel'). For *Ecce* the MS. has *Cite*, a scribe's error.

703. *Patriarkes, &c. :* cp. Luke x. 24.

729. *A bob of cherys.* Only the Shepherds of the Coventry Cycle bring no gifts ; in the other plays some imagination is shewn in the choice of rustic presents. Thus in the first Towneley Play the gifts are a 'lytyll spruce cofer,' a ball and a bottle ; in the York, a brooch with a tin bell, 'two cobill notis uppon a band' (cob-nuts on a riband), and a horn spoon that will hold forty peas. In the Chester Play double gifts are offered, a bottle, hood and shepherd's pipe by the 'Boys,' and a bell, spoon and cap by the Shepherds. In the Coventry Play of the *Shearmen and Taylors*, the gifts are a pair of mittens, a hat, and a stick for hooking down nuts or plums.

735-36. *Haylle lytyll tyne mop, Of oure crede thou art crop.* These phrases are repeated from the corresponding scene in the *Prima Pastorum*.

747. *The tenys.* Tennis was a fashionable game in France at the end of the 14th century (cp. the Dauphin's gift of tennis balls to our Henry V.), and was well known in England and Scotland about the same time. In the romance of *The Turke and Gawin* it is alluded to as having been played by Arthur's Knights !

> Thou shalt see a tennisse ball,
> That never knight in Arthur's hall
> Is able to give it a lout.

749. *That sett alle on seven:* that put all things in order. The phrase is repeated from the *Prima Pastorum*, in an earlier part of which it occurs slightly altered as 'to cast the world in seven.' In the play of *Magnus Herodes* the King threatens to 'sett alle on sex and seven.'

765. *Let take on loft:* let us deliver on high, let us sing out loudly.

'COVENTRY' PLAY.

THE SALUTATION AND CONCEPTION.

SUBJECT.—There is no counterpart to this play in any of the other cycles, and it is to this fact rather than to any special merit, whether literary or dramatic, that its selection is due. We have here a personification of the heavenly virtues of Truth, Mercy, Justice and Peace, and we thus advance a step towards the dramatic allegory of the earliest Morality Plays, such as the *Castell of Perseverance*, which ends with a precisely similar scene.

METRE.—This play is written throughout[1] in stanzas of eight lines, riming ababbcbc, with the occasional substitution of two more A-rimes for the Cs in the second quatrain. This very undramatic metre runs through eleven of the Coventry Plays and appears also in twelve others. The chief variation from it is a still longer stanza, riming abababbcdddc.

DIALECT.—The chief scribal peculiarity is the appearance of x in such words as xal, xulde, etc. According to Mr. Halliwell-Phillipps this is in harmony with the traditional attribution of the Cycle to Coventry, or its neighbourhood, but xal, xulde, etc. are usually associated with the East-Midland dialect, and in the General Introduction (p. xxxviii) I have stated my belief in the East-Midland origin of this Cycle.

TEXT.—The text of this extract is taken from Mr. Halliwell-Phillipps' edition for the Shakespeare Society, the title of which runs as follows :

'Ludus Coventriae. A collection of mysteries formerly represented at Coventry on the Feast of Corpus Christi. Edited by James Orchard Halliwell. London : printed for the Shakespeare Society, 1841.'

[1] There are three half-stanzas of four lines each.

The proofs have been read with the unique Manuscript in the Cottonian Collection at the British Museum, dated 1468.

1. *Ffowre thowsand sex undryd foure.* (The MS. adds *yere*, but see l. 3.) As there are nearly 200 computations of the number of years between the Creation of Man and Birth of Christ it is hardly worth enquiring to whom this particular calculation should be credited. It is six hundred years longer than the reckoning of Archbishop Usher (4004 years), now usually inserted in Bibles. According to Jewish chronologists the length of the period is 3992 years, according to the Samaritan 4293, while other calculations vary between 3483 and 6984.

7. *Seyd by Ysaie:* Isaiah lxiii. 15.

10. *Into erthe:* a rime is wanted to 'fede.' We should rather read 'this stede,' and explain 'erthe' as a gloss.

13. *Thi thryste:* for 'thi' we should have expected 'their.'

21. *Balys.* Mr. Halliwell suggested this as an emendation and in deference to his authority I have so marked it. But the word in the MS. looks to me far more like 'balys' than 'babys.'

25. *Quod Jeremye:* Jerem. ix. 1.

38. *That ben in the fyrst ierarchie:* see note to York, l. 23.

48. *Of Locyfere to restore the place:* see note to York, l. 23.

49. *Propter miseriam, &c.:* Ps. xii. 5.

71. *Thou hast lovyd trewthe:* Heb. i. 9.

85. *Veritas mea, &c.:* Ps. lxxxv. 10.

87. *Byddyth:* imperative, 'Cry "Ho" to that hell-hound who hates thee.' Cp. Chaucer, *Knightes Tale,* 1796-98.

> And when that Theseus hadde seen his sighte,
> Unto the folk that foughten thus echon
> He cryde, 'Hoo! no more, for it is doon.'

93. *Therefore his endles punchement.* The argument is that because God is eternal, i. e. with an existence not conditioned by time, therefore any offence against Him partakes of His eternity, and provokes an eternal punishment.

95. *The devyl to his mayster he ches.* For the use of 'to' cp. Skelton's *Magnificence,* l. 1961—

> I sende ofte times a fole to his sone.

107. *Above:* i. e. in a greater degree than.

108. *He:* i. e. man.

Be feyth he forsook hym never the more: i. e. though man fell into sin and so forsook God and presumed on His mercy (l. 109), none the less he retained his faith in God.

114. *In vertuys:* i. e. among angels of the order of Virtues to which *Mercy* and *Justice* belong.

134. *Tyl wysdam:* the heavenly Wisdom, or Christ.

MARY MAGDALENE.

SUBJECT.—The importance of this play consists chiefly in its union of all the essentials of every kind of religious and didactic drama. It is a miracle play, according to the current definition, as treating of the life and death of St. Mary Magdalene. It is a mystery play, by virtue of the introduction of scenes from the life of Christ. It is a morality play, as exhibiting the contest between good and evil, and as introducing upon the stage such abstract personages as the King of the Flesh.

Dr. Furnivall has divided the play, which has the least possible dramatic unity, into two parts, with twenty scenes in the first, and thirty-one in the second. The play must have been an expensive one to produce, as there are upwards of forty different characters in Part I. and twenty-six in Part II. Probably only two pageants were used for its representation, for several of the scenes appear to be inserted only to give time for a 'shift' on the other pageant. But if any attempt were made to depict the burning temple or the incidents of the voyage of the King and Queen of Marcylle, realistically, the resources at the command of the stage manager must have been extensive.

The story of the play is adapted, with very few variations, from the account of St. Mary Magdalene in the *Legenda Aurea* of Jacobus de Voragine, of which an English edition was published by Caxton in 1483. The identification of Mary Magdalene with Mary the sister of Lazarus was accepted by Gregory the Great, and being supported by his authority was hardly questioned until the 16th century.

DIALECT.—According to Dr. Furnivall the dialect of the play is East-Midland, probably from the neighbourhood of Lynn in Norfolk, or from Lincolnshire. The most notable dialectal and scribal forms are xal (shall) and qwat (what).

METRE.—The metre is very irregular. It seems to have originally been written in 8- or 9-line stanzas, and to have remained so now and then. Other stanzas, alternates and couplets, also occur. The line numbers which are taken from Dr.

Furnivall's edition, show them to some extent. Pt. II. is mainly in alternates.

TEXT.—The text here given is from Dr. Furnivall's edition of the *Digby Mysteries* (see Introduction) for the New Shakspere Society. The Bodleian manuscript in which these plays are preserved was the work of three different hands, but the greater part was probably written between 1480 and 1490.

54. *Besyn of all other men:* for the use of 'of' after 'besyn' (beseen) cp. 1 Cor. xv. 5, 'And that He was seen of Cephas, then of the twelve.'

55. *Cyrus is my name.* The following is the account of the Magdalene's parentage in the *Legenda Aurea:*

'Mary Magdalene had her surname of magdalo a castell | and was borne of right noble lygnage and parentes | whiche were descended of the lygnage of kynges | And her fader was named Sirus & her moder eucharye | She wyth her broder lazare & her suster martha possessed the castel of magdalo: whiche is two myles fro nazareth | & bethanye the castel whiche is nygh to Iherusalem· and also a grete parte of Iherusalem. whiche al thise thynges they departed amonge theym in suche wyse that marye had the castelle magdalo. whereof she had her name magdalene | And lazare had the parte of the cytee of Iherusalem: and martha had to her parte bethanye.'

Legenda Aurea. De Worde's edition (1493), f. 184, ver. 80.

55. *Be cleffys so cold:* a meaningless tag; cp. 'in contree and cost,' l. 1212.

60. *Bothe lesse and more:* i.e. the whole of it; cp. l. 1202. For 'more' and 'sore' we should read 'mare' and 'sare.'

84. *Whyll that I am in good mynd:* i.e. in my right senses, in full possession of my faculties.

89–91. *Hys wyll ... a-gens hem.* There is here a confusion of pronouns past any certain unravelling. 'Agens hem' (i.e. with respect to them) probably refers to Lazarus' sisters.

93. *Thatt God of pes.* For 'Thatt' we should probably read 'Thou.'

106. *To your grace:* to your honour or credit.

269. *Bak and syde:* a phrase for the whole body, as in the famous drinking song, 'Back and side, go bare, go bare.'

285. *In-wyttissymus.* Dr. Furnivall glosses this word in his margin as 'infinitissimus,' most infinite; but it clearly stands for 'invictissimus,' most unconquered.

288. *He to bryng us :* the construction is altered at the end of the line and the pronoun repeated.

299. *Thys castell is owerys :* the reply of Martha shows that in 'ours,' Lazarus is using the royal plural. In l. 81 the 'castell' had been given to Mary, and in l. 303 she seems to claim it as hers.

308. *And that I jugge me to skryptur :* and as to this I refer my claim to Scripture.

359. *Satan ower sovereyn :* ? for 'yower sovereyn.'

362. *At my ryall retynawns :* in my royal train.

377. *We xal hyrre wynne.* This is the first intimation that the attack is to be specially against the Magdalen.

476. *Wynne of mawt, &c.* Even with the aid of Henderson's *Ancient and Modern Wines* it is difficult to identify all the different varieties mentioned in the lists in which medieval taverners delighted. Wine of Mawt is possibly Maltese wine rather than wine made from malted barley ; Malmeseyn came from Malvasia in the Morea ; 'clarry' wine (vin doulce et clarré) was red or white wine seasoned with honey (cp. Chaucer, *Knightes Tale*, 613) ; it seems to have been a mixture made as required, as opposed to 'claret' which was manufactured. 'Gyldyr' is Guelder ; 'Galles,' Galicia ; 'at the grome' stands for 'at the Groine,' the port in Spain. 'Wyan' is our English way of writing 'Guyenne' ; 'Vernage' a wine grown near Verona, and often mentioned, as in Chaucer's *Merchant's Tale*.

484. *The fynnest thou hast.* Note the change from the polite *your* and *you*, with which Satan addresses Mary, to his *thou hast* to the Taverner. So Harry Bailey speaks to the Shipman as *thou* and to the Prioress as *you*. In the dialogue in ll. 615–630 of this play, Simon addresses Christ as '*Ye*' and is addressed by Him as *Thou*.

507. *Lady, this man is for yow :* for you, at your service, cp. *Much Ado*, ii. 1. 387 ' My lord, I am for you, though it cost me ten nights' watching.'

590. *Agens God so veryabyll.* For 'against' meaning 'in regard to,' cp. Trevisa's tr. of Higden's *Polych.* vi. ' Merciable agenst pore men.'

610. *The prophett :* i.e. Christ, who, however, has not previously been mentioned.

612. *Be the oyle of mercy.* The softening and healing properties

of oil have caused it to be regarded as symbolical of mercy and forgiveness ; cp. its use in the Sacrament of Extreme Unction, and the legend, narrated in the *Cursor Mundi*, that Seth, when Adam lay dying, was sent to Paradise to seek the oil of mercy for him.

619. *That thou wylt me knowe :* because thou art minded to recognise Me.

638. *With the to stond :* the infinitive is probably explanatory of 'my hart and thowt' in the next line.

670. *With good entent*, text ' with good in entent.'

1140. *Mahond :* throughout the Miracle Plays Mahomet is the common god of all heathens ; cp. in the Coventry Plays the speeches of the soldiers who guard the sepulchre :

> PRIMUS MILES. My head dulleth.
> My heart fulleth
> Of sleep.
> Saint Mahound,
> This burying ground
> Thou kepe.

'Secundus Miles' calls on 'Mahound Whelp' and the third soldier on 'Mahound of Might.'

1146. *Lythly, chyld, it be natt delayd :* i.e. it may not lightly be delayed.

1186. *Glabriosum, &c.* It is impossible to extract any meaning out of this Mahound's Lesson, but the gibberish seems to have been intended to carry along with it a suggestion of bad words.

1200. *Ragnell and Roffyn.* In the Chester Plays of *Antichrist*, Antichristus at his death calls out :

> Helpe, Sathanas and Lucifer,
> Bellsabube, bolde Balacher,
> Ragnell, Ragnell, thou arte my deare.

And in *The Fall of Lucifer* Primus Demon calls on

> Ruffyne, my frinde fayer and free
> Loke that thou kepe mankinde from blesse.

1377. *Our lordes precepte, &c.* The story as given in the *Aurea Legenda* here shows some differences from the version adopted by the playwright. It runs as follows :

' Saint maxyme, marie magdalene : and lazar her brother martha her suster Marcelle chamberer of martha, and saint cedonye whiche was born blynde & after enlumyned of oure lorde | alle these to gydre and many other crysten men were taken of the mescreau*n*tes and put in to a shippe in the see without ony takell or rother for to be drowned, but by the puruyaunce of almyghty god they came all to marcelle | where as none wold receyue them to be lodged they duellyd and abode under a porche to fore a temple of the peple of that contree | And whan the blessyd marie magdalene sawe the peple assembled at this temple for to do sacrefyce to the ydollis she aroos vp pleasybly wyth a glad vysage & discrete tongue & well spekynge | And began to preche the faith and lawe of Jhesu cryst | and wythdrewe them fro the worshyppyng of thydollis.'—*Legenda Aurea.* De Worde's edition (1493), f. 185.

1435. *The lond of satyllye:* Satalie (Attalia), part of Armenia, was the scene of one of the campaigns of Chaucer's Knight.

1540. *How-pleʒeauntly they stond:* here the king points to his idols.

1553. *Dominus, illuminacio mea:* Ps. xxvii. 1.

THE CASTELL OF PERSEVERANCE.

SUBJECT.—The date of the *Castell of Perseverance* has been fixed by Prof. W. K. Smart, in the article quoted below, at about 1405, and is in any case much earlier than that of any Morality still extant in its entirety. A curious sketch at the beginning of the MS., reproduced in a plate facing p. 23 of Sharp's *Dissertation on the Coventry Mysteries*, gives us a good idea of the manner in which it was played and the machinery used for its performance.

'A reference to the plate,' writes Mr. Sharp, 'will shew a rude representation of a castle, raised some height from the ground, upon pillars or supports, and standing in the centre of a circle formed by two lines one within the other, in the space between which is written " + this is the watyre a bowte the place, if any dycke may be mad ther it schal be pleyed ; or ellys that it be strongly barryd al a bowte: & lete nowth over many stytelerys [marshalmen ?] be withinne the plase[1]." Over the castle we read : "This is the castel of perseveranse that stondyth in the myddys of the place; but lete no men sytte ther for lettynge of

---

[1] I write out the contractions in full.

syt, for ther schal be the best of all." Beneath the castle and within the supports to it stands a bed, below which are these words :—" Mankynde is bed schal be under the castel, & ther schal the sowle lye under the bed tyl he schal ryse & pleye." On each side of the castle is written the following direction:— " Coveytyse copbord schal be at the ende of the castel, be the beddys feet."

' On the outside of the circle five stations for scaffolds are marked out ; beginning at the top we read : " Sowth, Caro skaffold—West, Mundus skaffold—Northe, Belyal skaffold— North Est, Coveytyse skaffold—Est deus skaffold." Underneath the circle are the following directions to the performers :—" & he that schal pley belyal, loke that he have gunne powder brennyng in pypys in his hands and in his ers, etc. whanne he gothe to batayle ... the iiij dowters schul be clad in mentelys, Mercy in wyth, rythwysnesse in red al togedyr, Trewthe in sad grene, & Pes al in blake, and they schul pleye in the place al to gedyr tyl they brynge up the sowle." '

A week before the play was acted criers were sent round to the neighbouring villages proclaiming its subject, and an- nouncing its performance ' this day sevennyt' ' at N on the grene in ryall array.' The play was thus a travelling one like those of the ' Coventry ' or N-town cycle and like that probably belongs to the East-Midlands. There is, however, some ad- mixture of specifically northern words in its vocabulary, such as bedene (at once), boun and busk (get ready), byggyng (build- ing), gate (way), kettis (tangles), rakle (hurry), syke (a rill), tak (leasehold), &c., and on the strength of these Prof. W. K. Smart in the *Manly Anniversary Studies* (1923) suggested Lincolnshire rather than Norfolk as its home. A reference to the 'galows of Canwyke' (l. 2422) confirms this, as there is a Canwick a mile and a half SE. of Lincoln and references to its gallows, visible from a high hill to all the country round, occur in a poem on the martyrdom of Hugh of Lincoln (1255) and in the time of Edward III. For the date of the play Prof. Smart suggests *c.* 1405 on the ground of a reference to ' shrewdnes' both yn Ingelond and in Walys,' explained as pointing to the revolt of the Percies in 1403 and the revolt of Glendower (1402–11).

METRE.—The greater part of the play is written in stanzas of 13 lines, riming abababababaccca, the ninth and thirteenth lines having three accents, the rest four. But we find also a nine-line stanza, riming ababcdddc; an eight-line stanza, with two accents to a line, riming aaabcccb, and other varieties.

TEXT.—The text of these extracts is based on a transcript from Mr. Hudson Gurney's MS. (written about 1440), with whom I subsequently had the honour of editing it in the Macro Plays for the *Early English Text Society* in 1904, kindly placed at my disposal in 1890 by Dr. Furnivall.

5–7. *Lende . . . lende.* Here, as in Chaucer, who copies the French rule as to 'rimes riches' two words identically spelt may rime together if their meanings are different. Cp. Chaucer's *Prol.*

> The holy blisful martir for to seeke [seek]
> That hem hath holpen whan that they were seeke [sick].
>
> ll. 17, 18.

13. *Whow mankende is unchende.* 'Unchende' can only mean 'unkende,' unkind, unnatural; but the spelling is surprising and the sense hardly what is wanted. Prof. Skeat suggests 'unhende,' unserviceable, clumsy, as a possible emendation, and this exactly suits the sense.

16. *I am born and have ryth nowth:* i. e. now that I am born I have nothing, etc. It seems better to construe thus than to put a comma after 'wot' in l. 15, and connect together 'to woo and wepynge I am born.'

20. *Crysme.* The 'chrism' or 'chrisom-cloth' was properly a white cloth placed by the baptizing priest on the head of an infant to prevent the holy oil from rubbing off. It was afterwards enlarged into a white robe covering the whole body, as a token of the innocency conferred in baptism; but the words 'my hed hath cawth' show that the reference here is to the original chrisom-cloth.

28. *The ton.* The apparent doubling of the article is really a survival of the old *thet on*, that one; cp. l. 38, Hey. 579, and Chaucer's *Legend of Good Women*, A. text, l. 325.

Techyth me to goode. The presence of the preposition is explained by the old meaning of 'teach' = show, direct. Cp. *Piers Plowman*, i. 81, 'Tech me to no Tresour.'

32. *Be fen and flode:* the first of nearly a dozen periphrases for 'everywhere'; cp. be 'strete and stronde,' 'strete and stye,' 'downe and dyche,' 'sompe and syke' &c.

43. *Hevene trone:* 'hevene' is a genitive; cp. next line, and 'heven kynge,' Ev. 19.

78. *All in povert here thei stode.* The pronoun is inserted because of the intervention of 'all in povert' between the nouns and their verb. See Abbott, *Shaksp. Gram.* §§. 242, 243.

90. *Have thou, &c.:* conditional; cp. l. 126.

98. *Faryn wel at mete and mele:* an allusion to the inconvenience of fasting.

115. *Take the werld to thine entent:* take the world as the subject of your thoughts. The construction is as in the phrase 'take to wife.'

137. *Thou schalt thynke al be tyme:* 'schalt' here is equivalent to 'you are sure to'; cp. *Richard III*, v. 3. 201,

> And, if I die, no man shall pity me;

i.e. 'it is certain that no man will pity me.' See Abbott, *Shaksp. Gram.* § 315.

139. *Thou schalt holdyn hym inne:* you will easily keep *Bonus Angelus* in his place.

141. *With lofty lyvys fode:* with the food of a lovely life, i.e. with dainty living.

145. *Goode:* probably a misreading for 'Gode' (God); cp. 'fode,' l. 141.

146. *And so I may make mery.* The sentence should end 'I will do what I please yet a while,' but *Hum. Gen.* slightly alters his turn of thought in l. 148.

151. *Ryde be sompe and syke.* To be possessed of a horse to carry one dryshod through swamps and streams is taken as a mark of wealth.

158. *Other while thou muste be fals.* We are tempted at first to read 'otherwise,' as if *Mal. Ang.* were explaining that any failure of 'acord' with him would be treacherous to *Hum. Gen.'s* new allies. But l. 166 shows that 'other while' (occasionally) is right, though a little abrupt.

170. *Holt and hale:* 'hale' means a 'tent,' a 'pavilion,' and makes but poor sense in connection with 'holt,' but in these phrases everything is sacrificed to the alliteration. The distinction here is between 'land' and 'house.'

195. *And ther to here myn honde.* For the omission of the verb, cp. Ev. 150, 'Farewell, and there an end,' also l. 207 of this stanza.

201. *I recke nevere of hevene wonde:* I care not whether I turn aside from heaven.

231. *Je vous pry.* It has been contended that, inasmuch as from the reign of Edward III onward French ceased to be the language of the English Court, the fact that in the Chester and other Miracle Plays, and in the present Morality Play, the scraps of French fall exclusively to kings and courtiers, is to be disregarded, and we are to see in them traces of French literary originals. But stage traditions in such matters would be very conservative, and the coincidence is too strong to be explained away.

246. *With cursydnesse in costes knet:* in my manners made up of cursedness.

259. *Who so [nol] be lecherous.* I have ventured to substitute *nol* for MS. *now,* as the point of the remark is that if a man has not one sin he has another; if a man is *not* lustful he is proud, etc.

263. *Ther is pore nor ryche.* For the ellipse of 'neither' cp. Shaks. *Son.* 141—

> But my five wits nor my five senses can
> Dissuade one foolish heart from seeing thee.
>
> Abbott, *Shaksp. Gram.* § 376.

272. *Man doth me bleykyn blody ble:* man makes my countenance pale and bloody—a strong metaphor.

281. *Ffewe men in the ffeyth they fynde.* If the text is right, 'they fynde' must be used for 'men find' or 'we find,' i. e. one finds now few men in the faith.

286. *For that schuld cunne Cristis lessoun, &c.:* he who is to learn Christ's lesson must bind his body in penance. For the use of 'should' see Abbott, *Shaksp. Gram.* § 324.

309. *May any bote thi bale brewe.* The true phrase is given in l. 317, where Schrift says, 'I schal, if I cunne, Brewe the bote of bale,' i. e. concoct or devise for thee a remedy out of thy evils.

321. *He is in poynt to be spylt:* the transcript, my only authority for the text, reads 'iij poynt,' but the correction 'in,' suggested by Dr. Skeat, is certain.

323. *And wyl certes:* i. e. will continue to sit there. Cp. l. 353.

325. *He hath me forsake and I have no gylt.* For this use of 'and,' almost with the meaning of 'though,' cp. *Apol. for Lollards,* 40: 'And he was riche He was mad nedy for us.'

363. *slake.* This reading is required to rime with 'make' in l. 361. MS. reads 'slawe' = slay.

372. *ye me spelle :* imperative.

EVERYMAN.

The play of *Everyman* is perhaps the finest of all the Morality Plays that have come down to us. Its early popularity is testified by the fact that it was twice printed by Richard Pynson and twice by John Skot. Neither of the Pynson editions is now extant in a single perfect copy. Of one the British Museum possesses a large fragment containing from l. 305 to the end, of the other a few leaves only are preserved at the Bodleian. Skot's editions have been more fortunate. Of the one identified only by his device the Huth copy is now in the British Museum ; while of the edition bearing his imprint an example was formerly preserved at Lincoln, and from a transcript of this our extracts have been made. The original till lately at Britwell, is now in the United States.

Like the *Castell of Perseverance*, the play of *Everyman* was written to persuade men to a life of good deeds and morality, and it inculcates the sacramental teaching of the Catholic Church. In 1892 Dr. Henri Logeman shewed that, with the exception of the prologue, it is a translation, made probably towards the end of the fifteenth century, of the Dutch play *Elckerlijk*, attributed by Dr. Logeman to a certain Petrus Dorlandus, a native of Diest. (See *Elckerlijk and Everyman*, edited by Dr. H. Logeman. Gand, 1892.) The metre of the play is the rimed couplet with sometimes four, sometimes five, beats to the line. But for the couplet is sometimes substituted a quatrain with alternating rimes, and in the Messenger's prologue after each couplet comes a line of three beats with rime in *-aye.*

3. *By figure :* i. e. as to its form.

7, 8. *Mater . . . entent :* the 'matter' is the play, the 'intent' its didactic purpose.

19. *Heven kynge :* cp. CP. (43) note.

45. *In all the haste.* For the presence of the article where we should now omit it, cp. 'at the lengthe,' l. 828.

77. *Fro heven to departe :* to separate *him* from heaven.

104. *With the thou brynge:* cp. Ch¹. 21, 22.

> Littill chamberes therin thou make,
> And byndynge slyche also thou take.

111. *Ado:* the reading is from the 'Salisbury' Skot; the Lincoln reads 'have I do.'

116. *Spareth.* The termination is influenced by 'dredeth' in the previous line.

132. *I may saye deth gyveth no warnynge:* for the form of the assertion cp. l. 182, and Bale's *King John,* 2078, 'a lovynge person thou mayst seeme for to be.' Cp. also Aesch. *Agam.* 737—

> Παρ' αὐτὰ δ' ἐλθεῖν ἐς Ἰλίου πόλιν
> λέγοιμ' ἂν φρόνημα μὲν νηνέμου γαλάνας, κ.τ.λ.

145. *Of nature:* i.e. in accordance with nature; cp. the still current phrase 'of necessity.'

179. *Without ony advysement:* Dethe scornfully refers to Everyman's 'with good advysement' in l. 175.

194. *Ago:* gone by. The prefix *a-* here answers to the German prefix *er.* (A.S. *agán,* agangan = Ger. ergehen.)

245. *Adonay:* the Hebrew name for the Deity, a plural form of *Adon,* 'lord,' with the pronoun of the first person.

248. *Promyse is duty:* a poor version of the old proverb 'behest is debt.'

272. *And yet:* i.e. and even now. 'Yet' here is purely temporal.

290. *To brynge me forwarde:* to escort me; cp. *Rich. II,* i. 2. 2. 'How far brought you high Hereford on his way?' Cp. also l. 675.

315. *For kynde will crepe where it may not go:* a proverb; cp. T. 602.

495. *And you do by me:* if you will act by my advice.

500. *I may thanke you of all:* not 'of all people I may thanke you,' but 'I may thank you for everything.' In A.S. the verb *thank* takes a genitive of the thing and dative of the person; cp. *Alis.* 7576: 'And thanked him of his socour.' (Mätzner, ii. 235.)

522. *Thy gyde ... to go by thy syde.* For the use of the gerund cp. Ch¹. 10: 'Beaste, worme and fowle to flye.'

640. *Before God:* not an oath, but 'when ye come into God's presence.'

669. *Five Wyttes:* i.e. the Five Senses.

787. *Judas Machabe:* cp. 1 Macc. iii. 3, 4, etc.

795. *More and lesse:* great people and little. A common phrase in Chaucer for ' all.'

800. *I crosse out all this:* I make no account of this.

801. *I take my cappe in my lappe:* ' I doff my cap (so deep that it comes) into my lap.' Only Mr. Huth's Skot edition reads ' cappe,' the others having ' tappe,' for which no meaning can be found. The explanation is due to Dr. Logeman.

850. *Farewell, and there an ende:* for the ellipsis cp. CP. (195.)

902. *Doctour.* A Doctor or Expositor, who expounds the moral of the performance, appears occasionally in the Chester Miracle Plays (cp. page 30). In the Moralities, where he is more needed, his place is usually taken by one of the virtuous characters. But as late as the middle of the sixteenth century, in Ingelend's *Disobedient Child*, he reappears under a new name as the ' Perorator.'

903. *Take it of worth:* i.e. value it. ' Take *in* worth ' was the more common phrase ; cp.

> When a poore friend a small gift gives to thee
> Take it in worth, and let it praysed be.
>
> > Baker's *Cato Variegatus* (1636).

RASTELL'S THE FOUR ELEMENTS.

In November 1917 (*Bibliographical Society's Transactions*, xv. 58-82) Mr. Arthur W. Reed confirmed Bale's ascription of this play (under the title : *Natura Naturata*) to John Rastell, ' lawyer, printer, venturer, dramatist, and controversialist,' and in *The Library* for January 1919 (3rd series, vol. x) established Rastell's authorship also of *Gentleness and Nobility* and the English fragment from the Spanish *Calisto and Melibea.* Mr. Reed discovers Rastell as a Coventry man, born about 1495, who studied at the Middle Temple, was Coroner of Coventry 1501-1508, before 1504 married Elizabeth More, by 1512 had engaged in diplomatic service, and in 1515 was granted the estate of Richard Hunne (condemned posthumously for heresy). In 1516 he printed a *Grand Abridgement* of the Statutes in three fine volumes. An attempted voyage in 1517 to the New Found Lands, ended by a mutiny at Waterford, is alluded to in this interlude, which is dated by its reference to ' new lands ' ' called America, because only Americus did first them find,' as having been discovered ' within this twenty years,' i. e. counting from Amerigo Vespucci's voyage in 1497. In 1524 Rastell leased a house in Finsbury, and about 1527 built a private stage in the garden. He was also a deviser of pageants, introducing into them the astronomical features shown in his printer's device. In 1530 a controversy with John Frith as to Purgatory changed his religious views, and six years later he died, while in prison for opposing the payment of tithes to the clergy, a cause substantially the same as Hunne's.

14. *To regard his only intent and good wyll :* 'only' may here be an adjective (= sole), or we may regard it as an adverb transposed, as in Shaks. *Cor.* i. 1. 40—

> He did it to please his mother, and to be *partly* proud.

16. *What nombre of bokes . . . be made and imprintyd.* In 1517 the number of books printed since Caxton began work at Westminster (1476) would scarcely have reached 500. For Caxton is only known to have printed about a hundred, and the other English printers in the 15th century only about twice as many more, while early in the 16th century the output was small.

17. *Of toyes and tryfellys.* Caxton's tastes lay chiefly in the direction of works of morality and devotion, but he printed the works of Chaucer and Gower, and Malory's *King Arthur.* Wynkyn de Worde kept much on his master's lines, but added one or two interludes, some grammars and law books. To call these works 'toys and tryfellys' is unjust to our early printers ; but it is true that they shrank from the labour and expense of publishing editions of the classics or many of the great works of medieval learning. In the *Day Book* of John Dorne, an Oxford bookseller, for 1520, the entries of 'Balets' and Kesmes Kerrells (ballads and Christmas Carols) sold at a half-penny each, show a brisk trade in these 'trifles.'

25. *Our tonge is now sufficient, &c.* Contrast Chaucer, who refuses to descant on Canacee's beauty, in the tone of an artist working in an imperfect material, saying—

> I dar not undertake so high a thing.
> *Myn English eek is insufficient ;*
> It muste be a rethor excellent,
> That couthe his colours longing for that art,
> If he sholde hir discryven every part.

And he complains elsewhere of the poverty of the language which he himself so nobly enriched.

47. *Why shold not than, &c.* Our dramatist is of Juvenal's mind—

> Semper ego auditor tantum, numquamne reponam?

330. *Other causys there are wolde, be lernyd.* For the use of *would* for *requires to*, cp. l. 404—

> For cunnyng is the thynge that wolde be sought.

Also—

> Which would be howled out in the desert air.
>
> *Macbeth*, iv. 3. 194.

And for the omission of the relative—

> I have a brother is condemned to die.
>
> *Measure for Measure*, ii. 2. 33.

See Abbott's *Shaksp. Gram.* §§ 244, 329.

339. *In the myddes of the firmament.* According to the Ptolemaic system the earth was a sphere, immoveable in the centre of the universe, and the entire heavens revolved round it every four and twenty hours. The work of Copernicus (*De Revolutionibus*), which revived the Pythagorean doctrine of the sun as the centre of the planetary world, was not published till 1543.

367. *May be playne.* The earth was anciently believed to be a flat disc of land, surrounded by the river Oceanus. The discovery of its sphericity is ascribed to Thales (640 B.C.).

373. *The eclypse . . . is never one tyme, &c. :* e. g. an eclipse not visible at Greenwich until 6.10 a.m. would be visible at Dublin at 5.55, or a quarter of an hour earlier.

394. *How many myle :* the circumference of the earth at the equator is 24,899 miles, its equatorial diameter 7926.6 miles.

402. *Then myght I say :* i. e. if you were to bring him hither I should have reason to say, etc.

404. *Wolde be sought :* cp. note on l. 330.

417. *Synge tyrll on the bery :* a fragment of a song ; cp. *Ralph Roister Doister*, ii. 3. 36—

> Heigh derie derie Trill on the berie ;

and Browne's *Brit. Past.* i. 2. 'Piping on thine oaten reede upon this little berry (some ycleep a hillock).' [*Murray's Dictionary.*]

430. *Hym :* i. e. Studious Desire.

476. *Nought in regarde .* ..e. the feeling, for what pleasure there may be in it, is nothing to be esteemed, except it be due to me.

517. *Such wyse, me thynketh :* in such a manner that it seems to me my wits grow weary. For the omission of 'that' cp.

> I am so much a fool it would be my disgrace.
> *Macbeth,* iv. 2. 27.

529. *Poynt devise :* exactly, faultlessly ; cp. *As You Like It,* iii. 2. 351 ' Point device in your accoutrements.'

SKELTON'S MAGNYFYCENCE.

John Skelton was probably a native of Norfolk, and born about the year 1460. He studied at Cambridge, and has been identified with a 'Scheklton' who took his M.A. degree in 1484. Lines on the death of Edward IV (1483) and the Earl of Northumberland (1489) were probably among his earliest writings, and in 1490 Caxton describes him as having translated the Epistles of Cicero *Ad Familiares* and Diodorus Siculus. Caxton also mentions that Skelton had been 'late created poete laureate in the vnyuersite of oxenforde,' and the same distinction was conferred on him at Cambridge in 1493. In 1498 Skelton took Holy Orders, and soon afterwards was appointed tutor to the future Henry VIII. Before 1504 he had been given the rectory of Diss in Norfolk. By this time Skelton had engaged himself in literary quarrels with Sir Christopher Garnisshe, with Alexander Barclay, and with William Lily, the grammarian. As yet, however, he enjoyed the patronage of Wolsey. But the poet was a born satirist, and shortly after the Cardinal's appointment as Papal Legate (July, 1518), Skelton drew down on himself his bitter enmity by a series of scathing satires. Of these his *Colyn Cloute* touches Wolsey but slightly, and may possibly have been written before 1518, but *Why come ye nat to Court* and *Speke, Parrot,* are full of bitter invective, and Skelton was obliged to take sanctuary at Westminster against the Cardinal's vengeance, and remained there till his death, June 21, 1529. Another satirical work, an allegorical poem entitled the *Bowge of Court,* was written quite early in his career. Skelton also wrote a charming lament of a nun for her pet bird (*Phyllyp Sparrowe*), and a coarsely humorous description of an ale-wife (*The Tunnyng of Elynour Rummyng*). *The Garlande of Laurell,* a poem of sixteen hundred lines in his own honour, was composed late in life. Of his four dramatic compositions, the *Enterlude of Vertue*, the *Comedy callyd Achademios*, the *Nigramansir* (Necromancer) and *Magnyfycence*, the first and second have utterly perished, the third was seen by Warton (in an edition by Wynkyn de Worde, 1504) in the possession of William Collins, the poet, but has since disappeared, while *Magnyfycence* survives in a folio edition, assigned to the press of John Rastell, with the title : ' Magnyfycence, A goodly interlude and a mery deuysed and made by mayster Skelton poet laureate late deceasyd.'

Magnyfycence was edited in 1908 for the Early English Text Society by Dr. R. L. Ramsay, who suggested early in 1516 as its probable date, while Alexander Dyce, the first editor of Skelton's works (1843), put it four or five years later.

Mr. Dyce entertained a higher opinion of the merits of *Magnyfycence* than the present editor finds it easy to share. It is distinctly inferior to the earlier plays, such as *Everyman*, and except in a few scenes does not tower greatly above *Hickscorner*, *Lusty Juventus*, and the like. The play begins with a controversy between *Liberty* and *Felicity*, who both submit themselves to *Measure* (Aristotle's virtue of the ' mean '), and all three are taken by *Magnificence* as his counsellors. They are superseded, however, by the vices *Fancy, Counterfeit, Countenance, Crafty Conveyance*, and others, under false names. These new advisers bring *Magnificence* to ruin, and he comes under the blows of *Adversity*, and is visited by *Poverty, Despair*, and *Mischief*. Only the entrance of *Good Hope* saves him from suicide, but by the help of *Redress, Sad Circumspection*, and *Perseverance* he is eventually restored to his high estate. Our extract exhibits the fall of *Magnificence* and his visitation by *Adversity* and *Poverty*, and certainly shows Skelton at his best.

1879. *Ye sente us a supervysour.* In l. 1808 Magnificence had appointed Clokyd Colusyon his supervisor, to direct Largesse and Liberty in the management of his affairs.

1885. *Clokyd Colusyon, &c.* A rather distracting feature in these plays is the habit of the evil characters taking to themselves the names of their contrary virtues. Thus Clokyd Colusyon went by the name of Sober Sadnesse, Crafty Conveyance as Surveyance, Counterfeit Countenance as Good Demeynaunce, Courtly Abusyon as Lusty Pleasure, and Fansy as Largesse.

1893. *The letter:* a forged letter by which Fansy had won the favour of Magnificence.

1909. *I make them overthrowe:* 'overthrowe' is here intransitive.

1923. *That folowe theyr fansyes in foly to fall.* For the use of 'to' to express a result, cp. Gen. iii. 22, 'Man is become one of us to know good and evil.'

1938. *I vysyte to bataylle.* In ll. 1927, 1934 and 1951 we have 'vysyte *with*,' and this, as Dyce suggests, is probably the true reading here.

1955. *To spare the rod.* The writers of Morality Plays were devout adherents of this text, see *The Nice Wanton,* which begins by quoting it ; compare also *The Disobedient Child,* who dilates on the cruelties of schoolmasters at great length, and persuades his father not to send him to school, to his own subsequent misery. But the brutality of the schoolmasters of old is well established.

1960. *A fole to his sonne.* For the use of 'to' cp. Mark xv. 23, 'The seven had her to wife,' and Co. 95 'The devyl to his mayster he ches.'

1967. *I am Goddys preposytour :* 'preposytour,' i. e. a scholar appointed by the master to overlook the rest. 'I am preposyter of my boke, *Duco classem.*' Hormanni *Vulgaria,* ed. 1530. [*Dyce's* note.]

1973. *Of him hath frounde.* I can find no instance of 'frown' used with the preposition 'of,' nor does such usage seem reasonable. Dyce queries *on,* and probably rightly.

1989. *Have envy at me.* For the use of 'at' as 'introducing what is at once the exciting cause and the object of active emotions,' cp. Metr. Hom. 78, 'The fende at him had grete envye.'

2006. *For, though you were sometyme a noble estate:* i. e. a person of rank ; cp. l. 311, 'Syr, yf I have offended your noble estate.'

2042. *Shertes of Raynes :* i. e. shirts of fine linen from Rennes in France ; cp. the *Romance of Eger and Gryme,* l. 305—

She gave me 2 shirts of Raines in fere.

2070. *In manus tuas.* The beginning of the text 'In manus tuas, Domine, commendo spiritum meum' (Lord, into Thy hands I commend my spirit), used by repentant criminals at their execution.

HEYWOOD'S THE PARDONER AND THE FRIAR

John Heywood was born in 1497, perhaps at Stock, near Chelmsford. He is said to have studied at Broadgate Hall, now Pembroke College, Oxford. From 1519 to 1528 he was employed at Court as a musician, retiring with a pension of £10. About 1523 he married John Rastell's daughter Joan. After 1528 he earned a living as a teacher of music, and his 'children' acted plays under Edward VI and Mary ; he was again attached to the Court, and his pension was increased. A staunch Catholic, despite his dislike of Friars, Heywood had narrowly escaped hanging in 1544 for complicity in an intrigue against Cranmer. In 1564 he fled from England, was befriended by the Jesuits, and died at Louvain some time after 1578.

Heywood wrote some *Centuries of Proverbs* and *Epigrams*, and an allegory entitled *The Spider and the Flie*. The dramatic or semi-dramatic works which may be assigned to him comprise the Dialogue of *Witty and Witless* (or *Wit and Folly*), first printed by the Percy Society from Harley MS. 367 in the British Museum, and five interludes, four of them printed by his brother-in-law William Rastell in 1533-4, and one (*The Foure PP.*) of which the first extant edition is some years later, though the play itself is probably early work. It has been suggested by Mr. A. W. Reed (see his two articles in *The Library*, 1918), that in *Wit and Folly*, in *The Play of Love* which deals with the contrarieties of lovers, and *The Play of the Weather*, telling of the troubles of Jupiter in bringing the elements into accord with the wishes of contending petitioners, we have Heywood working unaided, while in the three other plays assigned to him we can trace the hand of his uncle by marriage, Sir Thomas More. Of these *A Play between John the husband, Tyb the wife, and Sir John the priest*, takes a hen-pecked husband as its subject, while of *The Foure PP. : a very mery enterlude of a Palmer, a Pardoner, a Potecary and a Pedlar*, the humour is in the rivalry of the first three characters as to which can tell the greatest lie. Of the third piece, *A merry Play between the Pardoner and the frere, the curate and neybour Pratte*, perhaps enough is here printed, from a facsimile (about 1830) of William Rastell's edition of 5 April 1533, to render superfluous any analysis of Heywood's plot. For his conception of the play he was undoubtedly greatly indebted to the characters of the Pardoner and the Frere in Chaucer's *Prologue*, from which he borrows freely. Further illustrations of the ill practices of the Pardoners will be found in Jusserand's *English Wayfaring Life in the Middle Ages*.

9. *To poll nor to shave :* not to bestow the tonsure, for this ceremony, being part of the rite of ordination, could only be performed by a bishop, but to shear and shave people of their money, or, as we should say, to ' fleece' them.

23. *Wylfull poverte.* In the decadence of the Mendicant Orders this vow was evaded by means of an arrangement with the Pope, in whose name the Friars held property.

36. *On the gospell :* cp. Mark xvi. 15, and Luke x. 5-12.

79. *Saint Leonard :* Deacon and Martyr, roasted alive at Rome, A.D. 258.

97. *I com from Rome :* cp. Chaucer's Pardoner, whose mail or bag was ' bretful of pardons com from Rome al hot.'

98. *All and some :* 'each and all'; cp. Chaucer, *Anelida and Arcite*, l. 26—

> For which the people blisful, al and somme,
> So cryden, etc.

104. *These holy relyques.* Lists of impossible or ridiculous relics formed a favourite weapon of satirists against the Pardoners. Chaucer selected as typical absurdities a veil worn by the B. Virgin, and a piece of the sail of St. Peter's boat ; but other lists, and Heywood's among them, are full of medieval light-hearted irreverence.

173-82. *But one thynge, &c.* These ten lines, with some verbal changes, are lifted bodily from Chaucer's Pardoner's Prologue, ll. 377-86.

192. *Pope Leo X :* Giovanni de' Medici, born 1475, raised to the papacy March 11th, 1513, died December 1st, 1521. This allusion makes it probable, though by no means certain, that the play was composed during the pontificate of Leo X, i.e. at least ten years before it was printed.

195. *As departe :* for ' as' used to introduce an imperative, cp. Chaucer, *Troilus*, 522—

> 'For love of God,' ful pitously he seide,
> 'As go we seene the paleis of Creseide.'

262. *Accurst in the greate sentence.* This may refer either to the Final Judgment or to the sentence of Greater Excommunication, but probably to the former.

289. *Yf they fall ones, &c.* There is no reference here to the

subject of Article XVI of the Church of England (Of Sin after Baptism). The Pardoner does not mean that from sins against knowledge there is no recovery, but that the knowledge remains, and there would thus be no help in the Friar repeating his instructions.

300. *And lede them thyther by the purse strynges:* cp. Chaucer. *Prologue,* 225-232 (character of the Friar)—

> For unto a poure order for to give
> Is signe that a man is well i-schrive.
> For if he gaf, he dorste make avaunt
> He wiste that a man was repentaunt.
> For many a man so hard is of his herte,
> He may not wepe although him sore smerte.
> Therfore in stede of wepyng and preyeres
> Men moot give silver to the poure freres.

552. *Ragman's rolles:* a long, unintelligible story. 'Ragman was the name of an old medieval game in which characters of persons, good or bad, were written on a roll, and a string with a seal appears to have been attached to each character, so that when it was rolled up the persons engaged in the game might draw characters by chance.' (Halliwell.) Hence the application to any document with many signatures and seals, such as the roll offering their allegiance to Edward I, subscribed by the Scots nobility in 1296, and always quoted as the *Ragman's Roll.* But *Ragman* or *Rageman* was also a name for the Devil, and this seems to have given an almost uniformly opprobrious turn to the phrase, which is quite in keeping with our text.

557. *Mayster parson gave me lycence before the.* In the ' Merie Tales of Skelton,' the eighth tells us *How the Fryer asked leave of Skelton to preach at Diss, which Skelton wold not grant.*

' There was a fryer the whych dydde come to Skelton to have licence to preach at Diss. What woulde you preache there? sayde skelton : dooe not you thynke that I am sufficiente to preache there in myne owne cure ? Syr, sayde the freere, I am the lymyter [=district-beggar] of Norwych, and once a yeare one of our place dothe use to preache wyth you, to take the devocion of the people ; and if I may have your good wil, so bee it, or els I will come and preach against your will, by the authoritie of the byshope of Rome, for I have hys bulles to preache in everye place, and therfore I wyll be there on Sondaye nexte cummyng.'

Skelton routed this particular friar with a stupid joke about bulls and calves, but the tale suffices to show that the leave of the parish priest was merely asked by way of form and could be dispensed with.

574. *Eggetoles.* Mr. Hazlitt in his modernized edition quite rightly renders ' egoteles' of the text by edgetools. Two lines of Chaucer give the right spelling :

> No flesh ne wiste offence of egge or spere.
>
> Former Age, l. 19.

> But yet it maketh sharpe kervynge toles.
>
> Troilus, l. 632.

579. *The tone :* see CP. (28).

596. *Within your lybertye :* i.e. within the district in which Pratt acted as a constable. Liberty = ' a place or district within which certain privileges or franchises were enjoyed.'

620. *Wylt thou be there ?* is that what you are after ?

635. *More tow on my dystaffe, &c. :* more work than I can get through.

THERSITES.

The original of part of the English play of *Thersites* has been found in one of the *Dialogi* of Jean Tissier de Ravisy, better known as Ravisius Textor, Professor of Rhetoric at the Collège de Navarre, and from 1520 to his death in 1524 Rector of the University of Paris. (See J. Vodoz, *Le théâtre latin de Ravisius Textor*, Winterthur, 1898, and review by Creizenach in Zeitsch. für Franz. Spr. und Litt., Bd. 21.) Comparison, however, of the two plays will show that the anonymous adaptor handled his materials very freely, and added much more than he took. Thus the prologue (ll. 1-21), the punning passage on the two meanings of ' Sallet' (32-69), the scriptural allusions in ll. 91-101, and the English in ll. 109-119, 121-143, 149-167, 171-187, 212-220, 314-322, 410-414, and the greater part (l. 894 to end) of the Epilogue are all new, and the entire episode (524-874) of Telemachus coming to the mother of Thersites to be cured of the worms has no counterpart in the Latin text. The anonymous English adaptor must have been an Oxford man, since the allusion to the ' proctoure and his men ' in l. 154

points to a University performance ; and that in the next line to
Broken Heys, a piece of waste land between the Castle and the
City Walls (my knowledge of this is due to Mr. Falconer Madan),
localizes it definitely in Oxford.   The Epilogue shows that the
text used by John Tysdale (who began to print about 1561) was
that prepared for a performance between the birth of Edward VI
on October 12, 1537, and the death of his mother, Jane Seymour,
on the 24th of the same month.   Whether the play was then
acted for the first time, or whether (as is more likely) an old
play (perhaps originally written for a New Year festival, see
l. 478) was revived with a new epilogue, cannot easily be proved.
The earliest complete edition of the *Dialogi* of Ravisius was
printed in 1530, and it is probable therefore that the English
play was composed subsequently to this.   In *The Library*
(Fourth Series, vol. vii, Sept. 1926) Mr. A. R. Moon, on the
evidence of a long note in verse on *Thersites* in Nicholas
Udall's translation of the *Apophthegmata* of Erasmus (published
in 1542), and of parallels in his *Ralph Roister Doister*, makes
a good case for regarding *Thersites* as an early interlude by
Udall, who was paid £5 for a play performed by his Eton boys
before Thomas Cromwell on 3 Feb. 1538.   Our text, which
gives substantially the whole play save for the Telemachus
episode, is taken from a facsimile-reprint made by Mr. Ashbee
(1876) from a copy of Tysdale's edition formerly in the library
of the Duke of Devonshire.

The play opens with three seven-line stanzas riming ababbcc.
A fourth is begun, but after the quatrain is abandoned for
couplets, which form the normal metre of the play, though
occasionally relieved by quatrains and triplets.   The number of
accents in a line varies from two to five.   Occasionally we get
two lines that might be read as a perfect heroic couplet, e. g.

> If Malvern hills should on thy shoulders light,
> They shall not hurt thee, nor suppress thy might.

But the succeeding line—

> If Bévis of Hámpton, Cólburn and Gúy,

is of a much more typical nature.

5. *In Homer of my actes ye have red.*   The story of the
attempt of Thersites to excite the Greeks against their leaders,
and his reproof and chastisement by Ulysses, is given in the
second book of the *Iliad*, but the Latin Homer is almost
certainly referred to.

20. *To play cowch quaile.* In the sarcastic Envoy to Chaucer's *Clerkes Tale* (E. 1206) a wife is promised that she shall make her husband 'couch [i.e. cower] as doth a quaile.' Shak. (*Lucr.*, 506) uses the verb transitively (' Which, like a falcon towering in the skies, coucheth the fowl below'). The word 'play' suggests that 'couch quail' may have been a cry in some children's game.

21. *Mulciber :* another name for Vulcan.

24. *Office :* officina, a workshop. Tysdale's edition prints the line—

Come forth, of thy office I the desire,

which may be forced into meaning 'I desire the help of your craft.'

30. *Lemnos and Ilva.* It was at Lemnos that Vulcan touched ground when hurled from Olympus, and here was his workshop. Ilva (Elba) is mentioned on account of its iron mines. Mr. Hazlitt proposes to read Ithalia (better Aethalia), another name for Elba, for the sake of the rime to 'galea.'

31. *Condatur mihi galea :* a helmet may be fashioned for me.

37. *A sallet, nowe all the herbes are dead.* For the play on the two meanings of 'sallet,' cp. Jack Cade's speech at the beginning of scene 10, act. iv, King Henry VI : ' Now am I so hungry, that if I might have a lease of my life for a thousand years, I could stay no longer. Wherefore o'er a brick-wall have I climbed into this garden, to see if I can eat grass, or pick a sallet another while, which is not amiss to cool a man's stomach this hot weather. And I think this word " sallet " was born to do me good : for many a time, but for a sallet, my brain-pan had been cleft with a brown bill ; and many a time, when I have been dry and bravely marching, it hath served me instead of a quart-pot to drink in ; and now the word " sallet " must serve me to feed on.'

88. *Hercules.* The references are to the twelfth, first, second, and fourth labours of Hercules, viz. his bringing Cerberus from the lower world, his fight with the Nemean lion, with the Lernean hydra and Erymanthian boar.

90. *Bere so wylde.* Bere, i.e. bear, is a misprint or mistake for bore or boar.

95. *Have take :* cp. l. 102, ' have do.'

116. *Bevis of Hampton, Colburne and Guy.* Three old English heroes. Bevis of Southampton performed his exploits chiefly in Armenia ; Colburn, or Colbrand, was a giant of Danish

O

descent, slain by Guy of Warwick ; and Guy, his slayer, fought the Saracens, killed the boar of Windsor, the dun cow of Dunsmoor, and other ferocious beasts. See Drayton's *Polyolbion*, Books II, XII, XIII, and Copland's chapbooks of Bevis of Hampton and Guy, also Ward's Cat. of Romances, i. 471 sqq.

124. *Lyons on Cotsolde.* 'Cotswold lions' was a cant term for sheep. Cp. Heywood's *Proverbs—*

> He semeth like a bore, the beaste should seme bolde,
> For he is as fierce as a lyon of Cotsolde.

130. *Gawyn the curtesse,* was Arthur's nephew, and was slain in error by his friend Lancelot. Cp. *Carle of Carlile*, l. 28.

> Sir Gawaine was steward in Arthur's hall,
> Hee was the curteous knight amongst them all.
>
> *Percy Folio*, vol. ii.

'Kay, the crabbed,' was Arthur's foster-brother, and a mean, unpleasant person, disliked at Court for his habit of giving nicknames.

132. *Syr Libeus Disconius:* Li Biaus Desconneus (The Fair Unknown), whose name is thus corrupted, was a son of Sir Gawain. He is the subject of an English Romance printed in the *Percy Folio*, vol. ii, of which the French original was written by Renauld de Beaujeu.

136. *Syr Launcelot de Lake.* Lancelot was the son of Ban, King of Benwick, but was brought up by Vivienne, the Lady of the Lake, from whom he derived his epithet.

150. *They geve me the wall:* i. e. as a mark of respect, the road next the wall being cleaner. Cp. Scott's *Fair Maid of Perth*, ch. ii. 'More than once, when from chance, or perhaps from an assumption of superior importance, an individual took the wall of Simon in passing, the Glover's youthful attendant bristled up with a look of defiance.'

154. *The proctour and his men:* the police of an English University.

155. *Broken Heys,* now Gloucester Green, Oxford. Wood writes of it as 'full of hillocks and rubbish.' It would thus offer good cover for rogues to hide in.

181. *Olde purgatorye:* 'olde' is here a 'colloquial intensive' ; cp. *Macbeth*, ii. 3, 'If a man were porter of hell-gate, he should have old turning the key.'

183. *No pardons:* i. e. no pardons such as were sold by Pardoners.

200. *Typhoeus :* a monster with a hundred heads, killed by Jove's thunderbolt and buried under Etna.

201. *Enceladus,* like Typhoeus, son of Tartarus and Ge (Hell and Earth), shared his brother's rebellion and fate.

216. *Whyle pardoners can lye :* see preface and notes to the extract from Heywood.

233. *Let us departe :* i. e. separate; cp. 'till death us depart' in the old form of the Marriage Service.

339. *Cacus,* a giant, son of Vulcan, dwelt in a cave on Mount Aventine, and stole some of the oxen which Hercules had taken from Geryon. For the story of his theft and its punishment see Virgil, *Æneid,* viii. 193-279.

246. *Good godfather :* apparently addressed to some one in the audience. 'Gaffer' (i. e. 'godfather') was till lately still a rustic mode of address to any elderly man.

247. *A man to be borne in the vale :* i. e. of the kind who would be born in a valley. Dwellers in mountainous districts have always regarded their neighbours of the valleys as dull-witted, as the Athenians the Bœotians.

297. *Goddes of battayle :* Bellona.

315. *All to-rent :* tear in pieces; cp. Chaucer, *Parl. of Foules,* 432, 'That with these foules I be al to rent.' So also 'to-torn,' 'to-shivered,' etc.

316. *Syr Isenbrase :* a gallant knight of whom his chronicler tells us—

> He was lyvely large and longe,
> With shoulders broade and armes stronge.

He fell into the hands of 'the Sowdan,' and nearly suffered martyrdom for the faith, but eventually by his prowess gained not only liberty but a kingdom. A romance of 'Syr Isenbras,' with a very humorous picture of the knight on the title-page, was published by Copland.

318. *Robin John and Little Hode.* Hazlitt is probably right in thinking the transposition is intentional.

324. *Busyris :* a king of Egypt, who sacrificed strangers to Zeus, but was slain by Hercules.

399. *I had craked to tymely here :* had boasted too opportunely, i. e. when there was some one at hand to accept his challenges.

421. *Dares.* See Virgil, *Æneid,* v. 362-484, for the story of how Dares, after conquering the boxers of his own age, provoked

the veteran Entellus to fight, and drew down on himself heavy punishment.

430. *They had better have fette me an errand at Rome.* The allusion is probably only to the length of time which any business at the Papal Court was protracted. It is possible, however, to read the line as a threat, inasmuch as appeals to Rome, without the king's leave, were severely punishable under the statutes of *Præmunire.*

470. *Now, where is any mo?* Thersites as yet has not heard the challenge.

477. *Tyll some bloude apeare.* Miles challenges Thersites to try a hit with him (assaye the a towche) to see who can draw first blood, the usual terms of a match with single-sticks or quarter-staves.

503. *There came none in my sight.* If readiness to fight was of the essence of the description of the foe, Thersites certainly did not answer to it, and Mater's reply was strictly accurate.

882. *Cowardes make speake apase :* there appears to be some confusion between ' may speak ' and ' make speech.'

913. *Lovely Ladie Jane :* see preface to this Extract.

BALE'S KING JOHN.

LIFE OF BALE.—John Bale was born at Cove, near Dunwich, in Suffolk, on Nov. 21, 1495. At the age of twelve he was sent to a Carmelite monastery, and subsequently studied at Jesus College, Cambridge. Although in Holy Orders, he took to himself a wife and preached against the celibacy of the clergy. He was protected by Thomas Cromwell, and given the living of Thornden in Suffolk. But on Cromwell's execution he was obliged to flee to Germany, where he remained till 1547. On his return he was made Rector of Bishopstoke, and in 1552 became Bishop of Ossory, where his stringent measures against the adherents of the old religion nearly cost him his life. On the accession of Mary he was again obliged to flee, this time to Basle, where he remained till the close of her reign. Returning to England in 1559 he was given a Prebend's stall in Canterbury Cathedral, and died peacefully in 1563, after an eventful and turbulent life.

Distinguished in a century of bitter controversy for his

unseemly virulence, which earned him the epithet of 'Bilious,' Bale gave the best of his strength to polemics. While in Germany he published an attack on the monastic system entitled *The Actes of Englyshe Votaries*, and also Lives of Sir John Oldcastle, William Thorpe and Anne Askew and the scurrilous Pageant of Popes. Another controversial work, *The Image of both Churches*, appeared while he was Rector of Bishopstoke, and after his stormy experiences at Ossory he printed an account of his 'Vocacyon' to that see. To a different category belongs his *Illustrium Majoris Britanniæ Scriptorum Summarium* (1548), an account of five hundred British authors, which though full of mistakes and largely founded on the labours of Leland, yet entitles him to the gratitude of all students of the history of English literature. But our own interest in Bale has mainly to do with his plays, of which five out of twenty-two mentioned in his *Summarium*, have been preserved. Of these *The three Lawes of Nature, Moses and Christ* has been printed in *Anglia*, Bd. v, and *The Temptacyon of our Lorde* by Dr. Grosart in the 'Fuller Worthies Library.' *A Tragedy or Interlude manifesting the chief promises of God unto man by all ages in the old law, from the fall of Adam to the Incarnation of the Lord Jesus Christ*, and the *Life of John the Baptist*, were published in 1538, and are said to have been greatly admired by Cromwell. They have been reprinted respectively by Dodsley and in the *Harleyan Miscellany*. Plays on 'God's Promises' or 'Processus Prophetarum' have left their traces on each of the four great cycles of Miracle Plays, but Bale's sermon in seven acts has a tediousness all its own. The play on St. John the Baptist, on the other hand, is enlivened by much party spirit and invective against the Old Church.

KING JOHN.—Bale's fifth surviving play is of later date than its predecessors. There is a reference to Darvell Gathyron, a Welsh image supposed to possess miraculous powers, which was burnt in 1538 ; in the Interpreter's speech at the end of act i, Henry VIII is alluded to as 'our late Kynge Henrye,' and the Epilogue, beginning—

> Englande hath a queene, thankes to the Lorde above,
> Whych maye be a lyghte to other princes all,

clearly alludes to Elizabeth. On the other hand, the play is mentioned in the edition of Bale's *Illustr. M. Brytan. Script.*

Summarium, and must therefore have existed in some form
when that work was written. The most probable supposition is
that the first draught of *King John* should be dated about
1547, when Bale returned from abroad, and that it was revised
in the reign of Elizabeth.

The play opens with a speech by the King, in which he
declares his determination to do justice. England, as a widow,
implores his help against the clergy, but their conference is
interrupted by Sedition, who is strongly clerical in his sym-
pathies. Nobility, Clergy, and Civil Order, come in and discuss
the state of the kingdom, and Clergy makes a hypocritical
submission. Dissimulation and Sedition take counsel, and
bring in Private Wealth and Usurped Power to their aid. They
procure the election of Stephen Langton as Archbishop (here
we touch history), and soon after we have the Pope cursing
King John for his attacks on the Church. This closes act i.
In the second act we find the clergy preparing to resist the
King, and then follows our first extract. In a subsequent scene
we are shown John's submission to Pandulph and the hard terms
exacted of him, but Sedition is not satisfied, and procures a
fanatic monk to murder the King. The scene in which he
effects this forms our second extract. But now come on Verity
and Imperial Majesty. The memory of the King is vindicated,
and the play ends with compliments to Queen Elizabeth.

That Bale took his views of King John and his reign from
any previous historian is unlikely. Holinshed, whose *History*
was published in 1577, distinctly tells us that all previous
historians had been prejudiced against the King, and that he
had been obliged to base his facts on the testimony of hostile
witnesses. He inclines to Bale's view, though somewhat doubt-
fully. Yet he can write of John : ' Certeinlie it would seem that
the man had a princelie heart in him, and wanted nothing but
faithful subjects to have assisted him in revenging such wrongs
as were done and offered by the French king and others.'
Quite, too, in Bale's tone is his mention of ' The sawcie speech
of proud Pandulph the pope's lewd legate to King John, in the
presumptuous pope's behalf.'

TEXT.—The text of our extracts is taken from the edition
printed in 1838 for the Camden Society, and edited by Mr. John
Payne Collier, from the unique manuscript, part of which is in
Bale's autograph, in the Library of the Duke of Devonshire.

1273. *Constytute.* For other instances of Bale's use of this unanglicized form of the Latin past participle, see l. 1357, convyt (convictus); l. 1358, interdytt (interdictus); l. 2141, excommunycate (excommunicatus); l. 2144, intoxycate intoxicatus).

1287. *A ster apared crowne.* Bale probably wrote these words intending them to mean 'a star-adorned crown.' But Mr. Bradley has pointed out to me a verse on the martyrdom of Becket in No. 46 of the *Songs and Carols*, edited by Thomas Wright from Sloane MS. 2593, which runs as follows—

> Beforn his awter[1] he knelyd adoun,
> Ther they gunne *to paryn his crown*,
> He sterdyn the braynys up and down,
> *Optans celi gaudia.*

The prefix a- (= ge-, y-) was not very uncommon in the 15th century in the formation of past participles, and 'ster apared' may thus mean 'star-clipped.' In either case the reference is to Becket's head when covered with wounds, and Bale may have intended some kind of pun.

1288. *Upon it :* in consequence of it.

1289. *The Pope's renowne :* cp. 'the king's majesty.'

1292. *Stand with :* is consonant with ; cp. l. 1381—

> Yt stondyth not with your avantage.

1294. *To helpe Jerusalem cyte.* According to Holinshed's account the third, fourth, and fifth clauses of the agreement ran as follows.

3. 'Item that within three years after the nativity of our lord next ensuing he [Henry II] should take upon him the crosse and personallie passe to the Holie Land.

4. 'Provided that if upon any urgent necessitie he chanced to go into Spain to warre against the Saracens there, then so long space of time as he spent in that journie he might defer his going to the East parts.

5. 'Item he bound himselfe in the meantime by his oth, to emploie so much monie as the Templers should thinke sufficient for the finding of two hundred knights or men of armes, for one yeares terme in the defense of the Holie Land.'

1314. *With the more :* i.e. with the additional amount payable as compensation.

---

[1] Misread by Wright as 'aunter'.

1318. *As for ther taxe :* cp. Holinshed, 'Moreover in this year [1207] about Candlemasse the K[ing] caused the 13 part of everie man's goods, *as well of the spiritualtie as of the temporalitie*, to be levied and gathered to his use.'

1320. *Quyck in sentence :* i. e. hasty of judgment.

1340. *As saith Solomon :* 'The king's heart is in the hand of the Lord, as the rivers of water : he turneth it whithersoever he will,' Prov. xxi. 1.

1359. *The bysshope of Norwyche and the bysshope of Wynchester.* Bale seems here to be drawing on his imagination, as the Bishop of Norwich was appointed in 1210 John's Lord Lieutenant of Ireland, and three years later brought 500 men to his aid, while the Bishop of Winchester also is expressly mentioned as having been of the king's party. The Bishops to whom the Pope's bull was directed were those of London, Ely and Worcester, who with Jocelyn, Bishop of Bath, and Giles, Bishop of Hereford, subsequently fled from John's vengeance over sea.

1366. *Any mayntenance pretend :* offer you any support.

1374. *Absolucyon a pena et culpa, and also clene remyssyon.* Absolution a *pœna* removes the penalties imposed by the Church; absolution *a culpa*, or 'clean remission,' removes guilt and reconciles the sinner with God.

1385. *Your curssys we have that we never yet demanded.* Bale, who took a great interest in Wyclif's movement, may have been thinking of the story he tells in the *De Officio Regis* of the man who told his priest that, since excommunication was such an excellent medicine, he might keep it for his own use.

2065. *Wassayle, wassayle.* 'This is probably,' says Mr. Collier, 'the oldest drinking song in our language.'

2075. *Now forsooth and God.* Probably the word 'wold' or 'would' has dropped out of the text (now of a truth if God so willed), or we may suspect Bale of confusing the 'for' in 'forsooth' with the 'fore' in the common oath 'fore or before God.

2076. *Alevyn.* The number appears to be dictated only by the necessities of rime and metre.

2078. *Thu mayest seme for to be :* a polite affirmative ; cp. Ev. 130 and note.

2082. *I am taken of men for monastycall Devocyon :* a very undramatic line, only to be excused as a kind of clumsy aside to the audience. 'Taken of men for' = interpreted by men as, taken as the type of.

2087. *Malmesaye, capryck, tyre or ypocras.* Malmsey or malvoise is a sweet white wine from Malvasia in the Morea ; capryck came from Capri near Naples, Tyre from Tyre in Phœnicia ; hippocras was a mixture of wine, spices and sugar, said to have derived its name from *Hippocrates' Sleeve*, the name for the strainer through which it was passed.

For another list of wines compare the Taverner's speech in the interlude of the *Four Elements*—

> Ye shall have Spanish wine and Gascon,
> Rose colour, white, claret, rampion,
> *Tyre, Capric and Malvoisin,*
> Sack, raspice, Alicant, rumney,
> Greek, *ipocras,* new-made clary,
> Such as ye never had ;
> For if ye drink a draught or two,
> It will make you, ere ye thence go,
> By [Jupiter], stark mad.

Also MM. 470–480, and note.

2090. *I praye the drynke half to me.* The dozen lines that follow show that Bale was not quite destitute of dramatic power. The poor fanatic does what he can for himself, and, when escape is hopeless, repeats the king's 'there is no remedye' in a wistful aside.

The alternative account of John's death given in Higden's *Polychronicon* comes nearest to Bale's version. 'John, kynge of Ynglonde,' he writes, ' diede of the flix at Newerke . . . Nevertheless the commune fame is that he was poysonede at the monastery of Swynyshed of White Monkes. For as hit is seide, he seide ther at a dyner that he sholde make a loofe, that tyme was worthe an halpenny, to be worthe xij^d. by the ende of the yere, yf he myghte have lyve. Oon of the brethren of that place, familier with the kynge, herynge that, ordeynede poyson, and receyvynge the sacrament afore, toke that poyson to the kynge, and so they dyede bothe by the drynkynge of hit.' In Holinshed the monk poisons some of a dish of pears, and knowing himself which to avoid, escapes. In Hardyng the poison is given in plums.

2107. *A masse of Scala Celi.* The reference is to a chapel dedicated to the Blessed Virgin outside the walls of Rome on the road to Ostia, to which special indulgences were attached.

It derived its name from a vision of St. Bernard, who, while celebrating mass, saw the souls for whom he was praying ascending to heaven by a ladder. See *Academy*, 974 (Jan. 3, 1891), where a will is quoted, dated 13 Hen. 7, in which the testator leaves money 'for j honest prest to syng att Rome att scala cely by the space of iiij yeres contynually for the soule of the seid John herwarde,' and references there given.

2110. *Provyde a gyldar, &c.* Another dramatic passage. Bale doubtless wrote it as a part of his polemic against the old religion, but the curious detail of the monk's dream suits well with his fanatic character.

2115. *To the than will offer, &c.* 'Sedition' speaks in contemptuous irony.

2120. *Where became the monke?* Another good touch. The monk has not been mentioned by England, but the King's thoughts turn to him on the word 'betrayed.'

2127. *So many masendewes, &c.* Bale was probably applying his remarks to his own times, of which they were fairly true. Holinshed gives no mention of any such benefactions made by John, but alludes to his building or repairing Beaulieu Abbey and six other monasteries, as a proof that 'he was not so void of devotion towards the Church as divers of his enemies have reported.'

2134. *Voluntarye workes:* cp. the XIVth Article of the Church of England, 'Voluntary works, besides, over and above, God's commandments, which they call Works of Supererogation, cannot be taught without arrogancy and impiety.'

2135. *Sacrifice of the Turke:* cp. Article XIII. 'Of Works before Justification.'

2171. *Report what they wyll, &c.* Bale here shows himself uneasily aware that his view of King John was not the one generally accepted. Holinshed, as has been noted, in summing up John's reign, alludes to the hostility of the witnesses on whom he had been obliged to rely.

ADDITIONAL NOTES.

—◆◆—

[For the majority of the notes here added I am indebted to the printed suggestions of Dr. Kölbing (K.) and those privately communicated to me by Prof. Logeman (L.).]

CHESTER PLAYS.—I. NOAH'S FLOOD.

101-2. *Reade . . . bydde,* read *rede . . . bede,* **K.**

135. *Ys,* B. *ye,* E. *is.*

185. *Kites,* B. *kitte.*

195. *One Godes halfe,* B. *one Godes name, halfe, &c.,* where *name* is plainly a marginal gloss of *halfe.*

209. *Wrawe,* read *wrowe* for the rime, L.

272-3*. A line has dropped out, as K. notes, but I should be sorry to supply it, as he proposes, by [*I hope, however, so it be*]! The rimes show that the whole stanza is corrupt.

285. *Grasse,* B. *treeyes.*

290. *Rouge:* Dr. Logeman proposes *ronged,* 'bitten, gnawed.'

CHESTER PLAYS.—II. THE SACRIFICE OF ISAAC.

310. *Leane,* read *layne,* K.

336. *On thee lighte:* Dr. Kölbing would change to 'come the tille' to rime with 'grylle' in l. 340. But the correction of 'grylle' into 'gryghte' proposed in the Notes is less violent.

446. *Ever,* read *ere,* K.

455. *Bonere,* 'metre would profit by reading *debonere,*' L.

461. *Th[e]*: K.'s correction for *thys* of MSS.

472. *Had broughte us to:* K. would read *had us with bounde* to rime with *confounde.* The text is certainly corrupt, but the emendation is not convincing.

492. *Abyde,* read *tarrye* to rime with *prophescie,* K.

TOWNELEY PLAY:—

28-36, 37-45. Dr. Kölbing proposes to reverse the order of these two stanzas, and the improvement is so great that it can hardly be doubted that he is right.

335. *Twelmothe:* K. would print *twelmonthe,* but the dropped *n* probably represents the pronunciation, cp. York Plays, IX. 251 (L).

521. *That ye wore :* K. would read *that it ye wore*, i. e. that it was you who did it. But Mak has just cried *had I bene thore—*, and the shepherd remarks drily *som men trowes that ye wore.—*

582. *Gaf ye the chyld any thyng ?* the preceding lines read—

SEC. PAST. Mak, freyndys will we be, for we ar all oone.

MAK.   We! now I hald for me, for mendys gett I none.
        Fare well all thre! All glad were ye gone.

TERT. PAST. Fare wordys may ther be, bot luf is ther none this yere.

Dr. Logeman thinks that the gift to the 'child,' which causes Mak's downfall, is the direct result of his complaint 'for mendys gett I none.' It is possible, so I quote the lines, but the shepherd's generosity was more probably inspired by custom.

658. *A qwant :* K. would read *the qwantest*, mending the construction at the expense of the rhythm.

690. *Oure kynde from wo :* K. would prefix *to free* or *to kepe*.

702. *Mener :* K. would read *meke*.

722. *Maker, as I meyne, of a madyn :* K. would insert *born* after *maker*.

COVENTRY PLAY :—

The first version of this colloquy in Heaven is found (see Miss Hope Traver, *The Four Daughters of God*, Bryn Mawr, 1907) in the Midrash, a rabbinical commentary of the tenth century, where it is applied to the Creation. It was transferred to the Redemption by Hugo de St. Victor (c. 1120) and developed (c. 1140) by St. Bernard of Clairvaux in his famous first Sermon on the Annunciation. In this is set forth how Man by his Fall lost Truth, Justice, Pity, and Peace, but that the two latter had compassion upon his misery and entreated the Almighty for his pardon. Hence resulted a heavenly conference : —

'Forte enim interpellantibus tale dicitur dedisse responsum : Usquequo preces vestrae? Debitor sum et sororibus vestris, quas accinctas videtis ad faciendam vindictam in nationibus; Iustitiae et Veritati. Vocentur, veniant, et super hoc verbo pariter conferamus. Festinant ergo legati coelestes, et ut viderunt miseriam hominum et crudelem plagam, ut propheta loquitur, *Angeli pacis amare flebant* (Isa. xxxiii. 7). Qui enim fidelius quaererent aut rogarent quae ad pacem sunt, quam angeli pacis? Sane ex deliberatione communi ascendit Veritas ad constitutam diem, sed ascendit usque ad nubes : necdum plane lucida, sed subobscura et obnubilata adhuc zelo indignationis. Factumque est ut legimus in Propheta : *Domine, in coelo misericordia tua, et veritas tua usque ad nubes* (Ps. xxxv. 6). Medius autem Pater luminum residebat, et utraque pro parte sua utilius quod habebat loquebatur. Quis, putas, illi colloquio meruit interesse, et indicabit nobis? quis audivit, et enarrabit? Forte inenarrabilia sunt, et non licet homini loqui. Summa tamen controversiae totius haec fuisse videtur. Eget miseratione creatura rationalis, ait Misericordia, quoniam misera facta est, et miserabilis valde. Venit tempus miserendi eius, quia iam praeteriit tempus. Econtra Veritas: Oportet, inquit, impleri sermonem, quem locutus es, Domine. Totus moriatur Adam necesse est, cum omnibus qui in eo erant, qua die vetitum pomum in praevaricatione gustavit. Utquid ergo, ait Misericordia, utquid me genuisti, pater, citius perituram? Scit enim Veritas ipsa, quoniam misericordia tua periit, et nulla est, si non aliquando miserearis. Similiter autem e contrario et illa loquebatur: Quis enim nesciat quod si praedictam sibi praevaricator sententiam mortis evaserit, periit, nec permanebit iam in aeternum veritas tua, Domine?' (Migne's *Patrologia*, tom. clxxxiii, p. 387.)

In the end the controversy is referred to Solomon, who ends it by the prophetic solution, 'Fiat mors bona et habet utraque quod petit.'

There are numerous references to this colloquy in heaven in writers of the fifteenth century, and it forms the subject of one of the pictures in some of the French editions of the *Hours of the Blessed Virgin* which often illustrate the Miracle Plays.

MARY MAGDALEN :—

93. K. proposes *pryncipall counsall* or *counsell pryncypall*, so as to secure the rhyme to *ryall*.

113. I might have added the stage direction *Here xal they be servyd with wyn and spyces.*

301. *And :* K. would read *all*, but *and on this wise* refers to the sisters' willingness to remain with Lazarus as their head.

303. *Systyrs : systyr*, K., but the slip may be the author's.

475. *Cleyr :* L. suggests *cleyn* to rhyme with *malmeseyn.*

613. *Syth :* perhaps we should emend to *nyth.*

1136. Two lines, containing a subject to *his* and rhymes to *presens* and *demure*, appear to have dropped out here.

1200-1. *Wavys . . . galows :* L. emends *wowes, galowes.*

1535-37. *War . . . more* may be corrected to *ware . . . mare.*

1538. *Atendaunt : atendaunts*, K.

1548-50. *Gentylnesse . . . blysch* may be corrected to *gentilisse, blisse.*

ADDITIONAL NOTES.

The Castell of Perseverance :—

9. *And schende :* K. proposes *all schende,* perhaps rightly.

54. *Of woful wo :* L. queries *of wo ful wel.*

87. *He :* K. proposes *It.*

105. *As wynde in watyr I wave :* in previous editions, from misunderstanding a correction in the transcript of the MS., I misprinted this line *I wave as wynde in water.* K. proposes *As watyr in wynde I wave,* which is certainly more exact.

125. *Lyven :* transcript reads *lyvng.* K. proposed *lyve.*

179. *Man :* K. ingeniously suggests that *man* may stand for m. an. i. e. malus angelus ! But this rather disregards the metre.

185. *To worthy wede :* K. proposes 'to [me] worthy [in] wede,' but the text ('you are welcome to a good livery') seems simpler unemended.

222. *Slothe :* K. proposes *clothe,* taking 'ryve' as an adjective (abundant).

272. *Man doth me bleykyn blody ble :* K. proposes *man doth bleykyn mi blody ble.*

336. *Fatt :* K. proposes *statt* (state) probably rightly.

Everyman :—

87. *Asketh,* for 'askest,' cp. *spareth,* l. 114.

113. *Gyve :* K. would add *now* to make a rime with *thou.*

133. *Seke,* K. *syte* (be sorrowful) to rime with *respyte.*

243. *Daungerous :* K. would add *y-wis* to make a rime with *is.*

301. *Ende :* K. *endynge* to rime with *mournynge.*

Skelton's Magnificence :—

2043, 2045. *Ye :* K. *yt.*

Heywood's the Pardoner and the Frere :—

608. I follow K. in assigning this line to the Frere, instead of the Pardoner.

Thersites :—

139. *Take :* the sense is 'he who made you a knight never expected that your courage would be put to the proof, and so knighted you recklessly.' K. proposes *forsake.*

182. *Cleane that so :* K. *that so cleane,* perhaps rightly.

GLOSSARIAL INDEX.

ABBREVIATIONS EMPLOYED.

Ch¹. = Chester Play of the Flood.
Ch². = Chester Play of the Sacrifice of Isaac.
Co. = 'Coventry' Play.
CP. = Castle of Perseverance.
Ev. = Everyman.
FE. = Interlude of the Four Elements.
Hey. = Heywood's Parson, Pardoner, and Neighbour Prat.
Hh. = Harrowing of Hell. (Appendix.)
KJ. = Bale's King John.
MM. = Play of St. Mary Magdalene.
Sk. = Skelton's Magnificence.
T. = Towneley's 'Secunda Pastorum.'
Th. = Thersites.
Y. = York Play of the Creation.

Also *adj.* adjective; *adv.* adverb; *num.* numeral; *pr. p.* present participle; *pp.* past participle; *sb.* substantive; *sb. pl.* substantive plural.

The following abbreviations are used in a particular sense:—*v.* verb in the infinitive mood; *pr. s., pt. s.* the *third person* singular of the present or past tense; *pr. pl., pt. pl.* the *third person* plural of these tenses, except when the numerals 1 or 2 are added; *imp. s., imp. pl.* the *second person* singular or plural of the imperative mood.

A.

A, *prep.* of; 'maner a way,' manner of way. Ch². 400.

A *for* he. FE. 529.

A *for* have; *a be* = have been, Co. 97; *God a mercy.* MM. 619.

A, *for* ah. Ev. 304.

A-baffe, *v.* turn aside, waver. MM. 1437.

Abasse, *imp. s.* abase. MM. 1376.

A-baye, *sb.* surrender. MM. 363.

Aboht, *pp.* paid for, atoned for. Hh. 59, 61, 158.

Abowndans, *sb.* abundance. MM. 381.

Abowne, *prep.* above. Y. 87.

Abrode, *adv.* abroad. Th. 522.

Abydande, *pr. p.* abiding. Y. 7.

Abye, *v.* pay for, atone for. T. 283; Th. 275.

Abyll, *adj.* sufficient. MM. 99.

Accompt, *v.* count, reckon. FE. 385.

Acord, *sb.* agreement, judgment. CP. (157.)

Acqueynt, *sb.* acquaintance. Ev. 156.

Adeu, Adewe = adieu, farewell. Hey. 640; Ev. 300, 800.

Adoun, *adv.* down. MM. 492.

Adreade, *pp.* dismayed. Ch². 260.

Aferde, *pp.* afraid. Ev. 251; Th. 197.

Afyauns. *sb.* affiance. MM. 383.

Agane, *prep.* against. T. 29.

Agaste, *pp.* afraid. Ch¹. 227.

Agens, *prep.* against. MM. 61, 91, 590, 632.

Ago, *pp.* gone, past. Ev. 194.

Ai, *adv.* aye, ever. Hh. 147, 233.

Al-beledande, *pr. p.* all-shelter-ing. Y. 21.

Alder, *in phr.* 'our alder,' of us all. Ev. 771.

Alevyn, *num. adj.* eleven. KJ. 2076.

Algatys, by all means, all the same. Hey. 622.

All and some, anybody. Hey. 98.

All-be, *conj.* although. Y. 26.

Almyght, *adj.* almighty. Hey. 68, 547.

Alonly, *adv.* only, solely. MM. 1382.

Als, *adv.* as. Y. 4, 13, etc.

Alys, *pr. s.* ails. T. 515.

Ambes as, double ace, the worst throw of the dice, and so sym-bolical of ill-luck. Hh. 110.

Amytted, *pp.* admitted. MM. 1381.

An, *conj.* and. MM. 69, 81, 286.

And, *conj.* if. Commonly in Ev. and Th., also Co. 113; Ch¹. 204; T. 27; MM. 1548; KJ. 1379, etc.

Ane, one. Y. 103.

Anon, *adv.* at once. MM. 1180; CP. (73).

Anoye, *sb.* harm. Ch². 294.

Anoynt, *pp.* anointed. Ch¹. 75.

Antychrysts, *sb. pl.* antichrists. KJ. 1293.

Anythynge, as an *adv.*, in any manner. Hey. 268.

Apas, *adv.* apace, quickly. Th. 472, 882.

Apere, *v.* appear. FE. 351.

Aply, *v.* apply. MM. 383, 672.

Apon, *prep.* upon. Y. 66.

Appayreth, *pr. s.* becomes worse. Ev. 44.

Appeles, *sb. pl.* appeals. KJ. 1293.

Apply, *v.* apply oneself to. Ev. 278.

Appose, *v.* dispute with. Th. 383.

Approbate, *adj.* approved. FE. 33.

A-prise, *s.* enterprise, achieve-ment. MM. 1133.

Aquyte, *v.* pay. MM. 267.

Aray, *sb.* attire. MM. 1183; CP. (135).

Arayd, *pp.* arrayed. MM. 1143.

Are, *adv.* ere, before. Y. 100.

Aren, have pity on. Hh. 29.

Armony, *sb.* harmony. FE. 466.

As, *sb.* ace. *See* Ambes as. Hh. 110.

Asay, *v.* try, assay. Ch². 251; CP. 120.

As now, *phr.* as things are. Ev. 295.

Aspecyall, in aspecyall, espe-cially. MM. 137.

Assaye, *v.* try, prove. Th. 117, 477.

Asse, *conj.* as. Hh. 168.

Assoyle, *pr. 1. s.* absolve. KJ. 1369.

Assoylynge, *pr. p.* absolving. KJ. 2143.

Asspy, *v.* espy, see. MM. 1392.

Astore, *v.* repair. CP. (310), (336).

Asynyd, *pp.* assigned. CP. (27).

At, *dem. and rel. pron.* that. Y. 73, etc.

At, *prep.* to. Y. 12, 47, etc.; T. 654.

Ather, *pron.* either. Y. 155.

Atter, *sb.* otter. Ch¹. 170.

Atwayne, *adv.* asunder. Ev. 655 *note*.

Atwynne, *adv.* asunder. CP. (300).

Atyred, *pp.* prepared, equipped. MM. 359.

Auctour, *sb.* author. FE. 47.

Aungelys, *sb. pl.* angels. CP. (40).

Autoryte, *sb.* authority. KJ. 1360.

Avant, *imp. s.* avaunt. KJ. 1337.

Avertyce, *pr. s.* advertise, warn. KJ. 1306.

Avoyde, *v.* decamp, run away. Th. 504; avoyded, *pp.* Th. 488.

Avoydyt, *pr. s.* goes out. MM. 276.

A-wansyd, *pp.* advanced. MM. 107.

Awayle, *sb.* avail, profit. MM. 1432.

Awctoryte, *sb.* authority. KJ. 1371.

Awe, *sb.* fierceness, rage. Th. 173.

Awne, *adj.* own. Y. 140.

Awter, *sb.* altar. MM. 1143, 1182.

Ayre, *sb.* heir. T. 615.

Aythor, *conj.* either. T. 529.

Aȝen, *prep.* against. Hh. 134.

B.

Bable, *sb.* a fool's bauble. Th. 129.

Bable, *v.* babble. Hh. 12.

Babys, *sb.* a scribe's error for balys, bales, evils. Co. 21.

Bake, *sb.* back. Hh. 54.

Balates, *sb. pl.* ballads. FE. 39.

Bale, *sb.* evil. CP. (309), (317); Y. 102.

Balk, *sb.* ridge. T. 49.

Ballyd, *adj.* bald. CP. (282).

Balys, *sb. pl.* bales, evils. Co. 21.

Ban, *v.* curse. T. 636.

Bandogge, *sb.* a bound or chained dog, a mastiff. Th. 89.

Barne, *sb.* child. T. 586.

Bawmys, *sb. pl.* balms. MM. 613.

Bayne, *adj.* obedient. Ch¹. 145; Ch². 256, 311, 480.

Baynely, *adv.* obediently, directly; Y. 20, 35, 47, 160.

Be, *prep.* by. Ch¹. 103; Co. 108; M. 55, etc.

Be, *pr. s.* is. MM. 62.

Be, *pp.* been. Ev. 201, 502; Th. 459.

Beane, *adj.* obedient. Ch². 239.

Beare, *sb.* loud noise. Ch¹. 109.

Becum, *v.* become. KJ. 1351.

Bedden, *pp.* bidden. Ch¹. 51.

Beddyng, *sb.* bidding. MM. 62.

Bede, *sb.* bed. MM. 270.

Bedene, *adv.* presently, forthwith, but often without much force. Y. 14. CP. (55).

Bedys, *sb. pl.* prayers. CP. (96).

Beeldand, *pr. p.* living, abiding. Y. 61, 87.

Beelde, *v.* build, make, Y. 35, 47; *pp.* 107.

Beeldyng, *sb.* shelter. Y. 38.

Beestly, *adv.* like an animal. E. 74.

Behaver, *sb.* behaviour. KJ. 1329.

Behette, *pr. 1 s.* promise. Ch¹. 305; *behighte.* Ch¹. 324; *behitte.* Ch¹. 282.

Behetyn, *pp.* promised. CP. (119).

Behove, *sb.* behoof, profit. Ev. 638.

Beledande, *pr. p.* al-beledande, all-protecting. Y. 21.

Belive, *adv.* quickly. Ch¹. 120; CP. (221).

Bemes, *sb. pl.* beams, rays. Y. 50, 68; *bemys.* MM. 623.

Bemys, *sb. pl.* trumpets. CP. (215).

Bene, *pr. pl.* are. Ch¹. 317.

Benesown, *sb.* blessing. MM. 1208.

Benyng, *adj.* benign. MM. 626.

Benyngly, *adv.* benignly. MM. 616.

Berande, *pr. p.* bearing, behaving. Y. 40.

Berar, *sb.* bearer. Y. 36.

Berdes, *sb. pl.* maidens. MM. 51.

Besawnt, *sb.* a gold coin. MM. 1218; *besawntes.* CP. (186).

Besegyn, *v.* besiege. MM. 364.

Best, *sb.* beast. Th. 359; *beste,* Hey. 164.

Besych, *pr. 1 s.* beseech. KJ. 2152.

Besyn, *pp.* beseen. MM. 54.

Bet, *pp.* made amends for. Hh. 172.

Betake, *v.* commit. Ev. 298.

Betande, *pr. p.* flaming. Y. 102.

Bete, *v.* heal, amend. CP. (93); Hh. 224.

Beth, *pr. pl.* are. MM. 1528.

Better, *adj.* bitter. MM. 666.

Betternesse, *sb.* bitterness. MM. 604.

Be-tyme, *adv.* betimes, quickly. Ch¹. 223.

Beyn, *v.* be. MM. 56.

Bicam, *pt.* 1 *s.* became. Hh. 48.

Biggeth, *pr. s.* builds. Hh. 87.

Bihete, *pt.* 2 *s.* promisedst. Hh. 189, 197.

Bi-leven, *v.* remain behind. Hh. 233.

Bitte, *v.* bite. Ch¹. 58.

Bittor, *sb.* bittern. Ch¹. 182.

Blakkeste, *adj.* most black. Y. 101.

Ble, *sb.* colour, complexion, countenance. MM. 68 ; CP. (10), (272) ; *blee.* Y. 5.

Blendyng, *vb. sb.* blending. Y. 5.

Blendyd, *pp.* blinded. CP. (301).

Blent, *pp.* blinded, deceived. CP. (294).

Bleykyn, *v.* turn pale, blench. CP. (272).

Blinde, *adj.* confused, 'blind mater.' Ev. 102 ; 'blind rekeninge.' Ev. 508.

Blo, *adj.* blue, livid. Y. 101.

Blo, *sb.* blow ; 'bemys' blo', the blowing of trumpets. CP. (215).

Bloudsouppers, *sb. pl.* bloodsuppers. KJ. 2169.

Blynne, *v.* cease. Ch¹. 8, 134 ; CP. (299), (368).

Blys, *pr. s.* bless. MM. 276.

Blysoh, *sb.* bliss. MM. 1540.

Blyssyng, *sb.* blissfulness. Y. 5.

Blyve, *adv.* quickly. CP. (111).

Bob, *sb.* bunch, cluster. T. 729.

Bobaunoe, *sb.* pride. CP. (349).

Bobbyt, *pp.* cheated. CP. (294).

Booke, *sb.* book. KJ. 1355.

Boht, *pp.* bought. Hh. 112.

Boke, *sb.* book. Ev. 104, 136.

Bokell, *v.* buckle. Th. 108.

Bokys, *sb. pl.* books. FE. 39.

Bone, *sb.* boon, favour. CP. (41).

Bonere, *adj.* debonair, complaisant. Ch². 455.

Boost, *sb.* boast. Ev. 883.

Borde, *sb.* board. Ch¹. 75.

Bore, *pp.* born. Ch¹. 286.

Borowe, *v.* redeem. Ev. 644; *borwe.* Co. 21.

Bot, *conj.* but. T. 10.

Bote, *sb.* salve, remedy, healer. CP. (169), (309), (317). MM. 921, 1546.

Botte, *sb.* boate. Ch¹. 245.

Boune, *see* bowne.

Boute, *prep.* without. Ch¹. 63, 122.

Bouth, *adj.* both Ch¹. 234, 289.

Bower, *sb.* chamber. MM. 363.

Bowne, *adj.* ready, prepared. Ch¹. 52, 64 ; *boune.* Ch¹. 264.

Bowrde, *sb.* jest. T. 343.

Bowrys, *sb. pl.* bowers. MM. 336.

Bowth, *pp.* bought. MM. 589.

Brace, *v.* bluster. Sk. 1916.

Bragaunce, *sb.* boasting. T. 34.

Brage, *v.* boast, Sk. 1916.

Brast, *v.* break. Ev. 814.

Brayd, *sb.* haste. MM. 1148.

Breade, *sb.* breadth. Ch¹. 29.

Brede, *adj.* broad. CP. (187).

Brefes, *sb. pl.* short notes. T. 668.

Breke, *v.* open, declare. Ev. 224; break through. Co. 9.

Bren, *v.* burn. T. 606.

Brennynge, *sb.* burning. Sk. 1934.

Brent, *pp.* burnt. Y. 107.

Brewe, *v.* brew, concoct, prepare. CP. (309), (317).

Briggen yrons, *sb.* brigandines. Th. 170, 188.

Brighthode, *sb.* brightness. Y. 50, 68.

Bring forward, *v.* escort. Ev. 290.

Brode, *adj.* broad. Ch¹. 26; Th. 120.

Browth, *pp.* brought. MM. 279, 592, 1389; CP. (14), (52).

Brynande, *pr. p.* burning. Y. 102.

Bryst, *v.* burst. T. 640.

Bryth, *adj.* bright. CP. (82); *brygth.* MM. 669.

Bun, *pp.* bowne, ready. T. 764.

But, *conj.* except, unless. Ch¹. 7, 206; MM. 1529.

Buxomly, *adv.* obediently. Y. 40; Hey. 610.

By, *v. for* abye, suffer for. Y. 119.

Bydde, *v.* pray. CP. (41).

Byddyth, *imp. pl.* bid. Co. 87.

Byde, *pr.* 1 *s.* bid, command. Y. 22.

Byde, *v.* abide. Y. 47.

Bydene, *adv.* immediately. Ch¹. 132.

Bygged, *pp.* built, made. Y. 68.

Byggyngys, *sb. pl.* biggings, buildings. CP. (187).

Bygly, *adv.* powerfully. Y. 70.

Byleve, *v.* believe. Ev. 676.

Byn, *v.* be. MM. 623, 1381; *pr. pl.* are. MM. 1533.

Byrnande, *pr. p.* burning. Y. 50.

By-sydes, *adv.* besides. KJ. 1356.

C.

Cabbelles, *sb. pl.* cables. Ch¹. 90.

Cam, *pt. s.* and *pl.* came. CP. (23), (30); Hey. 63; KJ. 1285, 1379.

Capcyouse, *adj.* captious. KJ. 1299.

Carbuckyls, *sb. pl.* carbuncles. Sk. 1928.

Carde, *sb.* 'a sure carde,' a sure proof. Th. 888.

Careful, *adj.* full of cares. Co. 16, 23.

Carshaffe, *sb.* kerchief. Ch². 386.

Cast, *sb.* contrivance. T. 352.

Catyfes, *sb. pl.* caitiffs, rascals. Hey. 590.

Cawdels, *sb. pl.* caudels, possets. Sk. 2034.

Cawth, *pp.* caught. CP. (20), (90).

Caysere, *sb.* kaiser, emperor. CP. (69).

Caytyfys, *sb. pl.* caitiffs, rascals. MM. 58.

Cete, *sb.* city. MM. 473.

Charret, *sb.* car, chariot. Th. 210.

Charys, *sb. pl.* jobs. T. 315.

Cheiste, *sb.* chest, used of Noah's ark. Ch¹. 206.

Chere, *sb.* countenance, demeanour. Hey. 57; Th. 469.

Chered, *pp.* entertained. Ev. 501.

Ches, *pt. s.* chose. Co. 95.

Chesun, *sb.* enchesun, reason. CP. (284).

Childer, *sb. pl.* (northern form), children. Ch¹. 238.

Chriseten, *sb.* Christian. MM. 1547; *Chrisetyn.* MM. 1542.

Chrystene, *sb.* Christendom. Th. 123.

Chyldyrn, *sb. pl.* children. MM. 276.

Chyte, *v.* chide. T. 637.

Clary, *sb.* a sweet wine. MM. 477.

Clatter, *v.* talk, brag. Th. 523, Hey. 10.

Cleffys, *sb. pl.* cliffs. MM. 55.

Clergy, *sb.* science, learning. T. 686.

Clokys, *sb. pl.* claws, clutches. Sk. 1900.

Clowches, *sb. pl.* clutches. Th. 507.

Clower, *sb.* clover. MM. 294.

Clowtes, *sb. pl.* blows. Th. 505.

Clowtt, *sb.* cloth. T. 595.

Clyme, *v.* climb. KJ. 2108.

Clyped, *pp.* called. Hey. 35.

Clyr, *adj.* clear. MM. 600.

Coke, *sb. pl.* cocks. Ch¹, 185.

Colacyon, *sb.* homily, sermon. Hey. 70.

Combred, *pp.* cumbered. Ev. 60.

Comeryd, *pp.* cumbered. Co. 31.

Comliar, *adj.* comelier, handsomer. MM. 67.

Commynalté, *sb.* commonalty. KJ. 2155.

Compane, *sb.* company. T. 53.

Compas, *v.* surround. FE. 366.

Concertation, *sb.* conflict. Th. 365.

Conger, *sb.* a sea eel. Th. 381.

Connynge, *adj.* clever. FE. 327.

Connynge, *sb.* knowledge, ability, power. FE. 21; Hey. 39.

Connyngly, *adv.* skilfully. MM. 1397.

Consell, *sb.* counsel. MM. 375.

Conseyll, *sb.* counsel. MM. 382.

Conseyte, *sb.* conceit, imagination. FE. 44.

Contembtacyon, *sb.* contentation, contentment. FE. 399.

Contene, *v.* hold together. Y. 15.

Convey, *imp. s.* stow away. KJ. 2099.

Conveyed, *pp.* escorted. Ev. 816.

Convyt, *pp.* convicted. KJ. 1357.

Cop, *sb.* cup. T. 735.

Cors, *sb.* body. CP. (188).

Cors, *sb.* course, direction. MM. 1437.

Coryows, probably a transliteration from Greek κύριος, lord: ' Coryows Christe,' Lord Christ. CP. (46).

Cost, *sb.* coast. MM. 1212.

Costes, *sb. pl.* manners. CP. (246).

Coule, *sb.* cabbage. Ch¹. 172.

Counte, *sb.* account, reckoning. Ev. 104, 493, 502.

Courese, *pr. pl.* course, run. Y. 155.

Courtes, *adj.* courteous. MM. 490.

Covetyse, *sb.* covetousness. Hey. 204.

Cowch Quail, ' cower, quail!', perhaps a cry used in some children's game. Th. 20. *See* note.

Cowde, *pt. pl.* could. KJ. 1379.

Cowre, *pr. 1 s.* cower. T. 733.

Crake, *v.* boast. Th. 371.

Craked, *pp.* boasted. Th. 399 ; *pt. s. crakyd,* sang noisily. T. 667.

Crakynge, *sb.* boasting. Th. 880 ; as *pr. p.* Th. 889.

Craturs, *sb. pl.* creatures. FE. 455.

Creke, ' to cry creke,' to yield. Th. 100.

Croes, *sb. pl.* crows. Ch¹. 185.

Crop, *sb.* head. T. 736.

Crosse out, *v.* annul, make no count of. Ev. 800.

Crouche, *imp. pl.* kneel. Hey. 170.

Crousse, *adj.* brisk, lively. Ch¹. 178.

Croyne, *pr. 2 pl.* croon. T. 672.

Crysme, *sb.* a chrisom cloth. CP. 20.

Crystyndom, *sb.* Christendom. KJ. 1365.

Cum, *v.* come. KJ. 1325 ; *imp. s.* KJ. 2101 ; CP. (71), (100), (110).

Cumly, *adj.* comely. Y. 99.

Cunne, *v.* learn. CP. (286); know, be able. CP. (316).

Cunnyng, *sb.* knowledge. FE. 404.

Cunsell, *sb.* counsel. KJ. 1282.

Curlues, *sb. pl.* curlews. Ch¹. 187.

Curssys, *sb. pl.* curses. KJ. 1385.

Curteys, *adj.* curteous. MM. 1137.

Cust, *pp.* kissed. CP. (126).

Cyataca, *sb.* sciatica. Sk. 1982.

Cyte, *sb.* city. KJ. 1274.

D.

Dale, *sb.* dole, bounty. Y. 78.

Dalle, *sb.* fist. T. 744.

Damdpnyd, *pp.* damned, condemned. MM. 636 ; dampned, Ev. 310.

Dar, *pr. 1 s.* dare. T. 303.

Dasters, *sb. pl.* dastards. Th. 17.

Daynetethly, *adv.* finely. Y. 78.

Debate, *vb.* abate, diminish. Th. 412, 469.

Ded, *pt. s.* did. KJ. 1280.

Ded, *pp.* dead. Hh. 111 ; Hey. 631.

Dede, *sb.* deed. MM. 633.

Dedyst, *pt. 2 s.* didst. MM. 672.

Dee, *sb.* Dieu, God ; ' per dee,' par dieu. KJ. 2081.

Deed, *pp.* dead. Ev. 255.

Defe, *adj.* deaf. Ev. 803.

Defte, *adj.* clever, dexterous. Y. 92.

Delande, *pr. p.* dealing, distributing. Y. 78.

Dele, *sb.* part, bit. Y. 158.

Dele, *sb.* pity. CP. (25), (210).

Dele, *v.* deal, have part with. CP. (99).

Delectabyll, *adj.* delightful. MM. 593.

Dell, *sb.* part, bit, whit. Hey. 563.

Delycows, *adj.* delicious. MM. 335.

Delycyte, *sb.* delicacy. MM. 72.

Demden, *pt. s.* condemned. Hh. 56.

Deme, *v.* judge. Co. 124.

Demenour, *sb.* director. Sk. 1887.

Dent, *sb.* blow. MM. 272.

Departe, *v.* (i) depart, go away, separate. Ev. 96. 296; Th. 233. Hey. 549. (ii) divide, e. g. 'depart your goodes' = divide your wealth. Hey. 96. (iii) part with, e. g. departe with your riches. MM. 102.

Depnes, *sb.* deepness. FE. 356.

Deprave, *v.* depreciate, slander. FE. 436.

Dere, *adj.* precious. Y. 11.

Dere, *sb.* harm, injury. Y. 64.

Derand, *pr. p.* harming. Y. 37.

Derworth, *adj.* precious. Y. 92.

Descend, *v.* make descend. MM. 1558.

Desevyr, *v.* separate. MM. 301.

Dessetres, *sb.* distress MM. 104.

Desyplys, *sb. pl.* disciples. MM. 614.

Devoyd, *pr. pl.* go out. MM. 1132, 3.

Devyne, *adj.* divine. FE. 1.

Devyr, *sb.* devoir, duty. MM. 1180.

Dew, *adj.* due, fitting. Hey. 72; *dewe.* H. 314.

Dewes, *int.* the deuce. Y. 92.

Dewks, *sb. pl.* dukes. KJ. 1368.

Dewresse, *sb.* duresse, hardship. MM. 281; *duresse.* MM. 284.

Dewylys, *sb. pl.* devils. CP. (34).

Deyver, *sb.* devoir, duty. Y. 156.

De3e, *v.* die. Hh. 56.

Diewly, *adv.* dewly. Y. 11.

Diffynicion, *sb.* definition, limit. Co. 100.

Digges, *sb. pl.* ducks. Ch¹. 189.

Dighte, *v.* make ready, prepare. Ch¹. 79, 301.

Dilfull, *adj.* sorrowfull. Ch². 313.

Disese, *sb.* discomfort. CP. (219).

Do, *pp.* done. KJ. 1354; Th. 102.

Does, *imper. pl.* do. Y. 156.

Dold, *adj.* stupid. T. 2.

Dole, *sb.* sorrow, trouble. CP. (407); Y. 98.

Dome, *sb.* doom, judgment. Ev. 261, 885, 901.

Don, *adv.* down. MM. 1203.

Don, *pr. pl.* do. MM. 61.

Dore, *sb.* door. KJ. 1377.

Dowtles, *adv.* doubtless. FE. 358.

Douctors, *sb. pl.* daughters. MM. 68.

Dowtter, *sb.* daughter. MM. 79.

Doyne, *pp.* done. T. 291.

Drackes, *sb. pl.* drakes. Ch¹. 189.

Drawe, *pp.* drawn over, covered. Sk. 2040.

Dray, *v.* draw. T. 317.

Dresse, *v.* direct. MM. 1182.

Dreve, *pp.* driven. CP. (407).

Dyghte, *pp.* prepared. Th. 351; Y. 11, 109.

Dylfe, *sb.* devil. MM. bef. 305.

Dylles, *sb. pl.* devils. MM. bef. 358.

Dynt, *sb.* blow. Sk. 1904.

Dyscus, *imper. s.* spread abroad. MM. 1562.

Dyspare, *sb.* despair. Ev. 468.

Dysses, *sb.* decease. MM. 80.

Dystaunce, *sb.* distance, estrangement. CP. (384).

Dystres, *sb.* distress. Ev. 508.

Dyvers, *adj.* several. FE. 49, 328.

E.

Ech, *adj.* each. Ch¹. 191.

Een, *sb. pl.* eyes. T. 295.

Eft-whyte, *v.* requite again, restore. T. 305.

Eftyr, *adv.* after. Y. 125; *efter*, Y. 131.

Egge-toles, *sb. pl.* edge-tools. Hey. 574.

Eke, *conj.* also. Ev. 503; Hey. 208, 210.

Eldyth, *pr. s.* aileth. Th. 480.

Elfe, *sb.* oaf, lubber. Hey. 629.

Elles, *adv.* else. Ch¹. 66, 207; MM. 635; Th. 101, etc.

Elvysshe, *adj.* simple. Th. 74.

Emel, *prep.* among. Y. 146.

Emprise, *sb.* enterprise. CP. (198).

Encomberowns, *sb.* encumbrance, MM. 1533.

Enew, *adj.* enough. Y. 104 (former reading).

Enhanse, *v.* exalt. MM. 611.

Enmys, *sb. pl.* enemies. KJ. 1378.

Enquere, *v.* enquire. FE. 400, Hey 61.

Entendyd, *pp.* minded, determined. Hey. 68.

Entent, *sb.* will, purpose, meaning. Sk. 1946; MM. 670; Ev. **8.** CP. (115.)

Envy, *sb.* ill-will. Sk. 1989.

Es, *pr. s.* is. Y. **2,** 10, etc.; art. **Y.** 74.; am. Y. 9.

Est, *sb.* the east. FE. 351, 355.

Estate, *sb.* class or order in the commonwealth. KJ. 2143.

Everychone, every one. Ev. 840, 856.

Evyn, *sb.* evening. FE. 407.

Excommunycate, *pp.* excommunicated. KJ. 2141.

Exorte, *v.* go forth. Co. 56.

Expoun, *v.* expound. FE. 26.

Exprese, *adv.* expressly. MM. 82.

Exprese, *v.* express, read out, declare. MM. 298, 1184, 1383.

Eylytt, *pr. s.* aileth. MM. 1545.

Eynd, *sb.* end. MM. 599.

Eynes, *sb. pl.* eyes. Co. 25.

F.

Facyon, *sb.* fashion. Hey. 590, 609.

Fade, *v.* make faded. Y. 60, 132.

Fall, *sb.* case, plight. Ev. 514.

Famyt, *pp.* famished. Co. 11.

Fand, *v.* find. Ch². 470.

Fane, *adj.* fain, glad. T. 39.

Fang, *v.* take. T. 679.

Fantasyes, *sb. pl.* fancies. **Y.** **129;** *fantesye.* FE. 43.

Fard, *pp.* feared, afraid. T. 677.

Fare, *v.* go. T. 714; *pr.* **1** *s.* P. (4); *faren, v.* Hh. 175.

Farmerye, *sb.* infirmary. KJ. 2102.

Farne, *pp.* fared. T. 587.

Faryn, *v.* go. CP. (403).

Fastande, *pr. p.* fasting. Y. 80.

Fatherys, *sb. gen. case,* father's. MM. 298.

Fatt, *sb.* fate. CP. (336).

Faver, *v.* favour. KJ. 1330.

Fawor, *sb.* fervour. MM. 483. *fawour.* MM. 638.

Faworus, *adj.* desirous. MM. 673.

Faye, *sb.* faith. Ch¹. 290; Ch². 433; Ev. 298.

Fayer, *adj.* fair. MM. 669.

Fayn, *adv.* gladly. MM. 495; *fayne.* Ch¹. 147; Ch². 252; Ev. 515.

Fayne, *v.* feign. Th. 910.

Fayre, *adj.* fair. Y. 65; *adv.* Ev. 872.

Fayrear, *comp. adj.* fairer. Y. 53.

Fayrhede, *sb.* fairness, beauty. Y. 66.

Faythly, *adv.* faithfully. Y. 19.

Fe, *sb.* possessions. Sk. 1993.

Feare, *sb.* companion; *in fere,* together. Ch¹. 78, 289; Ch². 454.

Fearefully, *adv.* timorously. Th. 387. s. d.

Fectually, *adv.* effectually, truly. MM. 643.

Fee, *sb.* money, goods. MM. 299.

Feft, *pp.* endowed. T. 631.

Felande, *pr. p.* feeling. Y. 79.

Felawe, *sb.* fellow. Ev. 284.

Felde, *sb.* field. Th. 149.

Felescheppys, *sb. pl.* fellowships CP. (311).

Fell, *pr.* **1** *s.* fell, lay low. KJ. 1392.

Fell, *adj.* cruel. MM. 280.

Felyng, *sb.* feeling. Y. 60.

Femynyte, *sb.* womanliness. MM. 71.

Fende, *sb.* fiend. CP. (269); Ev. 883; *fendes.* CP. (303); Hh. 131.

Fende, *v.* protect. CP. (373).

Fendyd, *pp.* prevented, hindered. CP. (303).

Fere, *v.* make afraid. Ev. 253.

Fere, *sb.* companion. Hh. 69 ; *in fere*, together. T. 715 ; *feres*, 53.

Ferre, *adv.* far. Ev. 816.

Fest, *adj.* fast, fixed. T. 20 ; *feste, pp.* fastened. Y. 66.

Fet, *v.* fetch. Th. 185.

Fete, *sb. pl.* feet. MM. 667.

Fett, *sb. pl.* feet. MM. 640, 1.

Fette, *v.* fetch. Hh. 5, 30 ; *pp.* fetched. Th. 430.

Fetys, *adj.* neat, well-made, elegant. Y. 55. 65.

Fier, *sb.* fire. Ch¹. 78.

Fine, *sb.* end. Hh. 11.

Firrette, *sb.* ferret. Ch¹. 175.

Fleete, *v.* float. Ch¹. 281.

Fleetinge, *pr. p.* floating. Ch¹. 225.

Fles, *sb.* flesh. Hh. 194.

Fleshe-likinge, *sb.* fleshly lust. Ch¹. 6.

Fleye, *v.* flee. Ch¹. 293.

Florychyd, *pp.* flourished. MM. 334.

Fludde, *sb.* flood. Ch¹. 84 ; *flude*, Ch¹. 224.

Flum, *sb.* river. Hh. 206.

Flyt, *v.* remove, turn aside. CP. (84).

Flyte, *v.* scold. T. 636.

Fode, *sb.* food. Y. 76.

Fole, *sb.* fool. FE. 407 ; Y. 129.

Folwe, *imp. s.* follow. CP. (100).

Folysshe, *adj.* foolish. H. 213 ; Ev. 872.

Fonde, *adj.* foolish. CP. (225).

Fonde, *pr.* 1 *s.* try. CP. (403).

Fonded, *pp.* tried, made trial of. Hh. 75.

Fondnesse, *sb.* folly. Sk. 1892.

Fondon, *v.* find. Hh. 70.

Fonge, *imp. s.* take. Ch¹. 27.

Fonne, *sb. pl.* foes. Ch¹. 6.

Foo, *sb.* foe. CP. (32).

Forbode, *pp.* forbidden. Hey. 256.

Force, *no force*, no matter. FE. 538.

Fordo, *imp. pl.* destroy. T. 295.

Forgang, *v.* forego. T. 43.

Forgete, *pp.* forgotten. Ev. 86. 94.

Forgeyffe, *pr.* 1 *s.* forgive. MM. 676.

Forleten, *pp.* forego, abandon, Hh. 169.

Forloren, *pp.* altogether lost, cast away. Hh. 239.

Formarryd, *pp.* completely spoilt. Y. 139.

Formaste, *sup. adj.* foremost, first. Y. 4.

Forme, *adj.* first. CP. (1).

Forseth, *pr. s. it forseth not*, it matters not. Hey. 312.

For-shapyn, *pp.* transformed. T. 630.

For-spoken, *pp.* bewitched. T. 624.

Fortaxed, *pp.* overtaxed. T. 16.

Forthi, *adv.* therefore. Y. 131, 136.

Forthy, *adv.* therefore. T. 681.

Forthynkes, *pr. s.* repents, grieves. T. 521.

Forward, *sb.* covenant, agreement. Ch¹. 301.

Forwhy, *adv.* because. Hey. 630.

Fote, *sb.* foot. FE. 473 ; Ev. 293.

Fott, *pt.* 1 *s.* fetched. T. 528.

Fourme, *v.* form. Y. 142.

Fowle, *adv.* foully. Ch¹. 4.

Fowle, *sb.* a fowl. Ch¹. 306.

Foyde, *sb.* child. T. 731.

Foyne, *sb. for* fone, few. T. 292.

Fra, *prep.* from. Y. 95.

Franesy, *sb.* frenzy. Sk. 1958.

Frawth, *pp.* laden. CP. (94).

Fray, *sb.* fear. MM. 280.

Frel-nes, *sb.* frailty. Co. 110.

Frend, *sb.* Ev. 629, 655; *frendes*, Hey. 54.

Freres, *sb. pl.* friars. Hey. 15.

Fro, *prep.* from. Ev. 644.

Froring, *sb.* help. Hh. 164.

Fryke, *adj.* bold, brave. CP (153).

Frynde, *sb.* friend. KJ. 2080.

Frynishe, *adj.* polite, formal. Ch¹. 100.

Frysch, *adj.* fresh. MM. 491.

Full, *v.* foul. Y. 60.

Fullimartes, *sb. pl.* polecats. Ch¹. 170.

Fumishenes, *sb.* irritability. Th. 107.

Fun, *pp.* found. T. 762.

Furst, *adv.* first. FE. 351, 355.

Fygure, *sb.* form, image. Y. 140.

Fygured, *pp.* formed. Y. 65.

Fynnest, *sup. adj.* finest. MM. 484.

Fyr, *sb.* fire. MM. 597.

Fytt, *adj.* fit, pretty. Y. 65.

G.

Gaf, *pt.* 2 *s.* gavest. T. 582.

Gaither, *v.* gather. Ch¹. 73, 77.

Galand, *sb.* galant. FE. 417.

Gan, *pp.* gone. Hh. 4, 47, 74.

Gar, *v.* cause. T. 621; *gares*, pr. s. Y. 103; *gard*, *pt. s.* T. 661.

Gat, *sb.* gate, road. Hh. 218; *gates.* Hey. 43; Y. 155.

Gawde, *sb.* trick. T. 604.

Gayne, *v.* avail. Ch¹. 146.

Gaynesay, *v.* contradict. FE. 384.

Gaytt dore, *sb.* outer door. T. 339.

Gentlery men, *sb. pl.* gentry. T. 18.

Gere, *sb.* array. Th. 198.

Gest, *v.* jest. Hey. 311.

Gete, *pp.* begotten. Ev. 189.

Getten, *pp.* got. Ch¹. 130.

Getteth, *pr. s.* obtains. Ev. 646.

Getyn, *v.* get. MM. 370.

Geve, *v.* give. KJ. 1346; Th. 478; *pr.* 1 *s.* Ch¹. 288; *pl.* KJ. 1341; *imp. s.* Th. 233.

Gevyn, *pp.* given. KJ. 1274, 1339.

Ghoste, *sb.* spirit. Ch¹. 5.

Glad, *sb.* gladnesse. T. 679.

Glase, *sb.* slippery place, difficulty? T. 327.

Gle, *sb.* joy. Y. 82.

Gleteryng, *sb.* glittering. Y. 82.

Glose, *v.* speak smoothly. FE. 41; Hey. 10.

Go, *pp.* gone. Ev. 165.

Gobet, *sb.* piece, morsel CP. (90).

God, *adj.* good. MM. 1203, 1543; FE. 407.

Goddes, *sb.* goddess. Th. 297; *sb. pl.* gods. Th. 310.

Gon, gone, *v.* go. Ch¹. 202; Ch². 227; MM. 1142; Ev. 465.

Gon-stone, *sb.* bullet. Th. 72.

Goo, *imp. s.* go. MM. 1145.

Good, *sb.* goods. Ev. 121.

Goon, *v.* go. CP. (72).

Goote, *sb.* goat. Ch¹. 158.

Gore, *sb.* a gusset, 'under gore,' under the clothes, privily. CP. (312).

Gore, *sb.* filth. CP. (338).

Gost, *sb.* spirit. MM. 601, 1211; CP. (47).

Gostly, *adv.* spiritual. MM. 609.

Gothe, *v.* goes. Ev. 806, 835.

Gowlande, *pr. p.* howling. Y. 103.

Gramercy, many thanks. Ev 221, 861.

Gravyte, *sb.* seriousness. FE. 28.

Grawous, *adj.* grievous. MM. 293.

Gre, *sb.* pleasure; *take in gre*, take in good part. Sk. 2005.

Grede, *v.* cry aloud. CP. (285).

Grestle, *sb.* young pig. Th. 391.

Grete, *v.* weep. CP. (320); Hh. 82.

Grete, *adj.* great. Y. 1.

Gretter, *comp. adj.* greater. T. 36.

Gretynge, *sb.* weeping. CP. (314).

Grevys, *sb. pl.* groves. CP. (59).

Grill, *v.* grumble. Ch¹. 46.

Grith, *sb.* peace, treaty. Hh. 126.

Grocchyn, *vb.* grumble, murmur. CP. (181); *grochynge*, murmuring, groaning. CP. (312).

Groge, *sb.* grudge. KJ. 1298, 1332.

Grom, *sb.* man. MM. 489.

Grome, *sb.* for Groine, a port in Spain. MM. 478.

Grose, *adj.* gross, substantial. FE. 345, 357.

Grotes, *sb. pl.* groats. Hey. 22, 93, 132.

Grucche, *v.* murmur, grumble. CP. (47).

Grudge, *v.* grumble. Sk. 2016.

Grunde, *sb.* ground. Y. 74.

Grylle, *v.* be terrified. Ch². 340.

Grysly, *adj.* horrible, dreadful. CP. (47); *adv.* CP. (175).

Guardon, *v.* guerdon, reward. Hey. 200.

Gunne, *pp.* begun. CP. (314).

Gydde, *v.* guide. MM. 601.

Gyde, *sb.* guide. Ev. 522, 780.

Gyde, *imp. s.* guide. MM. 1440.

Gyf, *imp. pl.* give. Y. 147; *pr. 1 s.* Y. 160.

Gyldar, *sb.* gilder. KJ. 2110.

Gyler, *sb.* beguiler. T. 724.

Gylt, *sb.* guilt. CP. (325).

Gynnyt, *pr. s.* begins. MM. 621.

Gyrnande, *pr. p.* grinning. Y. 103.

Gyrth, *v.* protect. Y. 133.

H.

Habergyn, *sb.* coat of mail. Th. 104, 108, 111.

Hade, *pt.* I *s.* had. Ch¹. 99.

Haile, *sb.* health. Ch¹. 198.

Hakt, *pt. s.* 'chopped away at,' and so 'had his will of,' 'mastered'? T. 668.

Hale, *sb.* tent, pavilion. CP. (170).

Hall, *v.* haul, drag. Th. 493.

Hals, *sb.* neck. CP. (156).

Haly, *adv.* wholly. Y. 27.

Hamer, *sb.* hammer. Ch¹. 62.

Hamyd, *pp.* crippled. T. 15.

Han, *v.* have. MM. 509; *pt.* Co. 35.

Happe, *v.* wrap. Sk. 2063.

Happyd, *pp.* circumstanced. Sk. 2010; wrapped up. T. 1.

Harbarow, *sb.* harbourage. MM. 1398.

Hard, *pt.* I *s.* heard. T. 658, 667; *harde, pt.* I *s.* KJ. 2084; *pp.* Hey. 257.

Hardely, *adv.* surely. Hey. 605.

Harnes, *sb.* armour, accoutrements. Th. 9.

Harnessed, *pp.* armed. Th. 16.

Harrowe, *interj.* a cry for help. Y. 97.

Hart, *sb.* heart. MM. 74, 640; FE. 501; *harte.* Ch¹. 234; KJ. 2098; *hartt.* MM. 1138; *harts, hartys,* hearts. KJ.1340. Hey. 571.

Hast, *sb.* haste. MM. 382.

Hast, *v.* hasten. Ev. 141; *imp. s.* MM. 1384.

Hat, *pr. s.* has. MM. 602.

Hatt, *v.* be called. T. 614.

Haunt, *v.* frequent. Ev. 273.

Havi, have I. Hey. 43.

Haveth, *pr. s.* has. Hh. 152.

He, *pron. pl.* they. Hh. 53, 55, MM. 366, 370.

Heale, *sb.* health. Hey. 8.; *hele.* Hey. 272.

Heare, *adv.* here. Ch¹. 156, 180, etc.

Hearnes, *sb. pl.* herons. Ch¹. 182.

Hed, *sb.* head. MM. 1530; FE. 427; *headake,* headache. Hey. 163.

Hede, *sb.* head. FE. 411.

Hede, *sb.* heed. CP. (138). Hey. 54.

Heder, *adv.* hither. FE. 401.

Hedibus, *sb.* comic Latinized dative plural for 'heads'. Th. 133.

Hee, *adj.* high. T. 605.

Hefne, *sb.* heaven. Co. 9.

Hegges, *sb. pl.* hedges. MM. 1198.

Hegheste, *sup. adj.* highest. Y. 27.

Heiste, *sb.* promise. Ch¹. 305.

Hek, *sb.* inner door. T. 316.

Heldand, *pr. p.* descending, alighting. Y. 6; *heledande.* Y. 95.

Hele, *sb.* health. CP. (96); Ev. 648.

Helowes, *sb. pl.* hallows, saints. Hey. 154.

Hely, *adj.* holy. KJ. 1308.

Hem, *pron.* them. MM. 57, 91, 670; CP. (375); Hh. 6.

Hend, *adj.* meek, gentle. Ch¹. 276.

Henne, *adv.* hence. Hh. 146.

Hens, *adv.* hence. Ev. 130, 862; Hey. 94; Th. 400; MM. 109, 1535.

Hent, *pp.* seized. CP. (253).

Her, *adv.* here. MM. 66, 643, 1396, 1597; CP. (31); Hh. 140, 143.

Her, *sb.* hair. MM. 669.

Here, *poss. pron.* their. Co. 28, 36; CP. (266).

Here, *v.* hear. Ev. 19, 236, 634, 667, 867; Hey. 62, 65, 210, 314, 555; T. 298.

Herers, *sb.* hearers. Ev. 903.

Heres, *sb. pl.* hairs. Hey. 539.

Herre, *sb.* hair. MM. 640, 1.

Herynge, *sb.* hearing. FE. 467.

Herwe, *sb.* harrow. Hh. 145.

Hese, *poss. pron.* his. Co. 45.

Het, *pr.* 1 *s.* promise. Ch². 451.

Hete, *pt.* 2 *s.* orderedst. Hh. 224.

Hether, *adv.* hither. Hey. 63.

Hetyng, *sb.* promise. T. 728.

Hevede, *pt. s.* had. Hh. 7.

Heviar, *comp. adj.* heavier. MM. 272.

Hevynes, *sb.* heaviness. MM. 488; Ev. 505.

Hey, *adj.* high. MM. 107.

Heydes, *sb. pl.* heads. T. 294.

Heyle, *imp. s.* hail. MM. 381.

Heynd, *adj.* gentle. T. 649.

Heys, *sb.* hedges. Th. 155.

Heȝe, *adj.* high. Hh. 31.

Hie, *imp. s.* hasten. Ch¹. 115.

Hied, *pt. pl.* hastened. Ch¹. 223.

Hight, *sb.* height. T. 295, 310.

Hihte, *pt.* 1 *s.* ordered. Hh. 227.

Hof, *interj.* ho! MM. 491.

Hol, *adj.* whole. Th. 145; MM. 677.

Hole, *adj.* whole. Ev. 632; FE. 377; Hey. 306; Th. 192.

Holsome, *adj.* wholesome. KJ. 2087.

Holy, *adv.* wholly. CP. (192); Ev. 525.

Honde, *sb.* hand. CP. (228); Ev. 777.

Hondon, *sb. pl.* hands. Hh. 54.

Hoost, *sb.* host. Ev. 884.

Horse, *adj.* hoarse. Sk. 1930.

Hote, *sb.* heat. Y. 97.

Hou, how. Hh. 70.

How, *sb.* a yearling sheep. T. 301.

Howe, *interj.* ho! Sk. 1979.

Hower, *sb.* hour, season. KJ. 1349.

Hows, *sb.* house. MM. 618, 620, 622.

Hunder, *adv.* under. T. 24.

Hur, *pron.* her. MM. 378, 380.

Hy, *v.* hasten. MM. 1391; Ev. 180.

Hydande, *pr. p.* hiding. Y. 6.

Hyder, *adv.* hither. Ev. 665, 669, 819; Hey. 4, 67, 255.

Hye, *v.* hasten. Ev. 159, 813; *imper. pl.* Ch¹. 49.

Hye, *adj.* high. MM. 617; CP. (239); *on hye*, aloud. FE. 543.

Hyed, *pt. s.* hastened. Hey. 67.

Hyen, *v.* hasten. CP. (239).

Hyest, *sup. adj.* highest. Ev. 799.

Hyght, *pr.* 1 *s.* am called. Sk. 1908; Ev. 660; *pp. act.* Y. 112.

Hyng, *v.* hang. T. 319.

Hyrre, *pron.* her. MM. 377.

Hys, *poss. pron.* his. KJ. 2133.

I.

I, *prep.* in. MM. 508.

Ich, *pron.* I. Hh. 65.

Iche, *adj.* each. Ch¹. 91, 92, 279.

Ichone, each one. Ch¹. 108.

Icoren, *pp.* chosen. Hh. 240.

Iich, *adj.* each. Ch¹. 155.

Ile, *sb.* isle. Y. 26.

Ilke, *adj.* each. Y. 125, 158.

Incontynent, *adv.* incontinently, at once. Ev. 667.

Indeure, *v.* endure. MM. 292; *induer*, MM. 308.

Indifferent, *adj.* equal, fair. Th. 486.

Indyte, *v.* indite, write. FE. 39.

Ingendryd, *pp.* engendered. FE. 332.

Inoh, *adv.* enough. Hh. 51.

Inquere, *v.* enquire, search out. Th. 467.

Interdytt, *pp.* interdicted. KJ. 1358.

Intoxycate, *pp.* poisoned. KJ. 2144.

Invy, *sb.* envy. MM. 362.

Invyron, *prep.* round about. FE. 2.

Inwyttissymus, *adj.* invictissimus, most unconquered. MM. 285.

Iwis, *adv.* certainly. Hh. 57; *iwys,* Y. 81; CP. (350); MM. 489; KJ. 1393; *iwysse,* Ch². 438.

J.

Jentylnesse, *sb.* gentleness. MM. 105, 114.

Joparde, *v.* jeopard, risk. Th. 435.

Joynte, *sb.* joint, limb. Th. 435.

K.

Kayser, *sb.* Cæsar, Emperor. CP. (188).

Kende, *sb.* kind, nature. CP. (1).

Kenne, *v.* show. CP. (383).

Kente, *pp.* taught. Ch². 222.

Kepe, *sb.* heed, care. Hey. 106.

Kinde, *sb.* nature. Ch¹. 92.

Knakt, *pt. s.* performed cleverly. T. 670.

Knet, *pp.* knitted, compounded of. CP. (246).

Knett, *v.* knit. MM. 58.

Knocked, *pp. knocked bread,* bread made of flour only roughly ground. Th. 245.

Knyth, *sb.* knight. CP. (69); *Knythtes, pl.* MM. 673; *Knyttes.* MM. 112.

Kylt, *pp.* killed. CP. (323).

Kynd, *sb.* nature. MM. 94; *kynde.* Y. 99; CP. (245); T. 602, 690; kinship. Ev. 315.

Kynnesmen, *sb. pl.* kinsmen. Ev. 313.

L.

Lache, *v.* catch. CP. (347).

Lackes, *sb. pl.* lakes. Ch¹. 190.

Laghe, *v.* laugh. T. 621.

Langyd, *pt. s.* longed, desired. T. 42.

Lante, *pp.* lent, given. CP. (61).

Lappyd, *pp.* lapped, enveloped. T. 4.

Lastand, *pr. p.* lasting. Y. 24, 46.

Lat, *imp. s.* let, do. Y. 46, 120.

Late, *v.* let. Co. 101; CP. (96), (222).

Lawe, *adj.* low. Y. 122.

Lay, *v.* wager. T. 304.

Layser, *sb.* leisure. Ev. 101.

Laytheste, *sup. adj.* most loathsome. Y. 100.

Lazars, *sb.* lepers. Sk. 1930.

Leane, *v.* conceal. Ch². 283, 310.

Lease, *comp. adj.* less. Ch¹. 287.

Led, *sb.* lead. MM. 272; a sounding-lead. MM. 1440; *lede,* a leaden seal. Hey. 71, 195.

Leden, *sb.* speech. Ch¹. 191.

Lef, *imp. s.* leave. Hh. 106.

Lefe, *v.* believe. T. 31.

Leffe, *adj.* glad. Ch¹. 99.

Leiste, *sb.* pleasure, desire. Ch¹. 207.

Lekyng, *adj.* liking, pleasing. MM. 617.

Lele, *adj.* leal, loyal. T. 532.

Lely, *adv.* leally, truly. Y. 77.

Lende, *v.* abide, linger. Y. 53; CP. 7.

Lende, *pp.* lent. Ev. 164.

Lende, *sb.* loin. CP. (5).

Lengar, *comp. adj.* longer. MM. 276; *lenger.* Co. 100, 131, 849.

Lenges, *imp. pl.* remain. Ch². 226.

Lengest, *sup. adj.* longest. MM. 309.

Lengore, *comp. adj.* longer. Hh. 140.

Lent, *pp.* granted, given. CP. (116).

Lere, *v.* learn. T. 299.

Lere, *sb.* countenance, features. CP. (190).

Les, *sb.* deceit. MM. 83.

Lese, *v.* lose. FE. 387.

Lesen, *v.* loose, release. Hh. 36, 213.

Leser, *sb.* leisure. FE. 390.

Lest, *sup. adj.* least. FE. 383.

Leste, *v.* last. Co. 65.

Let, *v.* hinder, delay. Hey. 273; Ch². 407; *pp.* hindered. CP. (337).

Lete, *v.* let, allow. Co. 8; CP. (363); *imp. s.* KJ. 2114; lett bren, cause to burn. T. 606.

Lette, *v.* refrain, abstain from doing. CP. (121); *imp. pl.* ye ne lette. Ch¹. 283.

Lettyth, *pr. s.* hinders; *lettyth of audience,* hinders from being heard. Hey. 261.

Leve, *v.* believe. CP. (88); *leven,* Hh. 232.

Leve, *v.* live. CP. (401); *leven.* MM. 65; levyn. Co. 11; CP. (131), (394); *levyth,* lives. CP. (394).

Leve, *adj.* dear. Hh. 16, 166; *lever,* more willingly. Sk. 2066.

Leve, *imper. s.* leave. MM. 595.

Leve, *sb.* leave, permission, FE. 428; Hh. 173.

Levedest, *pt.* 2 *s.* believedst. Hh. 60.

Levyn, *sb.* lightning. T. 661.

Lewd, *adj.* common, simple. T. 718.

Lewtye, *sb.* loyalty, faith. Ch¹. 276.

Ley, *imper. s.* lay. MM. 492.

Lidderyns, *sb. pl.* rascals. Sk. 1945.

Lighte, *pt. s.* alighted. Hh. 31.

Linge, *v.* linger. Ch¹. 5, 297.

Litterature, *sb.* knowledge of letters, learning. Hey. 192.

Lofly, *adj.* lovely. CP. (141).

Loke, *v.* look. Ev. 503; *imp. s.,* Hey. 42.

Lokys, *pr. s.* looks. Sk. 1899.

Lond, *sb.* land. MM. 1430; KJ. 1327; *londe.* CP. (70); *londes, pl.* KJ. 1312.

Longyth, *pr. s.* belongs. MM. 1185, 1207.

Lore, *sb.* teaching. Ch¹. 127; Hey. 49.

Lore, *pp.* lost. Co. 58; Th. 459.

Lorne, *pp.* lost. T. 650; Y. 108.

Lose, *imp. s.* loose. Hey. 538.

Losell, *sb.* rascal. Sk. 1905; *losyll,* Sk. 192.

Lothe, *adj.* loathsome. Ev. 268; Hh. 154, 175.

Louerd, *sb.* lord. Hh. 103, 149, 165.

Loven, *pr. pl.* love. Ch¹. 205.

Lowte, *v.* bow before. Y. 24, 46.

Loyn, *pp.* lain. Co. 3. (MS.)

Luf, *sb.* praise. Y. 46, 57.

Lufly, *adj.* lovely. Y. 43.

Lurden, *sb.* clown. Sk. 1914; Y. 108; *lurdans,* Y. 120.

Lust, *sb.* pleasure. CP. (125), (217); Sk. 1912.

Lybertye, *sb.* liberty, jurisdiction. Hey. 596.

Lyche, *adj.* like. CP. (70), (114).

Lydderyns, *sb. pl.* rascals. Sk. 1945.

Lye, *v.* used transitively for ' lay '. Hey. 541.

Lyf, *adj.* glad. FE. 424.

Lyfelod, *sb.* livelihood. MM. 87, 99.

Lyg, *pr.* 2 *pl.* lie. T. 291, 346.

Lyges, *pr. s.* lies. T. 655.

Lyght, *pp.* delivered. T. 348.

Lykes me, *v. impers.* I like. Y. 159.

Lykyng, *sb.* delight. CP. (125), (217).

Lyth, *sb.* light. CP. (337).

Lyther, *adj.* bad, inactive. Sk. 2066.

Lythly, *adv.* lightly. MM. 1146.

Lyvys, *sb. gen.* life's. CP. (141).

Lyyn, *v.* lie. MM. 597.

M.

Mad, *pp.* made. Co. 14; *pt. s.* MM. 1386.

Made, *adj.* mad. Ev. 168.

Maintenance. *sb.* support. T. 35.

Maiste, *pr.* **2** *s.* makest. Ch¹. 110.

Maiste, *pr.* 2 *s.* mayst. Ch¹. 267.

Maistre, *sb.* master. KJ. 2166.

Makar, *sb.* maker, creator. MM. 632.

Make, *sb.* mate, partner. Ch¹. 119.

Males, *sb.* malice. Co. 45.

Malmsine, *sb.* Malmsey wine. Ch¹. 233.

Mament, *sb.* Mahomet. MM. 1545, 1557.

Mammockes, *sb. pl.* leavings, fragments. Sk. 2035.

Maner, *sb.* manner. Ev. 185 ; no maner wyghte, no kind of man. Hey. 159 ; cp. 167.

Mankin, *sb.* mankind. Hh. 112.

Mannis, *sb. gen.* mans. MM. 364; *mannys.* KJ. 1328.

Manrede, *sb.* homage, vassalage. Hh. 90.

Manteyn, *pr. pl.* maintain. T. 632.

Marde, *pp.* marred, ruined. Hey. 209.

Markide, *pp.* designed, noted. Y. 49, 58.

Marmoll, *sb.* ulcer. Sk. 1932.

Marrande, *pr. p.* marring. Y. 92.

Marters, *sb. pl.* martyrs. KJ. 2170.

Mary, *sb.* by the Blessed Virgin, an oath. FE. 487.

Mas, *sb.* the Mass. Hey. 211.

Mase, *sb.* mace. Th. 323.

Masendewes, *sb. pl.* maisonsdieu, houses of charity. KJ. 2127.

Massenger, *sb.* messenger. KJ. 1304.

Mastry, *sb.* mastery, masterful behaviour. T. 30.

Mater, *sb.* matter. Ev. 102, 248.

Mawt, *sb.* Malta. MM. 476.

May, *sb.* maid, virgin. T. 695.

Mayne, *sb.* main, strength. Y. 92.

Mayntenance, *sb.* support. KJ. 1366.

Mays, *pr. s.* makes. T. 30.

Maystries, *sb.* masteries ; *to try maystries,* to try conclusions. Th. 515.

Meanye, *sb.* company. Ch¹. 113, 265 ; Ch². 225.

Meche, *adj.* great. Co. 28, 68.

Mede, *sb.* meed, reward. T. 679 ; CP. (329) ; *to medys,* by way of reward. CP. (197).

Medylle, *sb.* middle. T. 610.

Meete, *adj.* meet, fitting. Ch¹. 94.

Meke, *v.* make meek. Co. 8.

Mekill, *adj.* great. Y. 41.

Mekly, *adv.* meekly. MM. 106.

Mekyl, *adj.* much. CP. (249).

Mele, *sb.* meal. CP. (97).

Mell, *v.* meddle. Hey. 589.

Memoryall, *sb.* memory, thought. MM. 1134.

Mende, *sb.* mind. Co. 7.

Mene, *pr.* 1 *s.* mean, think. T. 647. FE. 408.

Mener, *adj.* handsome. T. 702.

Meneye, *sb.* company. T. 357.

Mente, *pt. pl.* thought. Y. 139.

Menytt, *pr. s.* meaneth. MM. 1544.

Merakyll, *sb.* miracle. MM. 1551.

Mercyabyl, *adj.* merciful. Co. 107.

Merour, *sb.* mirror. Y. 34.

Merrorys, *sb. pl.* mirrors, i. e. shining qualities. MM. 73.

Mery, *adj.* merry. FE. 416.

Merys, *pr. s.* grows merry. T. 725.

Mesels, *sb. pl.* lepers. KJ. 2116.

Messe, *sb.* the sacrament of the Mass. FE. 448.

Messuer, *imper. s.* measure. Ch¹. 28.

Mesure, *sb.* reward. MM. 296.

Met, *adj.* meet. CP. (250), (333).

Mete, *sb.* meat. T. 321.

Mete, *adj.* meet, fitting. Th. 38.

Meve, *v.* move. MM, 1134 ; *mevyd, pp.* Co. 43.

Meynye, *sb.* company. CP. (77).

Michel, *adj.* much, great. Hh. 7, 47, 67, 119.

Mightefull, *adj.* powerful. Y. 58.

Mightes, *sb. pl.* powers. Y. 33.

Mo, *comp. adj.* more. T. 686;

FE. **22**; Hey. 616; Th. 66, 467, 470; Sk. 1978.

Moche, *adv.* much. KJ. 1326.

Mockes, *sb. pl.* jests. Hey. 603.

Mode, *sb.* mood. T. 5, 14.

Moder, *sb.* mother. Hh. 193.

Moe, *comp. adj.* more. Ch¹. 122.

Molde, *sb.* mould, earth. CP. (154).

Mon, *sb.* man. Ch¹. 275. *mone,* dative. Ch¹. 5.

Mon, *pr.* 2 *pl.* may. Ch¹. 284.

Mone, *pr. pl.* may. Ch¹. 129, cp. Ch¹. 66; Ch². 463.

Mone, *sb.* moon. T. 673; FE. 374; Hey. 555.

Mone, *v.* moan. KJ. 2125; *sb.* T. 47; Ev. 461.

Moneth, *sb.* month. Hh. 207.

Mony, *sb.* money. MM. 487.

Mop, *sb.* young creature. T. 735.

Moo, *comp. adj.* more. MM. 477.

Mot, *pr.* 2 *pl.* must. MM. 107, 276.

Mow, *v.* may. Co. 64.

Moyn, *sb.* moon. T. 289.

Mustyr, *v.* show. Y. 145.

Myche, *adv.* much. FE. 505; *adj.* MM. 631.

Myddel earde, *sb.* the middle region, the world. Ch². 267.

Myddes, *sb.* midst. FE. 361.

Mykyll, *adj.* great. MM. 1140.

Myle, *sb.* mile. FE. 394.

Myn, *pr.* 1 *s.* mind. T. 685, cp. 756.

Myne, *v.* mind, think. Ch¹. 272.

Mynstrelly, *sb.* minstrelsy. MM. 1141.

Mynyshe, *v.* diminish, lessen. Ev. 878.

Myrkness, *sb.* darkness. Y. 146.

Mys, *v.* fail. Y. 83.

Myschevyd, *pp.* hurt. Co. 76.

Mytes, *sb. pl.* mights, powers. MM. 632, 1210.

Myth, *sb.* might. MM. 1140, 1541; *v.* CP. (151).

N.

Na, *adv.* no. Hh. 66.

Nacked, *adj.* naked. Ch². 279.

Nam, *pt. s.* took. Hh. 39.

Nan, *adj.* none. Hh. 77.

Nas, *for* ne was. Hh. 9.

Nat, *adv.* not. MM. 57, etc.

Natt, *adv.* not. MM. 1431.

Nawther, *conj.* neither. T. 514.

Ne, *conj.* nor. Ch¹. 18, etc.

Neemly, *adv.* nimbly. T. 282.

Ner, *conj.* nor. CP. (121).

Ner, *adv.* nearly. MM. 293, 482.

Nere, *for* ne were. Hh. 14.

Nerehande, nearly. T. 2; *nerehandes,* T. 10.

Neven, *v.* name, proclaim, speak. Y. 25, 85; *nevyn.* T. 659, 750.

Nexile, *sb.* an aisle. Y. 25. *See* note.

Ney, *conj.* neither, nor. Ch¹. 72, 306.

Nil, *for* ne will, will not. Hh. 62.

Nolden, *for* ne wolden, would not. Hh. 232.

Nomen, *pt. pl.* seized. Hh. 53.

Non, *adj.* none. CP. (138).

None, *sb.* noon. Th. 210.

Nones, 'for the nones,' for the occasion. Th. 217.

Not, *pron.* naught. KJ. 2146.

Not, *for* ne wot, know not. CP. (7) (109).

Note, *sb.* use. Ch¹. 246.

Note, *sb.* labour, work. T. 314.

Nother, *conj.* neither. Ev. 483; FE. 485, 506; Hey. 32; Th. 72, 85, etc.

Noutt, *adv.* not. MM. 1377.

Nowth, *pron.* naught. MM. 591.

Nowther, *conj.* neither. KJ. 1347.

Noy, *v.* annoy, distress. Y. 71, 85.

Noyn, *sb.* noon. T. 290; noyne, T. 54.

Noys, *sb.* nose. T. 623.

Noyther, *conj.* neither. KJ. 1374.

Noyttment, *sb.* ointment. MM. 640, 641.

Nyce, *adj.* foolish. Th. 215.

Nye, *adv.* nigh. Ev. 839.

Nye, *sb.* harm. Ch¹. 11.

Nyp, *sb.* approach thievishly. T. 300.

Nyse, *adj.* foolish. Hey. 577.
Nyth, *sb.* night. CP. (184).

O.

O, *prep.* of. Y. 5, 90.
Obeysauns, *sb.* obedience. MM. 364.
Occident, *sb.* west. FE. 372.
Of, *adv.* off. MM. 379, 1444; FE. 446; Th. 885; KJ. 2095.
Ofer, *v.* offer, sacrifice. MM. 1219.
Oferyng, *sb.* sacrifice. MM. 1204.
Off, *prep.* of. Ch¹. 125.
Oke, *sb.* oak. Th. 109, 226.
O-mys, *adv.* amiss. Y. 139.
On, *adj.* one. CP. (265), (275); Hh. 44, 91.
On-bynd, *v.* unbind. MM. 96.
Onder, *prep.* under. MM. 266.
One, *prep.* on. Ch¹. 11, 117.
Ones, *adv.* once. Ev. 150, 837; Hey. 283, 289, 553, 600; Th. 67, 143, 518; KJ. 2160.
Onest, *adj.* honest. Co. 114.
On-lyve, *adj.* alive. CP. (36).
Onstabyll, *adj.* unstable. MM. 588.
Onto, *prep.* unto. MM. 617.
Ony, *adj.* any. Ev. 71, 100, 157, 218.
Onymentes, *sb. pl.* ointments. MM. 668.
Onys, *adv.* once. MM. 52; CP. (126); Th. 29.
Oone, *adj.* own. T. 46.
Oones, *adv.* once. T. 45.
Opteyn, *v.* obtain. FE. 41.
Or, *prep.* ere, before. Ch¹. 103, 118; Hey. 87, 94. 295; Th. 449.
Oration, *sb.* prayer. Th. 364.
Ore, *sb.* grace, favour. CP. (26).
Oryent, *sb.* the East. FE. 370.
Other, *conj.* either. Th. 73, 286, 352, etc.
Other whyle, *adv.* occasionally. CP. (158).
Otys, *sb. pl.* oats. Hey. 131.
Ou, *pron.* you. Hh. 2, 28.
Oughte-wher, *adv.* anywhere. Ch¹. 296.
Ous, *pron.* us. Hh. 36.
Overall, *adv.* everywhere. Ev. 72.

Owles, *sb. pl.* owls. Ch¹. 174.
Owt, *prep.* out. MM. 96.
Owte, an exclamation of pain. Y. 104.

P.

Pacyens, *sb.* pacience. Hey. 69.
Palet, *sb.* palate. Th. 34.
Parais, *sb.* Paradise. Hh. 6, 167.
Parceyve, *v.* perceive, understand. Th. 58; FE. 337.
Parde, *for* pardieu. Ev. 270; *per dee,* KJ. 2081.
Parfytely, *adv.* perfectly. Ev. 501.
Parsayve, *v.* perceive. FE. 397.
Partriche, *sb.* partridge. KJ. 2168.
Parvert, *adj.* perverted, reprobate. Hey. 45.
Passande. *pr. p.* surpassing. Y. 56.
Passeth, *pr. s.* surpasses. KJ. 2088.
Passynge, *adv.* surpassingly. Ev. 647.
Pastaunce, *sb.* pastime. EF. 524.
Pay, *sb.* pleasure. MM. 1428.
Paynt, *pp.* painted. T. 28; *payntyd,* feigned. Sk. 1886.
Payre, *v.* fade, deteriorate. Y. 54.
Peas, *sb.* peace. Ev. 768, 803; Hey. 42, 554. FE. 441.
Pen, *sb.* pin. Sk. 1967.
Pende. *v.* suspend. CP. (251).
Pens, *sb.* pence. Hey. 22, 93, 132.
Peple, *sb.* people. KJ. 1369.
Pepyll, *sb.* people. MM. 1388.
Per, *prep.* by; *per dee,* par Dieu. KJ. 2081.
Perdon, *v.* pardon. KJ. 2157.
Peres, *sb. pl.* peers. Y. 56.
Perfyth, *adj.* perfect. MM. 611.
Perfythnesse, *sb.* perfection. MM. 603.
Perhenuall, *adj.* perennial. MM. 637.
Perpetuall, *adv.* perpetually. MM. 636.
Perse, *v.* pierce. Th. 71.
Persecute, *pr. pl.* pursue. Th. 482.

Pes, *sb.* peace. Co. 115; MM. 93, 625; CP. (66), (75).

Peynes, *sb. pl.* pains. MM. 96.

Peynfulnesse, *sb.* painfulness. MM. 608.

Pine, *sb.* pain. Hh. 12, 63.

Placys, *sb. pl.* places, benefices. KJ. 1312.

Pleien, *pr.* 1 *pl.* play. Hh. 70.

Plesauns, *sb.* pleasure. MM. 100, 361.

Pleson, *sb.* pleasure. Co. 116.

Plesowans, *sb.* pleasure. MM. 90.

Plete, *v.* plead. Sk. 2061.

Pleȝeauntly, *adv.* pleasantly. MM. 1540.

Ploghe, *sb.* plough. T. 38.

Ply, *v.* turn. Y. 12.

Plye, *imp. s.* apply oneself to. KJ. 2164.

Po, *sb.* peacock. T. 37.

Poll, *v.* cut short the hair, fleece. Hey. 9.

Pomped, *pp.* pampered. Sk. 2038.

Pope-holy, *adj.* hypocritical. FE. 423.

Pore, *adj.* poor. MM. 596; *porys,* of the poor. Co. 51.

Porsue, *v.* pursue. MM. 610.

Portatur, messenger, angel. MM. 306.

Post, *imp. s.* put. MM. 1558.

Poste, *sb.* might. MM. 1559.

Pottill, *sb.* pottle, flask. Ch¹. 233.

Potyt, *pr. s.* strives? MM. 606.

Pouste, *sb.* power. Hh. 7.

Povert, *sb.* poverty. CP. (78).

Poynt, *sb.* point; *in poynt,* about, ready to. CP. (321).

Prease, *sb.* readiness. Th. 234.

Predycacyon, *sb.* preaching. Hey. 563.

Prefytyth, *pr. s.* profits. CP. (360).

Prengnaunt, *adj.* pregnant. FE. 29.

Preor, *sb.* prayer. MM. 1561; *preors.* MM. 1137.

Preparate, *pp.* prepared. Ev. 631.

Preposytour, *sb.* officer, prefect. Sk. 1967.

Prese, *sb.* misprint for *presence.* Hey. 71.

Presens, *sb.* presence. MM. 1137.

Presone, *sb.* prisons. Y. 32.

Prest, *adj.* forward, ready. Th. 191, 878.

Pretend, *v.* offer. KJ. 1366.

Preve, *v.* prove, try. Ev. 142.

Prist, *sb.* priest. KJ. 1337; *pristes.* KJ. 1279.

Promtyt, *pp.* prompted. MM. 602.

Proves, *sb. pl.* proofs. Th. 380.

Provyd, *v.* provide. KJ. 1394.

Prykkyd, *pp.* adorned, set out. MM. 358.

Prynse, *sb.* prince. MM. 358.

Pryse, *sb.* prize. MM. 472.

Pryst, *sb.* priest. MM. 1544; *prystes.* MM. 1178; KJ. 1351.

Punchement, *sb.* punishment. Co. 93.

Purveance, *sb.* 'purveyance.' T. 33.

Pyche, *v.* pitch, tar. Ch¹. 74.

Pyghte, *pp.* pitched. Th. 238.

Pylt, *pp.* pushed, knocked. CP. (174).

Pynande, *pr. p.* torturing. Y. 72.

Pyne, *v.* pine, suffer torture. Y. 32.

Pyninge poyntes, *sb. pl.* torturing pricks. CP. (313).

Pynne, *sb.* pin. Ch¹. 61.

Pynsynesse, *sb.* pensiveness. MM. 606.

Pyrked, *pp.* proud, conceited. MM. 358.

Q.

Quecke, *adj.* quick. Sk. 2070.

Qued, *adj.* evil. Hh. 36.

Quod, *pst. p.* quoth, said. Co. 25; FE. 529.

Quycke, *adj.* quick, living. Ev. 255; Hey. 197.

Quyte, *v.* pay, requite. Sk. 1902.

Qwantte, *adj.* quaint. T. 604, 658.

Qwatt, *int. pron.* what? MM. 1539, 1544.

Qweme, *v.* please. Co. 122.

R.

Ramyd, *pp.* overreached. T. 16.

Rathely, *adv.* quickly. CP. (398).

Raumpinge, *pp.* ramping. Th. 85.

Rayle, *sb.* a rail, a small bird. KJ. 2168.

Raynes, *sb.* the town of Rennes. Sk. 2042.

Reade, *sb.* counsel. Ch¹. 101.

Reade, *pr.* 1 *s.* counsel, advise. Ch². 269.

Recche, *v.* reck, care. Hh. 120.

Recure, *v.* recover. MM. 311.

Red, *imp. s.* advise. T. 347.

Rede, *v.* counsel, advise. CP. (96), (111); Hh. 66.

Redshonckes, *sb. pl.* redshanks. Ch¹. 190.

Refe, *pr. pl.* deprive. T. 19.

Reke, *pr.* 1 *s.* reckon. KJ. 1315.

Relyff, *v.* relieve. MM. 488, 612.

Relykes, *sb. pl.* relics. Hey. 560.

Rendyt, *pr. s.* rends. MM. 271.

Renne, *v.* run. Ev. 72, 846; Th. 17, 154, etc.; Hh. 142.

Reprefe, *sb.* reproof. Hey. 52; T. 587.

Reprefe, *v.* reprove. T. 30.

Resonnes, *sb. pl.* reasons, arguments. MM. 1527.

Respeccyon, *sb.* regard. MM. 70.

Ressayve, *v.* receive. Y. 90.

Restoratyff, *sb.* restorative. MM. 486; return, payment. MM. 651.

Restore, *v.* refresh. Y. 143.

Restryne, *sb.* restrain. MM. 290.

Rether, *adv.* rather. KJ. 1344.

Retynawns, *sb.* retinue. MM. 362.

Reve, *v.* deprive. Hh. 122.

Rewle, *v.* rule. MM. 91; KJ. 1327.

Rewthe, *sb.* pity. CP. (203).

Reylle, *v.* ramble. T. 285.

Rightwysnes, *sb.* righteousness. Y. 124.

Rihte, *adj.* right, direct. Hh. 39, 201.

Rike, *sb.* kingdom. Hh. 176.

Rod, *sb.* rood. Hh. 38.

Rodde, *sb.* rood. Ev. 777.

Rode, *sb.* rood, the holy cross. Ev. 812; CP. (30); Sk. 1896.

Rombe, *sb.* room. Ch². 485.

Rome, *sb.* room. FE. 415; Hey. 20.

Ron, *v.* run. MM. 374.

Roninge, *pr. pt.* running. Ch¹. 190.

Roode, *sb.* the holy cross. Th. 174; Ch². 468.

Rotten, *sb.* rat. Ch¹. 179.

Rowe, *sb.* row, line; *on rowe,* in order, duly. Y. 124.

Rowfed, *pp.* roofed. Ch¹. 34.

Rown, *v.* whisper. MM. 495.

Rowte, *sb.* company. MM. 374.

Ruffle, *v.* shake. Th. 300.

Ruffled, *pp.* swaggered. Th. 180.

Ruffler, *sb.* swaggering bully. Th. 1.

Rughly, *adv.* roughly. Sk. 1910.

Ruth, *sb.* pity. MM. 274.

Ryall, *adj.* royal. MM. 95, 361.

Ryalte, *sb.* royalty. MM. 65.

Rybbys, *sb. pl.* ribs. MM. 271.

Ryche, *adj.* rich. CP. (74).

Ryche, *sb.* kingdom. CP. (81).

Rydy, *adj.* ready. MM. 1388.

Rype, *imp. pl.* rip, ransack. T. 526.

Ryst, *v.* rest. T. 641.

Ryth, *adj.* right. CP. (23), (48), etc.

Ryve, *v.* dress, robe. CP. (223).

S.

Sadly, *adv.* soberly, steadfastly. MM. 614; Sk. 1966.

Saffe, *adj.* safe. Ch¹. 86; MM. 1434.

Saggyd, *pp.* oppressed, encumbered. CP. (298).

Sagh, *pt.* 1 *s.* saw. T. 611.

Sagh, *pt.* 1 *s.* say. T. 617.

Sake, *sb.* cause. Hh. 53.

Sall, *fut.* shall. Y. 10, 15, 16, etc.

Sallet, *sb.* helmet. Th. 35, 43; etc; *sallett,* KJ. 1347.

Sallet, *sb.* a salad. Th. 37, 39.

Sam, *adv.* together. T. 631.

Santiflcatt, *pp.* sanctified. MM. 1555.

Save, *adj.* safe. Th. 363.

Saveryth, *pr. s.* savours. FE. 440.

Say, *pt.* said. Ev. 271.

Saynt, *adj.* holy. Ev. 148, 290, 921.

Saynt, *v.* give health to. KJ. 2098.

Schemerande, *pr. p.* shimmering. Y. 69.

Schende, *v.* destroy. CP. (395); used intransitively(?) CP. (9).

Schent, *pp.* destroyed. CP. (340).

Schewyng, *sb.* appearance. Y. 69.

Schreve, *pp.* shriven. CP. (406).

Schryfte, *sb.* absolution after confession. CP. (319).

Schul, *v.* shall. CP. (72).

Schynande, *pr. p.* shining. Y. 69.

Scrat, *v.* scratch. Hey. 542.

Scyens, *sub.* science, knowledge. FE. 393.

Se, *v.* see. Co. 19; MM. 507; Ev. 16, 42; Hey. 611; Th. 59, 99.

Se, *sb.* sea. Co. 29.

See, *sb.* sea. MM. 1391.

Sees, *v.* cease. Co. 93.

Sei, *v.* say. Hh. 40.

Seidest, *pt.* 2 *s.* saidest. Hh. 216.

Sekyn, *v.* seek. CP. (377).

Sekyr, *adj.* safe. CP. (399).

Sele, *sb.* time, opportunity. CP. (24).

Sely, *adj.* good, innocent. T. 10; CP. (20).

Semely, *adj.* seemly, comely. Y. 52; *semly.* CP. (182).

Sen, *v.* see. CP. (73).

Sen, *adv.* since. Y. 9.

Sendel, *sb.* thin silk. CP. (95).

Sene, *gerund,* see. MM. 51; *pp.* seen. CP. (53).

Sens, *adv.* since. KJ. 2128.

Sentence, *sb.* proposition. FE. 26; judgment. KJ. 1320; *the greater sentence,* probably 'the Day of Judgment,' but possibly 'the greater excommunication.'

Sentens, *sb.* opinion. Co. 123.

Sentt, *adj.* saint, holy. MM. 1205.

Sentur, *sb.* centre. MM. 312.

Serkylle, *sb.* circle. T. 289.

Sertes, *adv.* certes, certainly. CP. (307); *sertys,* CP. (208), (332).

Sestt, *pr.* 2 *s.* seest. MM. 1542.

Set, *v.* value at; *set not a strawe,* Ev. 222; cp. Th. 172; *set not a flye,* Th. 117; *sett the shakyng of a rod,* KJ. 1383; *set by,* Sk. 1915, 1945.

Sete, *sb.* seat. CP. (95).

Sett, *pr.* 1 *s.* sit. MM. 1217; *sette,* MM. 361.

Seven, *set on seven,* put things in order. T. 749.

Sewte, *sb.* suit. KJ. 1370.

Sey, *v.* say. MM. 1179; *pr.* 1 *s.* MM. 675; *seye, pr.* 2. *pl.* MM. 489.

Seyd, *pt.* 1 *s.* said. MM. 1531.

Seyle, *pr. pl.* sail. MM. 1427.

Seyn, *gerund,* say. MM. 644.

Seys, *pr.* 2 *pl.* seest. T. 316.

Seyst, *pt.* 2 *s.* sawest. Th. 501.

Seyth, *sb.* atonement. Co. 103.

Seyyst, *pr.* 2 *s.* saist. MM. 1539.

Shelde, *sb.* shield. Th. 405.

Shepe, *sb.* ship. MM. 1423, 1429.

Sheppyng, *sb.* shipping. MM. 1392, 1431.

Sheynd, *v.* reprove, shame. T. 651.

Sholde, *v.* should. Ev. 137, 146.

Shope, *pt.* 2 *s.* createdst. Hh. 156.

Shorte, *v.* shorten. Ev. 878.

Shortely, *adv.* quickly, without delay. Ev. 778.

Shote, *v.* shoot. Th. 105, 109.

Shrew, *pr.* 1 *s.* curse. T. 310; Hey. 573.

Shrewde, *adj.* malicious, ill. FE. 438; Th. 146.

Shryve, *v.* absolve after confession. CP. (38); *pp. shryven.* Hey. 176.

Shuld, should. KJ. 1387.

Shuyd, *pp.* shewed. MM. 86.

Sibnesse, *sb.* kinship. Hh. 204.

Siththen, *adv.* since. Hh. 48.

Sitten, *v.* sit. Ch¹. 164.

Skante, *adv.* hardly. Th. 431.

Skard, *pp.* scared. T. 300, 659.

Skawd, *sb.* scold. T. 607.

Skille, *sb.* wisdom. Ch². 362.

Skowte, *sb.* enterprise, scheme. MM. 375.

Skryke, ? misprint for 'stryke.' MM. 1395.

Slake, *v.* slacken. Ch². 247; *imp. s.* Ch¹. 18.

Sle, *v.* slay. Sk. 1939.

Slefe, *sb.* sleeve. T. 28.

Slo, *v.* slay. CP. (273).

Slokyn, *v.* slacken. T. 687.

Sloo, *v.* slay. CP. (244), (377).

Slowches, *sb.* lazy fellows. Th. 506.

Slowe, *v.* slay. Ch¹. 35.

Slyche, *sb.* plaster. Ch¹. 17, 73.

Slydder, *adj.* slippery. Hey. 296.

Slyke, *adj.* such. Y. 97.

Smoder, *v.* smother. Ev. 796.

Smore, *pr. 2 pl.* smother. Y. 117.

Snek, *sb.* latch. T. 317.

Soche, *adj.* such. KJ. 1366.

Sokor, *sb.* succour. MM. 286; *sokower*, MM. 481.

Solas, *sb.* solace, pleasure. MM. 63; Ev. 277.

Somekyl, *adv.* somewhat. CP. (267).

Somkyns, some kind of. T. 719.

Somoned, *pp.* summoned. Ev. 493.

Sompe, *sb.* swamp. CP. (151).

Son, *sb.* sun. Hey. 90.

Son, *adv.* soon. MM. 1529.

Sond, *sb.* sand. MM. 1439.

Sonde, *sb.* messenger. Hh. 150.

Sonde, *sb.* message, errand. CP. (397).

Sone, *sb.* sum. FE. 374.

Sone, *adv.* soon. CP. (74); KJ. 2146.

Sonest, *sup. adv.* soonest. Th. 903.

Sorde, *sb.* sword. Ch². 291.

Soroyng, *pp.* sorrowing. MM. 290.

Sort, *sb.* company, crew. Th. 250; KJ. 2169.

Sortes. *adv.* certes, certainly. CP. (65).

Sorwe, *sb.* sorrow. Co. 18.

Soth, *sb.* truth. MM. 100.

Sothfast, *adj.* truthful. Hh. 18.

Sotyllte, *sb.* subtlety. MM. 378.

Southly, *adv.* soothly, truly. Ch¹. 44.

Sowlys, *sb. gen. s.* soul's. MM. 286.

Sownd, *v.* take soundings. MM. 1397.

Sowth, *pp.* sought. MM. 307, 594.

Soyne, *adv.* soone. T. 50.

Spar, *v.* fasten. T. 338.

Spares, *pr. 2 s.* sparest. Ch¹. 43.

Speceows, *adj.* special, particular. MM. 628.

Spede, *sb.* progress. Hey. 205.

Spede, *v.* help, forward. Ev. 771; CP. (327).

Speede, *pp.* sped, despatched. Ch². 388.

Spelle, *v.* tell, relate. CP. (372).

Spere, *sb.* sphere. Ev. 899.

Spill, *v.* destroy. Ch¹. 43, 308; Ch². 287; Y. 110.

Sprete, *sb.* spirit. Y. 18.

Sprytes, *sb. pl.* spirits. MM. 483.

Spyll, *v.* kill. Th. 434.

Spylt, *pp.* destroyed. CP. (176), (321).

Spyttle-howses, *sb. pl.* hospitals. KJ. 2127.

Stale, *adj.* antiquated. Th. 246.

Stale, *pt. s.* stole. Th. 241.

Standes, *pr. 2 s.* standest. Ch¹. 193.

Starke, *adj.* stiff. KJ. 1283.

Starne, *sb.* star. T. 588, 665.

Stat, *sb.* state, condition. CP. (310).

Stavys, *sb. pl.* staves, cudgels. Hey. 573.

Steade, *sb.* place. Ch². 207, 264.

Stele, *sb.* steel. CP. (112).

Stere, *v.* stir. Ev. 488.

Sterris, *sb. pl.* stars. T. 658.

Steven, *sb.* voice. Y. 75.

Steylle, *sb.* steel. T. 710.

Stiche, *sb.* stick. Ch¹. 75.

Stodyys, *sb. pl.* studies. MM. 488.

Stokys, *sb. pl.* stocks. Hey. 602.

Ston, *sb.* stone. CP. (71).

Stond, *pr. s.* stands. KJ. 1358.

Stondyth, *pr. s.* stands. FE. 345; *stondyth not,* is not consistent with. KJ. 1391.

Stordy, *adj.* sturdy. KJ. 1283.

Stott, *sb.* young bull. T. 529.

Stounde, *sb.* time, occasion. Ev. 633.

Stower, *sb.* store. Ch¹. 307*.

Stownd, *sb.* time, occasion. MM. 1220.

Stowth, *adj.* stout. MM. 373.

Strate, *sb.* strait ; ' in a strate,' at a pinch. T. 322.

Straytway, *adv.* straightway, immediately. Hey. 615.

Strayte, *adj.* strict. Ev. 244.

Strete and **stalle,** CP. (42); *strete and stronde,* CP. (199), (226); *strete and stye,* CP. (7); *strete and style,* CP. (12); alliterative phrases with general meaning ' everywhere.'

Streytnes, *sb.* straitened circumstances. MM. 97.

Sty, *sb.* a narrow lane, contrasted with *strete,* a highway, in the phrases *stye and strete,* CP. (89), (189) ; *strete and sty,* CP. (7).

Stylle, *adv.* silently. CP. (71).

Substancyall, *adj.* full of matter. FE. 11, 18.

Sucke, *adj.* such. Ch². 259.

Suete, *adj.* sweet. Hh. 193.

Sum, *adj.* some. MM. 495.

Supportacyon, *sb.* tolerance, forbearance. FE. 5 ; Hey. 69.

Surely, *adv.* safely. Ev. 147.

Suspowse, *sb.* suspicion. T. 525.

Swane, *sb.* swain, fellow. T. 37.

Swearde, *sb.* sword. Th. 435, 455.

Swedylle, *pr. pl.* swaddle, wrap. T. 605.

Sweme, *sb.* sorrow. Co. 127.

Swerde, *sb.* sword. Th. 288.

Swyche, *adj.* such. MM. 58, 87 ; CP. (36).

Swynke, *v.* labour. T. 323.

Swythe, *adv.* quickly. CP.(160).

Sye, *v.* sigh. CP. (175), (222), (332) ; *syest,* CP. (306) ; *syinge,* CP. (315).

Syke, *sb.* stream. CP. (151).

Sykenesse, *sb.* sureness. Sk. 2054.

Symple, *adj.* simple, foolish. Ev 283.

Syn, *adv.* since. CP. (40), (77), (119).

Syt, *pr. s.* sitteth. CP. (242); is becoming. Co. 113.

Syth, *adv.* since. MM. 624; Ev. 312 ; Hey. 19.

Syth, *sb.* sight. MM. 69, 613, etc.

Syyng, *sb.* sighing. MM. 63.

T.

Take, *v.* give. T. 765 ; *take of worth,* regard highly. Ev. 904.

Tale, *sb.* count, reckoning. CP. (171).

Talents, *sb. pl.* desires, inclinations. Y. 144.

Tane, *pp.* taken. T. 337.

Tappe, *sb.* ? Ev. 801.

Taspysster, *sb. fem.* tapster, barmaid. MM. 495.

Tast, *sb.* taste. MM. 482.

Tastinge, *sb.* trial, proof. Th. 46, 343.

Tawth, *pp.* taught, given in charge, committed. CP. (92).

Te, *v.* go, run. Hh. 8 ; *tee.* CP. (398).

Techyd, *pp.* taught. MM. 1382.

Techyth, *pr. s.* shows, directs. CP. (28).

Teene, *sb.* sorrow. Ch¹. 319.

Tell, *adv.* till. Ch¹. 7, 134.

Telle, *v.* reckon. Co. 1.

Temtyd, *pp.* tempted. MM. 603.

Ten, *v.* go, run. Hh. 231.

Tene, *sb.* sorrow. CP. (57).

Tene, *pr. 2 pl.* trouble. T. 648.

Tenys, *sb.* tennis. T. 747.

Teres, *sb. pl.* tears. MM. 666.

Terestryall, *adj.* terrestrial. Ev. 155.

Termys, *sb. pl.* phrases. FE. 42.

Teyn, *sb.* sorrow. T. 724.

Than, *adv.* then, Co. 81, 86 ; Ev. 166 ; Hey. 44, 289 ; KJ. 2096, etc.

Thane, *conj.* than. Y. 113.

Thar, *v.* need (used impersonally). Y. 64. ; T. 318 ; MM. 1437.

Thare, *pron.* their. T. 360.

The, *pron.* they. Ch¹. 8 ; CP. (256), etc.

Then, *conj.* than. Th. 514.

Thenne, *adv.* thence. Hh. 13.

Ther, *adv.* where. MM. 621.

Ther, *pron.* their. MM. 79.

Tho, *adv.* then, when. Hh. 4.

Tho, *dem. adj.* those. Hh. 84.

Thole, *v.* suffer. T. 317 ; *pp. tholed.* Hh. 49, 58 ; *pt.* 1 *s. tholede.* Hh. 208.

Thore, *adv.* there. Hh. 65.

Thorowe, *prep.* through. Y. 84.

Thou, *conj.* though. CP. (344).

Thought, *sb.* sadness, anxiety. Sk. 1995.

Thowth, *sb.* thought. MM. 633 ; CP. (48).

Thoys, *dem. adj.* those. MM. 1388.

Thred, *num. adj.* third. KJ. 1303.

Threde, *sb.* thread. Hey. 260.

Threpe, *pr.* 2 *pl.* chide, dispute. Y. 114.

Threttye, *num.* thirty. Co. 11.

Thridde, *num. adj.* third. Hh. 45, 74.

Thrist, *sb.* thirst. Hh. 50.

Thritti, *num.* thirty. Hh. 45.

Throwe, *sb.* while, time. CP. (123), (147).

Thryfe, *v* thrive. T. 27.

Thryst, *v.* thrust. Ev. 825.

Thryst, *sb.* thirst. MM. 492 ; *thryste.* Co. 13.

Thu, *pron.* thou. KJ. 2078, 2100, 2105.

Thyder, *adv.* thither. Ev. 675, 918.

Thylke, *adj.* that. Hey. 44, 46.

Thynkes, *pr.* 2 *s.* thinkest. MM. 591.

Till, *prep.* to. Ch¹. 47.

To, *num.* two. MM. 68 ; CP. (34).

Tocken, *sb.* token. Ch¹. 311, 318.

Toddes, *sb. pl.* toads. MM. 1199.

To-dyghte, *pp.* committed to. Y. 98.

Togyder, *adv.* together. Ev. 666, 677 ; Hey. 285.

Toke, *pt.* took. Ev. 848.

Token, *sb.* parable. T. 331.

To medys, *conj.* provided that. CP. (197).

Ton, *adj.* the one. CP. (28), (38).

Tone, *adj.* the one, though used with the definite article, ' the tone.' Hey. 579.

Tong, *sb.* tongue. MM. 278; *tonge.* Ch¹. 234 ; MM. 1530.

Too, *sb.* toe. CP. (209).

Torke, *sb.* Turkey. MM. 1435.

Tother, the, i. e. that other. CP. (39).

Towe, *num.* two. Ch¹. 121.

To-whyls, *adv.* whilst. Y. 62.

Traysh, *sb.* trash. KJ. 1389.

Treey, *sb.* tree. Ch¹. 89.

Tremyll, *v.* tremble. MM. 1554.

Treubelacyon, *sb.* tribulation. MM. 1534.

Trew, *adj.* true. MM. 66, 603.

Trobylled, *pp.* troubled. MM. 269.

Trone, *sb.* throne. Ev. 637 ; CP. (43).

Trost, *sb.* trust. MM. 634, 1214.

Trotte, *sb.* old woman. Th. 501.

Trow, *adj.* true. CP. (212).

Trye, *adj.* pure, refined. CP. (81), (216).

Tryfellys, *sb. pl.* trifles. FE. 17.

Twyne, *pr.* 1 *s.* separate. Y. 153.

Tyde, *sb.* time, MM. 273, 1442.

Tympanye, *sb.* dropsy. KJ. 2117.

Tyne, *adj.* tiny. T. 735.

Tyte, *adv.* quickly ; *as tyte,* as quickly as may be. T. 638.

Tytte, *sb.* teat. Th. 73.

Tytyll, *sb.* title, name. MM. 603.

U.

Unbuxumnes, *sb.* disobedience. Y. 123.

Unchende, *adj.* unkind, unnatural? or for *unhend,* uncourteous. CP. (13).

Underfoe, *v.* undertake. Ch.¹ 67. 412.

Underfonge, *v.* undergo. Ch².

Unkende, *adj.* unnatural. Co. 67.

Unkynde, *adj.* unnatural. Co. 59; Ev. 23; unkind. Ev. 310.

Unlykynge, *adj.* in poor condition. Sk. 1984.

Unneth, *adv.* scarcely. FE. 19.

Unrightes, *sb.* unrighteousness. Ch¹. 142.

Unthryvandly, *adv.* in vain, unthrivingly. Y. 114.

Unyte, *sb.* unity. MM. 620.

V.

Vagys, *sb. pl.* strayings. Sk. 1947.

Vayne, *sb.* vein. Hey. 548.

Velyarde, *sb.* old man, dotard. Sk. 1903.

Vengeabyl, *adj.* vengeful. Co. 105.

Venter, *v.* venture. Ev. 484.

Vernage, *sb.* wine of Verona. MM. 480.

Veryabyll, *adj.* variable. MM. 590, 595.

Violatt, *pp.* violated, polluted, foul. MM. 1557.

Vyage, *sb.* voyage. Ev. 249, 674. 782.

Vyand, *sb.* food. FE. 465.

W.

Walter, *v.* welter, roll about. Sk. 1936.

Wane, *sb.* wain, waggon. T. 38.

War, *comp. adj.* worse. Y. 113.

War, *v.* were. MM. 1535.

Warande, *pr.* 1 *s.* warrant. Y. 96; KJ. 2105.

Ware, *imp. s.* beware. MM. 492.

Ware, *v.* wear. KJ. 1324.

Warke, *sb.* work. Y. 15, 17, etc. *warkes.* FE. 20.

Warloo, *sb.* warlock, wizard. T. 651, 723.

Warrye, *v.* curse. Ch¹. 273; *wary.* T. 19; *waryd.* T. 723.

Wassayle, *s.* wassail, 'good health.' KJ. 2165.

Wast, *sb.* waste. MM. 487.

Wat, *pr.* 1 *s.* know. Hh. 217.

Waus, *pt.* was. CP. (314).

Waxit, *pr. s.* waxeth, grows. CP. (144).

Waye, *pr.* 2 *pl.* weigh. KJ. 2166; *wayeth.* KJ. 1321.

Wayn, *adj.* vain. MM. 595.

Wede, *sb.* attire. CP. (183); Hh. 34.

Weder, *adv.* whither. CP. (177), (271).

Weders, *sb. pl.* weathers, storms. T. 1.

Wedyr, *adv.* whither. CP. (49).

Weeke, *adj.* weak. Ch¹. 67.

Weelde, *sb.* power. Y. 67.

Weendande, *pr. p.* wending. Y. 96.

Weete, *sb.* wet, rain. Ch¹. 95.

Wei, *sb.* way. Hh. 39, 209.

Weither, *sb.* weather. Ch¹. 323, 876.

Weither, *sb.* wether. Ch². 441.

Weke, *adj.* weak. Ev. 482.

Welde, *v.* wield, rule, enjoy. Y. 28, 73; Hh. 108.

Welde, *sb.* power. Y. 86.

Wele, *sb.* wealth, well-being. CP. (79), (335).

Wele, *adv.* well. KJ. 2137, 2145.

Weledyng, *sb.* wielding, rule. Y. 39; *weledande, pr. p.* Y. 86.

Well, *pr.* 1 *s.* boil, seethe. Y. 104, 131.

Welth, *sb.* well-being, salvation. Y. 3, 28, 85.

Wemen, *sb. pl.* women. Ch¹. 48, 67.

Wende, *pp.* thought. Ev. 163.

Wendest, *pr.* 2 *s.* weenest, thinkest. Hey. 179.

Wene, *v.* think. CP. (48); cp. Ch¹. 111; MM. 493; *wenest,* Ev. 161.

Wente, *pp.* gone. Y. 105.

Wepyn, *sb. pl.* weapons. T. 626.

Wer, *pt.* 2 *s.* wast. MM. 673.

Werd, *sb.* world. CP. (72); *werdes*, CP. (68).

Were, *v.* wear. Ev. 648; Th. 55, 129.

Werely, *adv.* verily. MM. 675.

Wery, *v.* weary, grow tired. FE. 518.

Weryauns, *sb.* variance. MM. 92.

Werye, *v.* war against. Th. 406.

Wes, *pt. s.* was. Hh. 4.

Westment, *sb.* vestment. MM. 1183.

Wete, *v.* know. Y. 67; Ev. 88, 112, 143.

Wete, *sb.* wheat. Hh. 131.

Weth, *prep.* with. FE. 522.

Wetyn, *v.* know. CP. (101).

Wexith, *pr. s.* waxes, becomes. FE. 460.

Weyle, *v.* wail. CP. (173).

Weylle, *adv.* well. T. 287, 709.

Weyn, *pr.* 1 *s.* ween. T. 706.

Weyscelles, *sb. pl.* weasels. Ch[1]. 175.

Whan, *adv.* when. Ev. 641; *whane*, CP. (45).

What, *adv.* how. T. 1, 298; CP. (405).

Wheder, *adv.* whether. Ev. 287.

Wheder, *adv.* whither. Ev. 297. 306.

Wher, *pt. pl.* were. MM. 369; *imp. subj.* MM. 1436.

Where, *conj.* whereas. Hey. 276.

Whyder, *adv.* whither. Ev. 802.

Who, *pron.* whoever. MM. 61.

Whorshep, *sb.* worship. MM. 384.

Whow, *adv.* how. CP. (13), (74)

Whypyng, *pr. p.* wiping. MM. 640.

Whytly, *adv.* quickly. MM. 376.

Whytt, *sb.* bit, atom. CP. (85).

Wiht, *sb.* wight, man. Hh. 23.

Wike, *sb.* town, place. Hh. 175.

Winde, *v.* escape. Hh. 146.

Wist, *pp.* known. Hh. 49.

Wite, *v.* know. Hh. 71.

With so that, *conj.* provided that. CP. (167).

Wo, *pron.* who. MM. 608.

Wod, *sb.* wood. T. 661.

Wode, *adj.* mad, furious. CP. (34); Y. 105.

Wold, wolde, would. Hey. 558; KJ. 1387; Ev. 274.

Wole, woll, will. Co. 14; MM. 488.

Won, *v.* dwell. Y. 28.

Wonde, *v.* turn aside from. CP. (201).

Wonders, *adv.* wondrously. Ev. 7; *wondersly*, FE. 329.

Wondydd, *pp.* wrapped, enveloped in. MM. 605.

Wone, *v.* dwell. Y. 137; Hh. 160; *wonen*, Hh. 233; *woned*, Hh. 46.

Wones, *sb. pl.* places, dwellings. Y. 28.

Wondyr, *adv.* wonderfully. CP. (51).

Woo. *pron.* who. MM. 609.

Wood, *adj.* mad. Ch[1]. 254.

Worche, *v.* work. Ch[1]. 50; KJ. 1382.

Word, *sb.* world. MM. 305, 381.

Worthely, *adj.* worthy. Y. 17.

Wo so, *pron.* who so. MM. 57.

Wost, *pt.* 2 *s.* knewest. Hh. 73.

Wot, *v.* know. Ev. 821; *wote.* Ev. 195, 271; wote, *pr. s.* Th. 150; *wolst.* MM. 1216.

Wounder, *adv.* wondrously. Ch[1]. 57.

Wrake, *sb.* harm. MM. 380.

Wrawe, *adj.* angry. Ch[1]. 209.

Wrocken, *pp.* wreaked. Ch[1]. 320.

Wrokyn, *pp.* avenged. T. 625.

Wrowth, *pp.* wrought. MM. 305, 631, 1387.

Wrytynge, *sb.* account. Ev. 187.

Wurkes, *sb. pl.* works. KJ. 2134.

Wyche, *pron.* which. CP. (107).

Wycke, *sb.* wickedness. CP. (39).

Wyhylles, *sb. pl.* wiles. MM. 377.

Wylddyng, *sb.* wielding, power. MM. 59.

Wylfull, *adj.* voluntary. Hey. 23.

Wyn, *sb.* wine. MM. 485.

Wynche, *v.* kick. Sk. 2049.

Wynde, *v.* turn, (go its own way). FE. 418.

Wyndowe, *sb.* window. Ch¹. 29.

Wyrk, *v.* work. T. 282.

Wyrschip, *sb.* worship. Y. 81.

Wyse, *sb.* manner. MM. 665.

Wyshyng, *pr. p.* guiding. Y. 157.

Wyssande, *pr. p.* guiding. Y. 152.

Wythly, *adv.* actively, swiftly. MM. 270.

Wytt, *sb.* knowledge, understanding Co. 115; MM. 1213; *wytte,* Ch¹. 29.

Wytte, know. Hey. 85.

Wytystsaff, *pr.* 2 *s.* vouchestsafe. MM. 624.

X.

Xall, *fut. s.* shall. MM. 64, etc.

Xulde, *pt. s.* should. MM.

Y.

Y, *pr.* 1. KJ. 1322; MM 292.

Ya, *adv.* yea, yes. CP. (53).

Yarde, *sb.* stick, rod. Ch². 290.

Yarde, *pp.* made ready. Ch¹. 91.

Yare, *adj.* ready, prepared. T. 715.

Y-beten, *pp.* beaten. Sk. 2043.

Ydolls, *sb. pl.* idols. KJ. 1352.

Yeinder, *adj.* yonder. Ch¹. 214.

Yender, *adj.* yonder. Ch². 250; MM. 1438.

Yer, *adv.* ere, before. Th. 328.

Yerth, *sb.* earth. FE. 332, 340.

Yf, *conj.* if. FE. 24.

Yinge, *adj.* young. Ch². 369.

Yle, *sb.* aisle. KJ. 2114.

Ylle, *adv.* ill. T. 1.

Ymagyn, *v.* imagine. Hey. 287.

Ynough, *adv.* enough. Th. 207; ynoughe. Ev. 816.

Yode, *pt. pl.* went, ran. T. 517.

Yone, *adj.* yonder. CP. (391), (404).

Yower, *pron.* your. MM. 86.

Yre, *sb.* ire, wrath. Hey. 59; Th. 77.

Yrons, *sb. pl.* irons. Th. 170, 188.

Ys, *pr. s.* is. KJ. 1313.

Ywys, *adv.* iwis, certainly. Th. 96, 510; Hey. 553.

Yys, *sb. pl.* eyes. MM. 640.

Yys, *adv.* yes. CP. (155), (164).

ȝ.

ȝaf, *pt.* gave. Hh. 91.

ȝates, *sb. pl.* gates. Hh. 135.

ȝateward, *sb.* porter. Hh. 137.

ȝeme, *v.* guard, take care of. Hh. 24, 167.

ȝer, *sb.* year. Hh. 45.

ȝerned, *pp.* yearned. Hh. 162.

ȝif, *imp. s.* give. Hh. 173.

ȝif, *conj.* if. Hh. 121.

ȝonge, *adj.* young. Hh. 132.

ȝoven, *pp.* given. Hh. 177.

THE END.

PRINTED IN GREAT BRITAIN AT THE UNIVERSITY PRESS, OXFORD
BY JOHN JOHNSON, PRINTER TO THE UNIVERSITY